SATA AUTO PAINT
FROM **PREP** TO **FINAL COAT**

By JoAnn Bortles

DanAm®

motorbooks

Dedication

To Barbara Wilson, the bravest and most thoughtful person I have ever known.
My hero, my friend. You live on in the work I do.
And to Simon, there will never be another like you.

First published in 2014 by Motorbooks, an imprint of Quarto Publishing Group USA Inc., 400 First Avenue North, Suite 400, Minneapolis, MN 55401 USA

Motorbooks titles are also available at discounts in bulk quantity for industrial or sales-promotional use. For details write to Special Sales Manager at Quarto Publishing Group USA Inc., 400 First Avenue North, Suite 400, Minneapolis, MN 55401 USA.

To find out more about our books, visit us online at www.motorbooks.com.

Library of Congress Cataloging-in-Publication Data
Bortles, JoAnn, 1960-
    Automotive paint from prep to final coat / by JoAnn Bortles.
        pages cm
    Summary: "In *Automotive Paint from Prep to Final Coat*, automotive paint expert JoAnn Bortles walks the reader through dozens of how-to lessons, tips, and tricks about repainting a car, whether for competitive show or just garage-time hobby. The book features over 500 how-to photos, as well as sidebars, walkthroughs, and informative text."—Provided by publisher.
    ISBN 978-0-7603-4278-7 (paperback)
    1. Automobiles—Painting. I. Title.
    TL255.2.B685 2014
    629.2'6—dc23

                                    2014003884

Editor: Jordan Wiklund
Design management and layout: Rebecca Pagel

Printed in China
10 9 8 7 6 5 4 3 2 1

On the front cover: Before-and-after paint job of a Pontiac Firebird Trans Am. *Kimballstock.com*

On the title page: Close-up of flame application.

About the author
JoAnn Bortles is a nationally recognized and award-winning custom painter. Her work has been featured in dozens of magazines, and she has written six books on custom painting techniques for Motorbooks, including the bestselling *How to Master Airbrush Painting Techniques*. She has won Best Paint of the Year four times since 2004, and has been featured on *The Today Show* and PowerBlock's *MuscleCar TV* show. She lives and works in Waxhaw, North Carolina, at her own custom painting shop, Crazy Horse Painting. On Facebook: http://on.fb.me/Z6KFf9On Twitter: @CrazyHorseFlame

Contents

Introduction

HOW TO SURVIVE A LIFETIME (OR A MONTH) IN AUTO BODY AND PAINT

Ask a handful of professionals who spend their time in an auto body and paint shop what makes a good painter, and the answer is sure to vary each time. Talent? Knowledge? Having a top-of-the-line shop to work in? The latest tools and equipment? A combination of all the above?

Those are all good answers, but there is one thing missing: call it common sense or ingenuity, but it's why sometimes a painter working in a dirty old shop, using outdated and handmade tools, will do a better job than a painter in a state-of-the-art body shop; why a painter with many years of experience and no schooling will outperform a painter fresh from a technical school armed with all the latest technology. They are either born with a great deal of common sense, or they learn it the hard way.

Here's an example of common sense in painting. Imagine you're rushing through your workday. Your mind is clicking away, multitasking, figuring out how much paint you'll need to mix up, what's the paint formula, do you have all the ingredients for the formula or formulas, did you remember to order the catalyst for the clearcoat, is the booth the right temperature, and where are you going to go for lunch? You open the cabinet and grab the gallon of black basecoat you're mixing. Except it's not the one you're mixing, because two containers look similar, and as you're pouring, you realize the paint going into the mix is clear. Oops! This is an easy mistake to make, and one made worse when you realize that most of the ingredients for the paint are

A number of elements combine to create this eye-catching paint job: properly done bodywork, color testing to create the basecoat color, pre-paint drawings to find the most effective design, and a thorough knowledge of the materials and tools used.

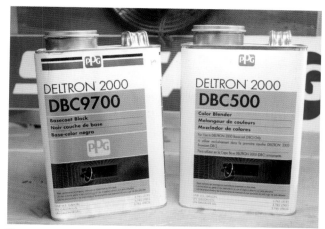

These two products look very similar. I wonder how easy it would be to grab the wrong can.

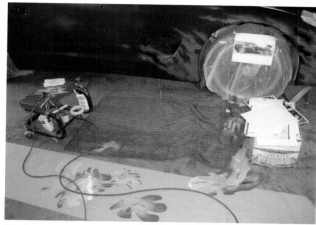

I don't work on Corvettes every day or every month. So when a customer needed a week's worth of artwork done to her car, I needed to be innovative with my setup. For example, I don't have a nifty low-level, roll-around airbrush cart. And even though I'm fairly short to begin with, this car is less than 6″ off the ground. Now the car could be put on a lift and airbrushed, but then I'd have to work around the structure of the lift. So I improvise with a towel or a Summit Racing mechanic's pad on the ground and a roll-around seat clamped in place with airbrush holders. Now I'm ready to paint fire.

The simple, cheap, and common sense solution is 30 seconds with a marker and masking tape. The brightness of the orange masking tape grabs your attention.

Remember to research. Things do not go as planned during many jobs. The painter has to *think* his way through the job. You have to think out of the box. You didn't order the paint you needed or the plastic filler isn't sticking to the soda-blasted metal surface. In the old days, you'd be on the phone, frantically calling your body shop buddies. Now, while this is still a good idea, we also have the Internet. The Internet is an amazing resource for I-need-to-know-this-immediately-or-I-will-

already in the mixing cup and you've added the wrong ingredient. Time to pour all that expensive paint into the used paint barrel. In other cases, sometimes the paint has been sprayed and it doesn't look right. Any number of things can go wrong with a momentary lapse in concentration.

Sometimes common sense involves the tools or equipment you need but don't have. Look around the shop of an old painter and you'll find many handmade tools—Allen wrenches that are cut down, and other various tools that are cut and welded together to fit into tight spaces. It would be wonderful to buy every nifty tool you'd ever need, but then you wouldn't have money to buy that lunch we were talking about. When you look at a roadblock, think your way through it. Maybe the tool won't reach, the stud is stripped, or like in this next picture, your back will be broken by the time you're done with the job.

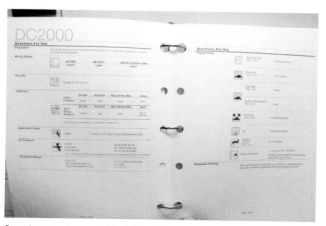

One of my most essential tools is my book of product sheets, or P sheets as they are known. For each paint product you have in your shop, you should also have the P sheet. After 33 years of painting, I still find myself opening up this book most every day.

Autobody101.com and other bodyshop forums are a great place to find help and answers, especially at night and on weekends when your paint store is closed or your paint representative is unavailable. Keeping a binder handy for the help you need can go a long way toward getting the job done right.

die kind of information. But much of what's out there is opinion. And each situation is as different as the factors that affect the problem (find more about "paint or die" situations in chapter 15).

Know the source of information on the Internet. Equipment or paint manufacturers usually give explicit information on their products, like how they should be used. Whenever I hear from painters about a problem, I ask them, "Did you look at the tech or P [*product* or *paint*] sheet for that product?" The answer is usually no. Paint stores don't automatically hand you a product sheet when you buy the product. The first thing a common-sense painter does when using a product is to obtain and read through the P sheet (technical information sheet) *before* using the product, not *after* the paint is solvent-popping all over the car because the wrong temp reducer was used. These sheets are easily

available on most paint companies' websites. If they are not, then you're using the wrong brand of paint.

After you have the P sheet and still need answers, another great source of information is an auto body and paint discussion website like www.Autobody101. com. Many experienced painters frequent the board and help other painters with problems, up to and including knowledgeable do-it-yourselfers and newbies. In the 33 years I've been painting, I still don't have all the answers—no one does. Heck, recently I got a call from one of the pioneers of custom painting asking me for advice on a problem he was having, illustrating another tenet of painting—never hesitate to ask a question. If you can't find what you're looking for here, I have my own expert area for questions and answers on Autobody101, but I still find lots of great information too. It feels good to know you are not alone and that there are others who need help.

Using common sense in the paint and body shop means having the sense to be prepared and informed before you start a task or use a product. It means not panicking when things go wrong and then making the problem worse, and slowing down when you feel you need to speed up. An old painter once told me if you hurry up, you'll fall behind. It took me a few years before I knew the true meaning of what he said. It took me even more years before I seriously practiced it. The paint and bodywork seen in this book are a result of getting the job done right, taking the time to think through it, stopping the process when something is not right and then making sure it's being done correctly instead of blazing onward. It's a great feeling when a project leaves the shop, knowing the customer will not

This job took many hours to get the best possible result, and no shortcuts were taken. As a result, the job went smoothly. Look closely at the sides of the car: note how straight the surface is and how regular the sheen of the paint. Over 600 hours of paint and bodywork went into this '33 hot rod (I put over 100 hours in on this project myself).

have a problem down the road because I did everything possible to make sure it was done right.

Keeping an Open Mind

Painting technology changes every year. Companies are always improving their products and coming up with new ones. A painter with common sense knows this and keeps informed and up to date on what's happening. How do you stay informed? Talk to your paint rep or the store you buy from, subscribe to a body shop publication like *AutoBody News* or read the latest news on their website, www.autobodynews.com. Find out what's going on and see if you want to try any new products. It's very tempting to simply stick with what works for you, but what can and has happened is that things change and the uninformed painters don't know until they try to buy a favorite product and find it's been discontinued, or as painters in California discovered, *outlawed.*

In 2008, all body shops in California became restricted to using low volatile organic compound (VOC), or waterborne paint. Painters who knew this were prepared for it, and those who had worked with waterborne paint had a much easier time than those who did not. Many painters like me had little experience with waterborne paint; since I was not required by law to use it, I didn't. But in 2012, I was presented with a great opportunity to use waterborne paint on a car; I took two classes to learn to use PPG's Envirobase line of paint, and I was amazed at the technology I had been missing. It sprays completely differently from solvent base, and the techniques took some getting used to. What's more, waterborne paint works better than solvent paint for some situations in the collision repair industry. And this brings up one last aspect of becoming comfortable with automotive paint.

Admitting You're Not an Expert

When I took the Envirobase class, I expected to see young body shop painters. There were many younger guys, but there were a few older guys too, grizzled veterans who had been painting longer than I. They were amazing painters, and part of what made them so good is that they kept up with the new technology. Unlike them, I had never taken a painting class before, and less than an hour into it, I asked myself why I had been so stubborn. Many of the painters in the class were regulars who attended as many classes as their schedules allowed. In fact, there's so much to learn, it's pretty much impossible to get all you want from a four-day

Here, Ron Payton teaches a PPG certification class at PPG's training center in Kissimmee, Florida. PPG has training facilities across the country.

class. It's better to come back and take it again because it's different every time, with different attendees who ask different questions. The four-day Envirobase class was an amazing experience for me. I learned so much, and not just from the instructors, but from discussions with the other painters as well. It was an exchange of information I had been missing out on for years. I knew that paint companies gave classes, but for some reason, I had never decided I needed to take one. What a mistake that had been—not very sensible! I now find myself trying to find time in my schedule to take each class PPG has to offer.

The bottom line is that the best painters are the people who use all their tools to their best ability and who know that the best tools you have aren't necessarily the ones in the toolbox. Patience, discipline, and a positive attitude will help anyone in his life and in his career. Another old painter also gave me some great advice that has stuck with me: when a project is going badly and you're freaking out, ask yourself, "Will this matter to me a year from now?" The truth is most of the time the answer to that question is no. Simply asking it helps me to calm down and figure out the best plan of action. It's not easy to step back from a project that is going wrong and reassess the situation when the customer is having a fit, but sometimes it's the best action to take. I always tell people to have fun when you paint. Or rather, try to keep it fun. Is that an easy thing to do? No. Do I have fun when I paint? Not all the time. But sometimes I do, and it's always an adventure. So relax and try to enjoy your journey through auto body and paint. I hope this book helps you in that quest.

Chapter 1
Paint and Materials

UNDERSTANDING PAINT

In order to paint your car, it's critical to understand how paint works as well as understand the different kinds of paint. People toss around terms like *primer, sealer, 2-part paint, tri-coat, lacquer, single-stage,* and more, and it can get confusing. This chapter explains the different kinds of paint and how paint works. Despite all the complex chemical names, paint is mostly composed of four major components: pigments, resin, solvents, and additives.

Pigments are finely ground powders. Some are naturally occurring minerals and some are synthetically produced. They provide the following:

- Color and special effects
- Opacity (coverage/hiding power)
- Filling properties
- Sand-ability
- Adhesion
- Durability and corrosion resistance

Resin is the backbone of the paint. It is what gives paint its strength. It's needed for the following:

- Film forming
- Pigment binding
- Durability
- Gloss
- Viscosity
- Adhesion

Solvents are sometimes referred to as vehicles because they "carry" the paint. They control the following:

- Reduce viscosity
- Change speed of dry-off

HOW PAINT WORKS

This drawing is very simplified, but for the most part, this is the quick and simple explanation of how paint works. The paint is sprayed onto a sanded surface. The sanded surface provides a "tooth" to help the paint stick. The solvents in the paint carry the pigments and resins to the surface, then as they evaporate, the layers bond together.

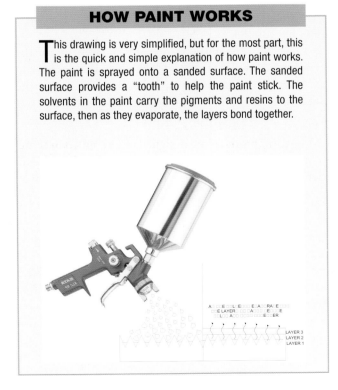

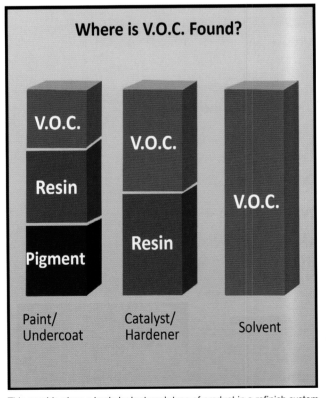

This graphic gives a basic look at each type of product in a refinish system and shows that each one contains VOCs. VOC is measured in pounds of VOC per gallon. VOC information for PPG products can be found on the product bulletin, both for the product itself and when it is ready to spray.

Additives are materials added in small quantities to give or improve certain characteristics, like the following:

- UV absorbers for durability
- Flow additives
- Anti-settle agents
- Driers and catalysts
- Plasticizers
- Anti-foaming agents

VOLATILE ORGANIC COMPOUND (VOC)

VOC is a class of materials that includes most evaporative solvents used in auto refinish products. VOCs are found in nearly all refinish products used in a collision center.

On September 11, 1998, a new regulation was put into effect that regulates the VOC level as applied for refinish paint products. Automotive refinish manufacturers can only sell undercoats, topcoats, and clearcoats that meet the law. Some states and countries have enacted VOC regulations that are stricter than the national rule. Technicians must follow the regulations in their area.

THERMOPLASTIC VERSUS THERMOSET

The vast majority of automotive refinish paints can be divided into two basic resin types: thermoplastic and thermoset. The table below shows the key characteristics of each type. For example, in this book, the basecoats being used are thermoplastic. The clearcoat urethanes are thermoset. But there are some products, like many aerosol paints, that exhibit characteristics of both and can be listed as mild thermoset because they have thermoset characteristics but don't cross-link like urethanes. Cross-linking is what happens when the two components of 2K products start to chemically react to each other.

Latex, or waterborne, materials are neither true thermoplastic nor thermoset, but show characteristics of both. Refer to chapter 11 for information on waterborne paints.

The Resin Rule Test

The steps below will quickly determine if the paint film or substrates are thermoplastic or thermoset. If you are working over old paint or making a repair, it's good to know what you're working over. Try this in an area that is already damaged or needs to be repaired. *Do not try this where the paint will not be worked on, as it may damage the paint.*

1. Soak a clean cloth in medium grade lacquer thinner.

Thermoplastic	Thermoset
Will reflow with heat or solvent	Will not reflow with heat or solvent
Cures by release of solvent, no chemical crosslink occurs. This means there will not be a "pot" life.	Cures by chemical cross-linking between product and a catlyst. This means there will be a "pot" life.
Generally less favored due to reduced retention of initial gloss, lowered long-term durabilty, and increased film shrinkage during curing cycle.	Are favored because they provide greater gloss rentention, durability, and very little shrinkage after reaching a cured state.
Considered "1K" products	Considered "2K" products

Thermoplastic and thermoset products do not always work well together. If the chosen products are not compatible, wrinkling or lifting can occur. This is why it's so important to get the P sheet for the products being used. For example, the P sheet for DBC Deltron basecoat will list what products can be under and over it.

2. Lay the soaked cloth on the paint film/substrate for approximately 5 minutes, then rub gently.

Lacquer thinner is a strong solvent and will cause a thermoplastic film to soften or dissolve. A weak or aged paint film/substrate may wrinkle, lift, or deteriorate quickly. Check the test area for any of these signs. If no effects are noted, the substrate could be considered sound and is most likely a thermoset paint film.

If the paint film/substrates are thermoset, the repair procedure can proceed as normal. If the paint film is in any way unsound, sand down to a sound surface or strip it to the metal or bare substrate before proceeding with any repairs or refinishing.

STANDARD CONDITIONS

Most paint products are designed to be applied in certain conditions. For instance, it's not a good idea to paint when it's very cold or very hot. Standard conditions are temperature, humidity, and air flow data under which an automotive paint product's dry time, cure time, pot life, and all general performance characteristics are determined. This information is usually found on the

WHAT'S A POT LIFE?

The term *pot life* applies to 2K products. The pot life is the amount of time a mixed 2K product can be used after the two parts, usually paint and hardener, have been mixed together.

Temperature	68-70 ºF / 20-22 º C
Relative Humidity	50%
Air Flow	Adequate to quickly and continuously remove all overspray during application and enhance the curing process. A recommended airflow is between 60 and 100 FPM.

Standard Conditions

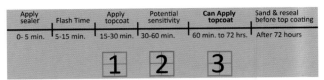

Apply sealer	Flash Time	Apply topcoat	Potential sensitivity	**Can Apply topcoat**	Sand & reseal before top coating
0- 5 min.	5-15 min.	15-30 min.	30-60 min.	60 min. to 72 hrs.	After 72 hours

To better explain, for example, sealer has been sprayed and basecoat will be applied next. This timeline is based on a 70ºF shop. This is just an example; all products will be different.

product's P sheet. The conditions used by PPG and most refinish manufacturers are as follows:

The 15º Rule
So what happens when you try to paint in colder or warmer temperatures? This is where the 15º rule comes in. This rule pertains to thermoset (2K) products and explains how temperature can affect a product's dry time and pot life.

- For every 15ºF (-9.4ºC) *increase* in temperature above standard conditions, a refinish product's dry time and pot life may be reduced by one-half.

- For every 15ºF (-9.4ºC) *decrease* in temperature below standard conditions, a refinish product's dry time and pot life may be doubled.

The Window Rule
This is a simple rule but it can *ruin* a paint job if you miss the appropriate recoat window. This rule has three parts and applies to thermoset (2K) coatings. Each 2K product goes through three stages (windows) as it cures. The windows open in the order explained.

1. Opportunity (OK to recoat)—chemically soft enough to accept more coats of the same product or a compatible product

2. Danger (not OK to recoat)—not chemically soft enough to accept nor hard enough to resist possible wrinkling caused by applying more coats

3. Stability (OK to recoat)—chemically hard enough to resist possible wrinkling that could be caused by applying more coats

The times necessary for each product to move from one window to the next will vary from product to product, so it's important to understand each stage for the products you are using. Film thickness can also affect the recoat window. Follow the recoat times on all product information or P sheets. Make sure to note the pot life of the product to anticipate when cross-linking will occur at your temperature. Remember the 15º Rule applies to these times.

SOLVENTS/REDUCERS/THINNERS
Most automotive undercoats and topcoats require the addition of a solvent. The amount of solvent type needed can be found in the product's P sheet. Remember to always use the correct solvent for the paint being used. For example, do not use lacquer thinner if the product requires reducer. Don't mix brands of solvent; if you are using one company's paint, make sure to use its recommended matching solvent. Do not use another company's solvent. A few fundamental facts need to be understood by painters regarding solvents:

- Reducers are made up of a combination or blend of solvents that provide different performance and application characteristics.
- They possess chemical strength to reduce the viscosity of a high-solids resin
- They evaporate at different rates during application process
- They alter the product's application characteristics
- Reducers are temporary tools needed during the paint application process.
- The ability to correctly choose, use, and understand reducers is a necessary skill for any painter.

	60º F	Standard Conditions	85º F	100º F	115º F
Dry Time	60 min.	30 min.	15 min.	7.5 min.	3.75 min.
Pot Life	120 min.	60 min.	30 min.	15 min.	7.5 min.

Note: All product cross-linking and curing in 2K products slows significantly or stops below 60ºF (16ºC). Thermoset (2K) paints will not cure properly if subjected to cool temperatures during the curing stages. Such conditions can result in a paint finish that may eventually dry but exhibit reduced durability, gloss, and reparability. This loss of performance is due to never having reached a fully cured state. Pay attention to the temperature in the paint area both during and after applying a two-part paint product. Think twice before turning off the heat in order to save on the power or fuel bill.

A PAINTING RULE

Once any kind of urethane paint (thermoset, 2K), including single-stage basecoats and urethane clearcoats, has dried or cured, it must be sanded or scuffed before any more paint is applied over it. Remember the Window Rule. This illustration shows what happens when a urethane surface is not properly sanded before it's recoated. The urethane surface was not sanded in the corner before the new urethane paint was applied. It looked great at first, but once the newly applied paint started to cure it pulled away from the unsanded surface below. This mistake is an extremely bad one that many painters make. Why do painters do this? Time is usually a factor. The painter is in a hurry and skips over things that may seem like small details, but in reality can ruin a paint job.

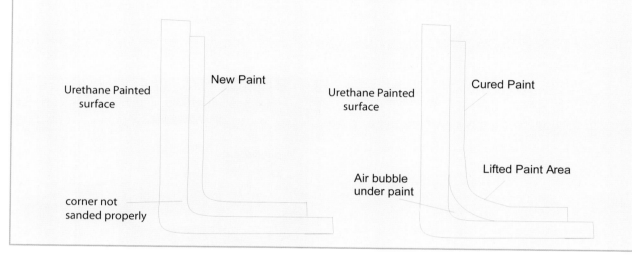

A reducer must perform three primary jobs:

1. Make the paint thin enough to apply easily through a spray gun

2. Act as a carrier or vehicle to get the paint to the part as well as provide initial leveling and adhesion

3. Allow the paint to achieve final leveling and begin the drying/curing process

The three primary jobs listed above are performed by the three blends of solvent used to make a reducer, front-end solvents, middle solvents, and tail solvents. The chart below shows each of these blends and their roles in the refinish process.

CHOOSING THE CORRECT TEMP SOLVENT

Picking the right temp solvent to go with your basecoat or clearcoat can make or break a paint job. When slower reducer is used, the paint dries slower. This means the top dries slowly, which allows the coats under it to dry out better.

Types of Solvent	Role of Solvent
Front End Solvents	Thins the resins in the paint product to allow it to be applied with refinish spray guns. Evaporates quickly after leaving the spray gun.
Middle Solvents	Remains with the atomized paint to provide initial adhesion and leveling of product once it reaches the substrate. Evaporates quickly after reaching panel.
Tail Solvents	Remains with applies product to finish the leveling process (flow) as well as insure chemical adhesion to previous products. Evaporates last during drying/curing process.

It's important to have a good understanding of the temperature range and evaporation rate of the solvents. This makes it easier to choose the correct reducer for a product and the painting conditions.

Fast reducer can dry too fast if used in warm temps. And if used with thick coats of paint, the top coat can skin over before the bottom layers have dried out. This traps the solvents in lower coats and causes a multitude of problems including peeling, bubbling, and tape marks when doing artwork.

A paint's product sheet will say what temp reducer should be used for certain temperature ranges. For example, PPG's DT 870 Reducer is a fast/medium reducer and should be used for temps around 70°F. DT885 is a little slower, and I use it for temps around 80°F to 85°F. But I also use it for cooler temps if I'm spraying a good number of coats as I want the lower coats to dry out well. Painting is mostly common sense—if I'm spraying more than just two coats of paint, I wait the maximum time in between coats to give each coat plenty of dry time before spraying the next coat.

TYPES OF AUTOMOTIVE REFINISHING PAINTS

Lacquer

Lacquer is very seldom used these days. In fact, many auto paint supply stores do not even sell it. If someone talks to you about using lacquer on your project or in your shop, think twice about using it. In fact, I have not used lacquer in over 25 years. Today's custom paints are urethane technologies. And never mix urethane and lacquer technologies. It's a formula for problems.

Single-stage Urethane

Single-stage paint, a 2K product, is urethane basecoat (not to be confused with regular 1K basecoat) that has been catalyzed with a hardener to provide quick dry, durability, chemical resistance, and chip-and-scratch resistance. These paints are usually sprayed as solid colors and are rich in resin to provide gloss and low in pigment, so they may need more coats to get total coverage.

Single-stage paint needs to dry overnight in warm temps, at least 70°F before any taping or sanding is done. They are medium-to-high solids, which means the film build or layer of paint may be fairly thick when spraying flames or graphics. This type of paint is usually used on single color paint jobs where no artwork will be done. In some cases, it can be used under the artwork as a base. In fact, the basecoat of the Trans Am hood seen in chapter 21 was done in single stage.

Single stage is thermoset (2K) paint. Thermoset resins must be sanded before more paint can be applied.

Basecoat or 1K Paints

Because most of the paint in this book has artwork on it, most of the basecoat paint seen here is done with acrylic basecoat. Basecoat is the best choice for custom paint work. Basecoats are thermoplastic resins unless a hardener is added. Now that can sound confusing, but in some instances, hardener can be added to basecoat. But this book focuses on basecoats that are not catalyzed.

Catalyzing basecoats provide a tougher film of resin and make repairs easier. But catalyzed basecoats have a strict window in which they must be recoated, and wait times for taping are increased. Thermoplastic resins reflow with solvent after they have dried. This means multiple coats can be applied on top of each other

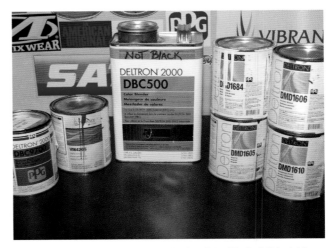

Some PPG basecoat paints from the shop's paint cabinets (left to right): Deltron DBC9700 black, a very commonly used product; Vibrance VM4205 Star Fire Orange, a specialty basecoat; DBC 500 Color Blender/clear basecoat into which pearl powders, candy toners, and metal flakes are mixed before application. On the right are a few colored mixing toners. Always know the paint system you are using. In the PPG Deltron system DBC means the paint is mixed and ready to be reduced and sprayed. DMD usually means it's just a mixing toner and needs to be mixed with other products before it's sprayed.

without having to sand for adhesion. The reducer used in the basecoat has the ability to soften the previous coat to obtain a chemical bond as long as a medium to wet coat has been applied.

Basecoats are made of urethane resins. Urethane resins have more pigment than resin. This means they give better and faster coverage but are low in gloss. They are also low in solids, which means the thickness of the paint coats is one-third less than single-stage or 2K urethane clearcoat. Because of this, they work great for doing artwork and most kinds of custom paint. The paint edge is thinner and levels out quicker when clearcoated. Custom paint tends to require more coats of paint than single-color paint jobs, which means more

Contrary to popular belief, when it comes to durability, less can be more. A paint job with 10 coats of thick paint will not be as durable as 10 coats of thin paint. The custom painter has to trick the paint surface into looking deep. The trick is to use your knowledge of paint to get great coverage but keep the coats down. For example, imagine the edge of a door: which will be more prone to chipping, a thick buildup of paint on it or a thin buildup? By using proper painting techniques when spraying a metallic or pearl base for candy, the painter can give the paint the illusion of being bottomless. This is a close-up photo of the basecoat paint done on the Firebird in chapter 10. The pearl paint was only three coats. Yet in the sun, the sparkle of the pearl flakes seems infinite.

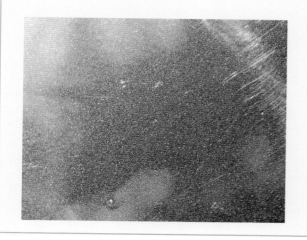

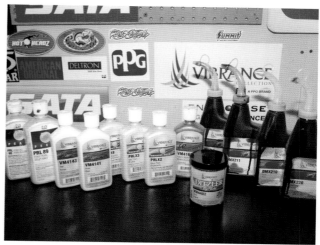

These products represent just a few of the many different PPG specialty products that can be mixed into basecoats, like PLR, Flamboyance, PLRX, Luminescence II pearl powders, Ditzler big flake, and Vibrance Radiance II candy dyes/toners.

coats of paint, and thick coats are not good when you are doing a custom paint job with 10 or more coats.

SPECIALTY PRODUCTS FOR BASECOATS

Candy dyes or concentrates, pearl powders, and metal flakes are specialty products that are added to basecoat paints to obtain a special effect. Pearl powders come in a number of differently sized and shaped particles. The effects are endless. PPG's Vibrance line features a few different kinds of pearl powders. The PLR pearls are the standard mica-type pearls used in OEM colors. They tend to have a warm side tone to them which is most noticeable over white paint.

The PLRX Crystal pearls are aluminum oxide–type pearls and are also used in OEM colors. They have a bright, crisp effect to them, and are much cleaner than mica-type pearls. For example, if you want a white pearl to look very white, a PLRX pearl would be whiter than a PLR pearl. The Miata in chapter 12 was painted with

a PLRX pearl. Flamboyance Pearls are much larger and sparkle more than PLRX pearls. They are mostly used for custom formulas.

Metal flakes come in various sizes and are much larger than any pearl or metallic. Spraying flake requires a very large nozzle in the spray gun (generally 1.7 or larger). The flakes are mixed into clear basecoat or top coat clear. They are best sprayed over a similarly colored metallic base, as it is difficult to get total coverage with metal flake paint. Chapter 13 shows how to use metal flake products.

Candy dyes or toners are added to clear basecoats to create a candy or colored transparent color. They should never be used alone without first mixing into a paint product. Chapters 10 and 12 show how to mix and use candy dyes and pearl powders.

CLEARCOATS

There are two main types of clear paint that a painter will use: clear basecoat (1K) and clear urethane (2K) topcoat. Basecoat clear or intercoat clear is not a topcoat and should never be used as one. It makes a great "wet bed" to spray first over a sanded finish before doing artwork, as it helps to eliminate overspray patterns and sand scratches. It also helps with adhesion when spraying over basecoats that have dried over 24 hours before applying more basecoat or a topcoat, as it helps the soften the surface. Mix pearl powders or candy toners/dyes in basecoat clear to create pearl or candy paint.

HIGH SOLIDS

What does *high solids* mean? High solids is a term for products that are, simply, high in solid ingredients. That means they are usually thick products that have good filling properties. For example, high build primer surfacers, which are used for leveling out areas of bodywork, are high in solids.

Clearcoat is usually mixed 1:1 with reducer. Basecoat clear is also used to protect airbrush artwork while it's in process. Do not spray heavy coats of basecoat clear. And never use it to build up and level paint edges; use a topcoat clear urethane for that.

CLEAR URETHANE

These days, there are a number of different kinds of urethane topcoat clears available. They vary from super-fast production clears to slow-drying, show-quality clears that look like glass. And depending on the clear, the dry times may be manipulated by using different hardeners and reducers. This is where P sheets come in handy—the P sheet for the clear will list the hardeners that may be used with it, plus the dry times for those hardeners. Take the time to research and find the topcoat clear that will be the best choice for your project and painting conditions. These are the PPG clear topcoats I use:

- DC2000, a very fast production clear. I use it over basecoat and as a finish clear for some projects. It buffs out great.
- DCU 2021, a slower clear with high solids. It's great for leveling out artwork and has an incredible, glass-like, show-quality finish. Another great buffing clear.
- Vibrance VC5200 is also high solids and great for leveling out artwork, as well as being a finish clear.

METAL CONDITIONER

Never leave unprotected bare metal parts sitting around or they will rust. One day they will look fine and next thing you know, there's rust everywhere. Bare metal starts to rust within 30 minutes in 50%-humidity, and the rust will not be visible when it starts. After metal parts have been sandblasted or stripped down, be sure to use a metal conditioner on them. PPG makes two products to help with this. DX 579 is a metal cleaner that cleans and neutralizes any rust. It leaves a phosphate coating on the metal to protect it. DX 520 is used after DX 579 to further protect the metal from rusting and leaves a gray, zinc-like coating. The zinc-like coating is much easier to paint over than the phosphate coating, so use both products together. Whatever you choose for a metal conditioner, be sure to get the instructions for the products and follow them closely.

EPOXY PRIMERS AND SEALERS

Bare metal should always be primed with a primer designed for painting over bare metal. Epoxy primers provide great adhesion to bare metal and give great corrosion protection. PPG's DPLV series of epoxy primers come in several tones from white to dark gray. DP50LV is a white primer while DP90LV is almost black. They are used with a catalyst, DP401LV. It's good to use a sealer in between the primer surfacer and the basecoat. Sealer helps smooth over minor imperfections and evens out the tone. This aids the basecoat in covering better. PPG recommends mixing their K36 urethane primer 2 parts to 4 parts of DCU2021 with

These are the PPG clear topcoat products that we use in my shop (left to right): Vibrance VC5200 Custom Clear and its hardener VH7990; DC2000 and its hardener DCH2015; and DBU2021 and one of its hardeners, DCX61. Note how the hardeners have red caps. This helps to identify which product is the hardener.

HOW TO AVOID PAINTING PROBLEMS

When using 2K products—products like body filler, primers, sealers, clearcoats—the best way to avoid problems is to use only the hardener or catalyst designed to go with that product. It doesn't matter if your buddy who has been painting for 15 million years tell you, "Sure, its ok to use that. I do it all the time." It may be the end of the day on a Friday, and the paint store is closed. You really need to get that job done. So you take a chance and use a hardener that goes with a different brand of paint or filler. Chances are something is going to go *very wrong*, and you will never know the real cause of the problem. If you do not have the correct hardener to go with the stuff you're using. *Stop and wait until you get the right hardener.* This is advice from a painter who has made this very mistake in her 35 years of painting and lived to tell others not to do it. It's never worth it!

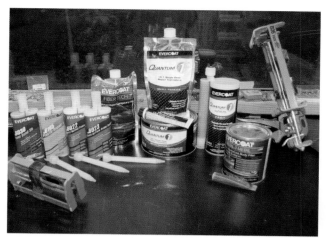

From left to right: Evercoat's 6030 Panel Bond 30, 6105 Plastic Bond, 6022 Heavy Bodied Seam Sealer, 6023 Control Flow Seam Sealer, Fiber Tech Reinforced Repair Compound Filler, Quantum 1 Single Step Body Filler, three kinds of dispensers (can, pouch, and cartridge), Metal 2 Metal metal reinforced filler, and the cartridge guns for the Quantum and the seam sealers, panel bond, and plastic repair.

2 parts DT reducer and 1 part DCX61 hardener. One coat of this is applied before basecoating. Epoxy primer can also be used. See Chapter 10 for more information.

PRIMER SURFACERS

Primer surfacers are 2K, two-part primers used for smoothing and leveling the surface. Polyester primers are very thick and are used when there is a good deal of bodywork. They are great time savers. While polyester primers are great for filling, they can be porous. When using a polyester primer, once the sanding is done, it's always a good idea to use a urethane primer over it, as urethane primers provide a better surface under basecoat. Think of polyester primer as pine and urethane primers as oak. The urethane primer is much denser and seals the polyester surface. The two products work great together.

Urethane primers come in standard and high build. Urethane primers also have great filling qualities. Follow the instructions for mixing and flash times (dry times in between coats). Primer surfacers shrink when flash times (usually 5–10 minutes) are ignored. Do not use a hardener meant for one product with a different product.

MATERIALS

This is a quick overview of some of the materials used during a painting project. Some are discussed in detail in the chapters where they are used.

Body Fillers

Good body fillers are always two-part products. Like anything, you get what you pay for, and it's always a bad idea to put cheap body filler under costly paint. Bad body filler causes a multitude of problems, and many times, those problems start to show up months after the paint is completed. A good paint job is only as good as the foundation under it. A few simple tricks will help you get the most out of the body filler products you use:

- Always knead the tube of hardener before removing the top and squeezing some out.
- Never mix in too much or too little hardener. Follow the directions for whatever product being used. What works for one product, might not work for another.
- Mix the two products thoroughly until it's all one color.
- Don't mix on cardboard as it absorbs the resin; always mix on a plastic palette or on tear-away palette sheets.
- Check the expiration date on products. The reactive chemicals in 2K products expire. When that happens, the product never gets as hard as it should.
- Give the filler applications plenty of time to dry out before applying another layer, even after sanding. I'll apply filler, sand it, then move to another section of the car and work, giving the first area plenty of time for it to get as hard as it can get before applying more filler over it.

Panel bond is easy to use. Clean and prep the metal. Install the mixing tube on the end of the two cartridge dispenser, load it into the gun, and pull the trigger. The two components mix as they run down the tube. Run a line of bond on a piece of paper until the tubes are equalized, then run a thin line of bond on both surfaces to be bonded. Brush the adhesive to a thin layer to cover the exposed metal. Clamp the parts together. The pressure should be evenly spread out. Here, wooden dowels run along the drip channel and the clamps press down on them. The dowels spread the pressure evenly along the seam. Leave the clamps in place for 1.5–2 hours.

Specialty Body and Paint Products

New specialty products hit the shelves regularly. The technology is constantly improving. Evercoat is one company that makes a wide variety of body fillers, adhesives, seam sealers, and plastic and fiberglass repair products. I use the following products in my work restoring and painting cars, trucks, and motorcycles.

When we installed the new roof on our Firebird, a long-time car restorer told us to "glue" on the new roof. He said the new panel bonding products were amazing, and he was right. The sides of the new roof were panel-bonded to the car as were various small parts like the quarter panel reinforcing plates. **Evercoat #6030 Panel Bond-30** is a two-component epoxy adhesive and can be used to bond SMC (sheet molded composite, a tech term for plastic used in auto body panels) to SMC, metal to metal, and SMC to metal. Panel Bond-30 has corrosion-inhibiting properties that eliminate the need for epoxy primer or self-etch primers. Chapter 3 has information on using panel bond.

Plastic Repair Products

New technology makes repairing plastic easier than ever. We use two products in our shop to repair plastic parts. Both can be used on most kinds of plastic. If there's a question or the plastic is severely damaged, we use a fiber-reinforced repair product. Chapter 7 has more information on how to repair plastic.

For small repairs and cracks, **Evercoat #6105 Plastic Repair-5** is a two-component epoxy repair adhesive that provides speed, incredible strength, and sandability. This fast-setting epoxy simplifies the plastic repair process by eliminating substrate identification and adhesion promoter. It's ideal for fixing tears, nicks, and gouges in plastic parts and for making other quick-fix applications.

Fiber Tech Reinforced Repair Compound Filler (#100633 from Evercoat) is what we use for repairing cracks in fiberglass and plastic. But it's also used to fill holes and repair severely damaged areas, and it works on just about anything, including metal. It's a unique repair filler formulated with a combination of Kevlar and high-tech short- and long-strand fibers. It offers superior strength and adhesion for repairing galvanized steel, aluminum, SMC, and rigid plastic body panels, such as ground effects, spoilers, running boards, fenders, and hoods. Fiber Tech is waterproof, which makes it ideal for filling weld areas, panel bond seams, and rust damage.

Seam Sealers

Seam sealer is the caulk-like stuff you see where two-piece panels of the vehicle connect. For example, that soft stuff in the drip rail of your car or truck is seam sealer. If you open the trunk of your car and look at where the trunk floor meets the wheel wells, that stuff along the corner is seam sealer. Seam sealer can be found over many of the joints in a vehicle, and anytime a welded-on panel is replaced, the old sealer must be removed and new sealer applied after the new panel is installed. Old seam sealer often cracks and chips off over time and has to be replaced.

There are two main types of seam sealer: single-component (1K) seam sealers and two-part (2K) seam sealers.

Single-component sealers come in a tube and are applied with a caulking gun. They usually have about a 7–10 minute work time before they are too hard to smooth out. They air-dry and may tend to shrink down as they dry. It can take anywhere from 2–24 hours for 1K sealer to fully cure, depending on the product used.

Two-component (2K) sealers come in a two-cartridge pack and require a special caulk gun that pressurizes both cartridges at once. They are also more expensive than the 1K seam sealers, but they are the way to go for the high-quality finishes. They are chemically curing and insoluble, resisting water, oil, fuel, thinner, and just about everything else. They have a shorter work time than 1K—5–10 minutes— and the cure time can run about four hours. They have virtually zero shrinkage, are very paintable, sand beautifully, and will probably outlast the car. Aside from the number of components, seam sealer is also available in several different types, including OEM type, control flow, self-leveling, and heavy bodied. OEM sealer can be tooled to look like seam sealer from the factory and is used on period-correct restorations. Self-leveling and control flow, like Evercoat's 6023, are great for areas like drip rails, trunk rails, and sloped areas. Heavy-bodied seam sealer, like Evercoat's 6022, is great for areas where you don't want the sealer to flow, like sealing the joint where the inner and outer wheelhouses meet so it doesn't sag. Chapter 3 has examples of using seam sealer.

Rust Preventer Paint

In a restoration, there will be times when inner structure metal that is prone to rust and may be rusting needs a protective coating. Now this is metal that will not be primed and finish-painted, but it still needs paint. POR15 is a great product for this. Chapter 3 has more information on using POR15 or rust-preventing paint.

Liquid Mask

Painters have been using liquid masking products for years. **SprayLat** is a liquid masking product that can be brushed on painted surfaces. Once it's dry, you can cut lines or shapes in it, peel the material out, and airbrush or paint on those areas. Once done, the rest of the mask can be peeled off.

MASKING MATERIALS

Here's another place where painters try to save money, but inexpensive tape and masking materials are no bargain. Cheap tape has cheap adhesive and is made of poor quality paper. Here's what happens when I use it. The tape tears apart as it's pulled up and leaves adhesive behind on the surface. Many times it does not stick well and tends to come up when air pressure from the spray gun hits it. Cheap masking paper sometime allows paint to bleed through it onto the surface of the vehicle and, depending on what is being masked, can cause damage, especially if it's applied over plastic trim.

Masking Tape

There are so many sizes and kinds of masking and automotive tapes, from $\frac{1}{16}''$ fine line to 2" heavy tape designed for using with waterborne paints. Tape for automotive paint applications is very different than what's used for painting a house. Try using house tape on a car project and watch it fly up with the first blast of air. Don't use it.

Some of the tapes and masking products used in my shop are shown here.

A number of great brands of automotive tape are available: 3M, FBS, and IP or American tape. I use a combination of all of them. Whatever you use, you will get the best result using one of these brands rather than a discount, generic brand of tape. Both 3M and IP have special tape just for use with waterborne paint products. I find that the waterborne-designed tapes are my favorites to use with solvent paint as well.

For artwork, these companies make plastic fine tape that is amazing. Some painters still prefer the traditional (crepe) tape for artwork, but many of us use the more maneuverable plastic fine-line tapes. FBS's ProBand fine line green is extremely maneuverable for laying down very tight curves when doing pinstripes and flames. Their fine line yellow is great for doing straight lines down the side of a car. But my favorite is their ProBand orange fine line; I use it for both curves and straight lines. The tapes come in widths from $\frac{1}{16}''$ to $\frac{3}{4}''$.

Masking Paper

You'll find a number of different kinds of masking paper, but it mostly comes down to two types: coated and uncoated. Coated paper has a satiny or shiny coating on it that adds an additional barrier to keep the paint from bleeding through it. If a good deal of paint is getting layered on the paper, it's better to use the coated paper. Summit Racing's Refinish Paper Logs (SUM-UPP18) are lint free and come in several different lengths. 3M makes some great masking films, as does Evercoat. 3M's Scotch Bold Brick and Scotchblock Bold are two of my favorites. I go through a lot of Evercoat's polycoated blue paper when I'm clearcoating.

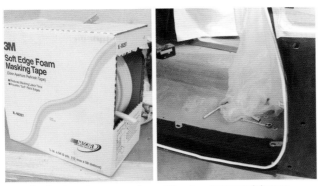

3M soft edge foam tape comes in a roll in a box dispenser. It has an adhesive strip along one side and can be rolled along door jams, trunk jams, hood jams, and any tight places that need to be taped off. It's the quickest way to mask off an interior when you're painting a car.

The ProMasker from FBS is a great product that combines the both masking paper and tape, and it's a real time saver. It comes in a refillable dispenser. One of my favorite timesavers and a must for anyone painting a car is 3M's Soft Edge Foam Tape. Many times during painting I would have given anything for a roll of this.

Overspray Plastic Sheeting

While tape and masking paper are used right along the edge of the paint area, overspray plastic sheeting is for use everywhere else, like over tires, engines, suspensions, and any large areas you need to protect from overspray. Do not use the plastic from a home improvement store. Plastic sheeting, like Evercoat's Plastic Sheeting, is designed to cling to a surface and comes in a variety of different sizes.

SANDPAPER AND ABRASIVE PRODUCTS

You can never have enough sandpaper when doing a project. Sandpaper comes in sheets, rolls, and discs. Some are better for dry sanding and some are better for wet sanding, and some are good for both. The chapters throughout the book show what kind of sandpaper or abrasive products I used with each project. Take

Plastic sheeting is a must when doing painting projects that do not involve disassembling the vehicle.

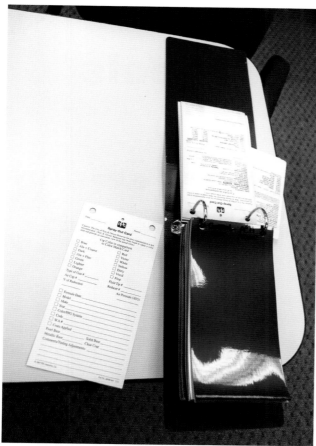

Here's a low cost way to save time, material, and your sanity. Get some sprayout test cards! They are a great way to test and get familiar with using unfamiliar products, testing and trying out new colors, and designing and testing custom colors. Once you have a master color sprayout card for a color being you use, write the name, color code, formula, and any other info on the back of the card. PPG even sells a handy little binder to keep them in. It's a great way to keep track of your colors.

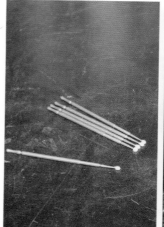

Touch up applicators are another one of the handiest things to ever come into a paint shop. These little guys make it easy to apply just a tiny touch of paint exactly where it's needed. For example, you're about to go into the spray booth and clearcoat the car. As you're tacking it, you spot a tiny sand-through on the end of a panel. Most of the time, you can just dab some of the color onto one of these applicators and touch up the sand-through. By the time the tacking is finished and the clear is mixed up and ready to spray, the touched up area is dry and good to go.

CLEANING PAINT FROM YOUR SKIN

Never, ever use lacquer thinner to remove paint from your skin! It is very hard on your skin as well as extremely bad for your health. In addition to causing skin irritation and maybe chemical burns, the solvents in thinner will absorb through your skin and pass into your body. Painters have become poisoned by this practice and have even gotten cirrhosis of the liver. Instead, use hand/skin cleaning products made especially for this task. 3M's Paint Buster is a nontoxic cleaner and is great at removing any kind of paint or auto body product from your skin. 5Star's Extreme Hand Cleaner is another product to remove paint without damaging your skin or your health. To remove hardened body filler that won't "chip" off of your hand, scrub the dried filler on your dry (not wet) hands with one of these cleaners. It will soften the filler enough for you to scrape it off your skin.

the time to get good quality sandpaper, and it will do a better job than the discount brands and last longer. Summit Racing has a great selection, and you can order it online and have it delivered. Plus, their prices are budget friendly. Their paint and body catalog is an awesome resource and makes it easy to look over the different kinds of paper and pick out the best ones for your project and budget.

PAINT MIXING CUPS

Mixing cups are another item you don't think of until you need them. Mixing paint at the correct ratios is critical. And these days, some mixing cups are also spray cups and fit on spray guns. This combination saves a step and time. SATA's RPS (Rapid Preparation System)

cup system gives the painter great efficiency, enhances a shop's productivity, and reduces the use of cleaning solvents. These cups have mix ratios for almost any amount of paint right on the side of the cups.

If a spray gun cup system is not in your budget, Evercoat makes a line of affordable mixing cups that come in a variety of sizes. They too have mix ratios on the sides to make it easy to mix the paint in whatever ratio is needed.

Chapter 2
Understanding the Tools and Equipment

For the gearhead, there is nothing quite like shopping for tools. It's like being a kid in a toy store. This chapter covers the tools that will be needed for prepping, bodywork, and painting. Some tools are essential; some tools make a task easier and save time.

You get what you pay for. Many years ago, I used bargain tools and whatever cheap stuff I could find. The thing about that $50 spray gun? It may work great for a month, but every time I bought one, it would die right in the middle of a paint job. With paint materials costing hundreds of dollars and when missing a paint window means the entire job might be ruined, what did that "bargain" gun really cost? Too much. Use common sense. If you cannot afford new, look around and buy very good quality used equipment. For example, you could buy a used spray gun and then buy a new nozzle set to go on it. A cheap tool will let you down at the time you can least afford it. Figure out your budget and plan accordingly. A good collection of tools is built up over time.

The SATA spray guns pictured here are the actual spray guns I use. They are not show guns. From left to right: my favorite basecoat gun, a 4000 HVLP with a WSB nozzle; a 4000 RP with a 1.3 tip that I use for transparent basecoats like candy and pearl; my 4000 RP 1.2, which features custom anodized artwork by Leah Gall and which I dedicate to spraying clearcoat; and a Minijet 3000B HVLP, which is used for spot repairs, door jams, and almost all of the motorcycle painting done in my shop.

SPRAY GUNS AND HOW THEY WORK

I didn't always use good spray equipment and my paintwork suffered because of it. I added hours and stress onto projects that could have gone much smoother and been easier had I used good quality spray guns. A number of different kinds of spray guns are available on the market, but I'm going to break them into the two main groups: HVLP and reduced pressure (RP) spray guns.

HVLP Spray Guns

HVLP spray guns are the most commonly used spray guns on the market. They produce a good finish and produce less overspray than reduced pressure, or RP, spray guns. Due to the way they spray, they require more air pressure. They need 15 cfm (cubic feet of air per minute) at the gun. What does this mean? It means you need a healthy compressor to keep up with them, which we'll learn about later in this chapter.

HVLP spray guns have great transfer efficiency (percent of materials that actually stick to the surface instead of going up in overspray), so there's less overspray, which means less wasted paint going into the air. I find I use about 20%–30% less paint when I use an HVLP spray gun. Less overspray also means less paint and solvent for the painter to breathe and absorb into his or her body. This is especially important for DIYers who are using homemade spray booths as they do not have the air flow of a commercial paint booth. In fact, the only time I don't use HVLP spray guns is when I'm spraying candy or clearcoat paint.

Reduced Pressure (RP) Spray Guns

For the average collision or custom painter, RP spray guns are primarily used for spraying candy and clearcoat as they have great atomization. Atomization is what happens to the paint when it hits the air at the air cap of the paint gun. Better atomization means smaller, finer droplets of paint. Better atomization equals a very evenly dispersed coat of paint.

The SATAjet 4000 B, perfect in every detail

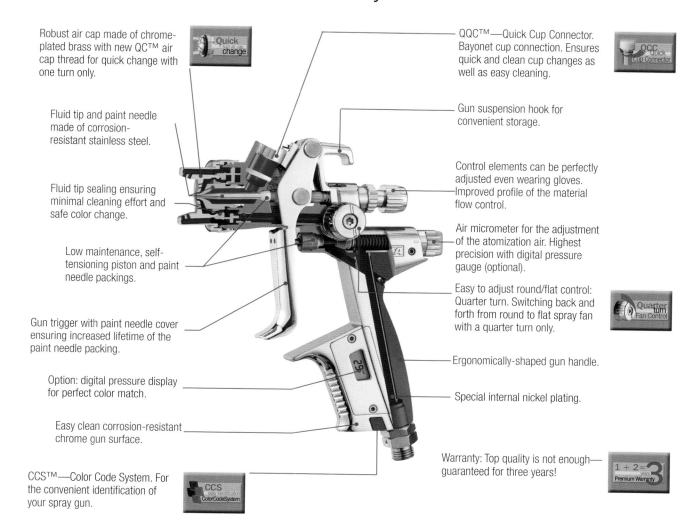

Robust air cap made of chrome-plated brass with new QC™ air cap thread for quick change with one turn only.

Fluid tip and paint needle made of corrosion-resistant stainless steel.

Fluid tip sealing ensuring minimal cleaning effort and safe color change.

Low maintenance, self-tensioning piston and paint needle packings.

Gun trigger with paint needle cover ensuring increased lifetime of the paint needle packing.

Option: digital pressure display for perfect color match.

Easy clean corrosion-resistant chrome gun surface.

CCS™—Color Code System. For the convenient identification of your spray gun.

QQC™—Quick Cup Connector. Bayonet cup connection. Ensures quick and clean cup changes as well as easy cleaning.

Gun suspension hook for convenient storage.

Control elements can be perfectly adjusted even wearing gloves. Improved profile of the material flow control.

Air micrometer for the adjustment of the atomization air. Highest precision with digital pressure gauge (optional).

Easy to adjust round/flat control: Quarter turn. Switching back and forth from round to flat spray fan with a quarter turn only.

Ergonomically-shaped gun handle.

Special internal nickel plating.

Warranty: Top quality is not enough—guaranteed for three years!

This illustration shows a state of the art SATA 4000 HVLP spray gun and its features. The blue areas on the gun show the air passages. The red areas show the fluid passages. The air comes in from the bottom of the handle, travels up through the body of the spray gun, and is adjusted along the way. Then the air travels through passages in the air cap at the front of the gun. These passages shape the air into an adjustable spray pattern. As the air is released from the outlets on the air cap, it picks up the fluid and together they form a paint pattern.

TRANSFER EFFICIENCY

While SATA's HVLP and RP spray guns both provide over 65% transfer efficiency, a number of other things that can affect that efficiency. The exact number varies upon viscosity, air pressure, gun distance, and the object being painted. Low viscosity products typically have lower transfer efficiency. Higher air pressure reduces transfer efficiency. Painting too far away creates far more overspray and reduces transfer efficiency, and objects that are large and flat will show higher efficiency than objects like a bike frame or a car's grill or trim pieces.

Many painters who can only afford one spray gun tend to use the RP. The RP is a great all-purpose gun. Besides laying down a smooth, wet coat of clear, it works great as a basecoat gun, spraying solids, pearl, and metallics with ease. The downside is they produce more overspray than an HVLP and use more paint. One advantage for the DIYer is that they require less cfm (about 10 CFM), meaning they do not need as big of an air compressor as an HVLP gun requires.

MINI SPRAY GUNS

Mini spray guns are smaller versions of the big spray guns. They produce a smaller, very efficient spray pattern and are perfect for painting motorcycle parts. They require far less air than a big spray gun; a SATA Minijet HVLP only needs 4.1 cfm. That means it can be run off a small compressor.

The SATAminijet 4400 B, mirrors the unique design of the standard size SATAjet 4000 B high performance spray gun is available in both HVLP and RP technology. Mini guns are also great for painting door and trunk jams. Their small sizes make it easier to work in tight areas where it would be difficult to maneuver a larger spray gun. And they are great for making spot repairs. SATA even has a special nozzle set up for doing spot repairs. The special SR nozzle sets come in sizes 0.8 SR, 1.0 SR, 1.2 SR and 1.4 SR for the HVLP. Most common size is the 1.2 SR HVLP. In this book, Minijet spray guns are used on a number of projects.

PRIMING GUNS

If you already have a good spray gun, why get a different gun for spraying primer? Because primer paints are much thicker than basecoat and clearcoat paints. That means they need larger nozzle openings than the 1.1 to 1.4 nozzles sizes that are found on the average spray gun. If you try to use a small size, say less than 1.7, for primer surfacers, it's very inefficient because the primer comes out of the gun in a spattery, coarse, thin, dry pattern. Primer is best applied in wet, even coats. Nozzle sizes 1.4 work great for applying sealers, epoxy, and some thin viscosity urethane primers. Most high build primer surfacers use 1.7 to 1.9 nozles. For spraying thicker polyester primer, choose a nozzle size of 2.5 These nozzle sizes are too big for using with basecoat and clearcoat. Basecoat and urethane clear are not designed to be sprayed that heavy, and you would be inviting many problems, including runs, sags, and solvent popping.

SETTING UP A SPRAY GUN AND PAINTING
How to Set the Air Pressure for the Spray Gun

One big mistake painters make is to set the gun pressure at the gun. By doing this, the air passage through the gun or gun regulator becomes smaller as the pressure is adjusted down. This means there is a high volume of air passing through the hose and into the gun. As it hits that small adjusted opening it speeds up, and by the time it's coming out of the spray gun, it's moving too fast to work effectively with the paint coming out of

These are my priming guns for urethane primers and sealers: the SATAjet 100 BF HVLP 1.7 nozzle, and for thick polyester primers, a SATAjet 100 BP with a 2.5 nozzle. Note how much smaller the air horns are on the jet 100 BP, the polyester spray gun. The polyester gun does not atomize the paint like the other guns. It produces a very sharp-edged fan spray pattern.

This picture shows the big differences between the various kinds of SATA spray guns when it comes to nozzle and air cap sizes and configurations. Note the difference in the amount of space between the nozzle tip from the 4000 RP and the 4000 HVLP. The primer guns are on the right; the jet 100 BF is the urethane primer and sealer gun. The jet 100 BP is the polyester gun, and the opening on it is huge compared to the jet 100 BF.

the gun. The best thing to do is open up the air adjuster or spray regulator on your gun, go over to the main regulator on the wall, pull back the trigger of the gun, and then adjust the pressure at that big regulator.

Using too much air or a flow of air that is too fast can override the regulator cap on the gun and overdry the coat of paint. So instead of laying down a nice flat coat of clear, the air forces the paint to hit the surface too hard, and the result is a light or worse orange peel surface. If the air had been traveling at the proper speed, the paint would be landing correctly on the surface and flowing out smooth.

For example, if you have 70 pounds of air coming up the gun, lower it to 40 at the main regulator. Some air pressure will be lost as the air travels through the length of the hose. Leave yourself about 5–10 pounds of air to play with at the gun. Then you can fine tune the pressure at the gun. It's like trying to breathe through

LARGER HIGH-FLOW FITTINGS VERSUS STANDARD (SMALLER) FITTINGS

Here's a low-cost way to improve the way your paint guns spray. I just explained why it's better to have larger openings for the air pressure to travel though the gun. But it also helps to have high-flow fittings in the spray gun. Larger openings equal better and more efficient air flow. You can be doing everything right and still have a poor paint job simply because of the fittings. Adding high-flow quick disconnect fittings to your air hose and spray guns usually cost less than $25.

WATCH THE PRESSURE

The max air pressure for an HLVP is 29 psi. For an RP, the max pressure is 32 psi. But that doesn't mean you have to use that much pressure, and in many cases, it's detrimental to use the max. It's better to use less. Many painters use 25 psi for an HVLP and 26 psi for the RP. In fact, those are the numbers I use. For hotter or dryer areas, manufacturers recommend setting the pressure even lower.

a coffee stirrer as opposed to breathing through a soda straw. Keep the adjusters on the gun as open as possible. This will give your gun an effective spray pattern and the gun will spray better.

GUN DISTANCE

Using the spray gun at the correct distance from the panel is critical, and doing this one thing will improve a paint job and make it easier. Having the spray gun at the spot where your atomization energy is perfect means better transfer efficiency. It cuts material losses, and everything improves. The recommended distance for most PPG products with a SATA HVLP or RP is 5-7 inches. The closer you are, the faster your gun's speed can be.

Holding the gun too close:

- loads solvent rich material on the surface, which provides poor film build,
- traps solvents that can lead to die back and solvent popping, and
- slows dry and cure times.

Holding the gun too far:

- loses too much material in overspray and in-flight solvent loss,

- dries the paint as it travels through the air to the surface for a dry, rough, bumpy film build,
- yields insufficient film build, and
- may require more coats to cover.

WALL OF AIR PRESSURE TEST

Here's a quick and easy way to see exactly how close the spray gun should be to the surface being painted. Every paint gun has a wall of air. To find it, have the spray gun set up with the amount of air pressure you'll be using to paint. Have the pattern set at the pattern being used. Now hold your hand about 2 feet in front of the spray gun and pull back all the way on the trigger. Move your hand forward until you start to feel a wall of air. The force of the air will be firm and evenly distributed over the surface of your hand. This is the optimum distance for painting—the distance between the spray gun and the surface, and is between 5 and 7 inches, in HVLP or RP.

CLEANING THE SPRAY GUN

Here's one of the easiest and simplest way to avoid painting problems. Take the time to clean your spray gun after you are finished painting. My spray guns get a good deal of use, and my ability to pay my bills depends on how well my equipment works. Each minute I spend working out spray gun problems is a minute that costs me money.

I find that not immediately cleaning my equipment after painting causes many of the problems that happen when I paint. SATA sells a complete gun cleaning kit (#64035) with soft brushes, cleaning needles, and gun lube. Each time you are finished painting, take a few minutes and remove the needle, air cap, and nozzle. Use soft brushes to clean them as well as the paint passages in the gun itself. Blow out the cleaned paint passages in the gun and the parts with air. Use a cleaning needle to clear out any blocked air passages in the air cap. Be sure to clean any paint buildup in the tip and tip opening on the air cap. Lightly lubricate the needle, spring, and

continued on page 26

SPRAY GUN ADJUSTMENT AND AIR PRESSURE

Creating test spray patterns is the best way to learn how your gun sprays, and knowing how it sprays will help you get the most of out of it. Use some black paint and tape up a few pieces of white masking paper. Turn the air cap on the gun 90°, and then intentionally spray too much paint. Depress the trigger until the paint begins to run down from the pattern. By looking at the runs you can tell how much paint is being applied across the length of the pattern and how even the flow is.

Too much air pressure yields a pattern that is narrow in the middle. So the first thing to do is to find the right air pressure for the spray gun.

Spray a test pattern and look at the edge of the pattern at the droplet size. Big droplets like this mean the air pressure is too low. The air pressure here was 7 psi at the gun. You never want to run your gun at too low a pressure or with too much air pressure.

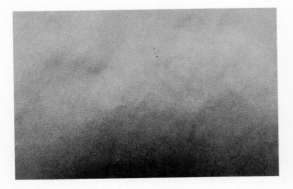

The pressure was turned up to 20 psi, and now the droplets are much finer. The gun is atomizing much better, which is why it's good to know the gun you're working with. Know the manufacturer's recommendations and use them as a starting point.

A HANDY TOOL FOR SPRAY GUNS

The SATA Cert is a pretty cool tool for keeping track of how your spray gun is operating. Using the SATA Cert monthly helps to see if your spray guns are operating at the optimum level, and it also helps to determine if they are developing any problems. The SATA Cert comes in a large binder that holds a pad of specially coated and calibrated tear-off sheets to create reference and control spray patterns. The binder mounts on a wall or spray booth. The current spray reference pattern slides into a handy transparent sleeve on the front of the binder, so it's easy to check the new pattern against the last to see if your gun has changed. There's also a single sheet holder that mounts inside the spray booth.

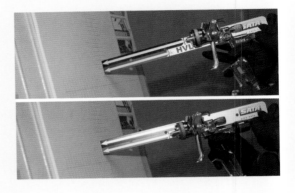

The SATA Cert comes with a spray distance marker to maintain the correct spray distance when creating spray patterns with measurements for both RP and HVLP spray guns.

Anytime a spray gun is serviced or parts are replaced, the SATA Cert makes it easy to keep track of knowing exactly how your gun is spraying.

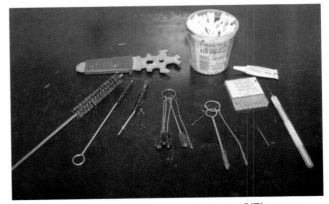

I use a number of tools to keep my spray guns clean: a SATA spanner wrench that is specially sized for the spray gun parts, round brushes of various sizes, cotton swabs, broaches or cleaning needles with a handle to hold them, and gun lube.

SPRAY GUN PATTERNS

Spray gun technique and its relationship to atomization of products is often understood by many automotive painters. Proper gun technique combines four factors: gun angle, speed, path, and distance. Before spraying paint with the gun, it's important to adjust the spray pattern properly and know the causes of improper spray patterns.

The proper spray gun pattern for solvent-borne paint is elliptical in shape (8 to 10 inches in length) with an even amount of material across the surface. Turn the gun's air cap to get a sideways pattern and pull back on the trigger long enough to make a series of runs. Your pattern should look like this when an even amount of paint hits the surface.

Heavy in the middle could mean too little air flow (not enough air pressure).

Divided or narrow in the middle could mean too much air flow (too much air pressure).

Too much paint at the top or bottom could mean a restriction in the fluid flow. Usually something in the air cap, fluid needle, or nozzle tip. Clean and retest.

A crescent-shaped pattern could mean a restriction at the fluid needle, nozzle tip, or air cap on one side. Clean and retest.

For waterborne basecoat, the test pattern should be 8 to 10 inches long and rectangular in shape. Test the pattern the same way as solvent-borne; pull back the trigger until a series of runs drips from the pattern.

Proper waterborne and solvent patterns after setting proper fluid flow.

Pressure Loss with 100 psi Inlet Pressure		1/4″ ID	5/16″ ID	3/8″ ID
35 Foot Hose	15 CFM	35 psi	12.6 psi	4.2 psi
	25 CFM	87 psi	31.5 psi	10.5 psi
50 Foot Hose	15 CFM	50 psi	18 psi	6 psi
	25 CFM	*	45 psi	15 psi

Check out this chart. Smaller diameter air hoses will result in significant pressure drop.

Minimum Pipe Size Recommendations

Compressor Size	Compressor Capacity	Main Air Line	Minimum Pipe Diameter
1-1/2 & 2 HP	6 to 9 CFM	Over 50 ft	3/4″
3 & 5 HP	12 to 20 CFM	Up to 200 ft	3/4″
		Over 200 ft	1″
55 to 10 HP	2 to 40 CFM	Up to 100 ft	3/4″
		100 to 200 ft	1-1/4″
		Over 200 ft	1-1/4″
10 to 15 HP	40 to 60 CFM	Up to 100 ft	1″
		100 to 200 ft	1-1/4″
		Over 200 ft	1-1/2″

Under no circumstances are we advising that correct air line piping reduces contaminates so much that you do not need a filtering system. A point of use filter is still strongly recommended.

Think about how big the pipe diameter should be based on the size of the air compressor and how long the main feed line will be.

This is the setup I use. It's a 3-step filtration system with a water and oil separator that also removes larger debris, a second filter that removes particles down to 0.01 microns, and a third charcoal filter that further cleans the air for use with fresh-air-supplied respirators.

Continued from page 23

material control threads with SATA High Performance gun lube (#48713). SATA has a video on its website that shows exactly how to clean a spray gun.

AIR HOSES

All air hoses are not created equal. For the most efficient and optimum painting, get a ⅜ ID (inner diameter) hose. If your hose is not ⅜ on the inner part of the hose then you are starving your gun for air flow. Spend a little more and get a good quality air hose.

FILTERING AND REGULATING SYSTEMS

You have to filter and regulate the air coming from the compressor. At the very least, a painter needs a good water separator and air regulator. It's best to have at least 25–50 feet of air line between the compressor and water separator. The air coming out of the compressor is hot, and as it cools condensation forms. You want the air to be as cool as possible when it reaches the water separator so the separator can do its job. If hot air gets past the separator, then condensation will form and the spray gun will spray water and harm the paint. Don't try to paint with just an air line from the compressor to the spray gun—some compressors come with regulators built into them. Make sure to get another one along with a water separator and set them up properly.

AIR COMPRESSORS

Chances are your spray gun is not the only piece of equipment that will require compressed air. Grinders, sanders, and impact wrenches all require air. For a small shop, it's great to have a two-stage unit with a 60-gallon tank. And these days, they are more affordable than you might think. For the DIYer, shop around and try to find a compressor with good horsepower and a decent-sized storage tank that puts out a minimum of 10 cfm. Also remember to check if the compressor is 110v or 220v.

Many shops keep their compressors outside because they can be loud. If you choose to keep the compressor outside of the garage, make sure there is a roof over it, and if you choose to build a shed around it, make sure there is adequate ventilation so the compressor does not overheat. And remember to drain the water from the compressor twice a month. There's a small drain at the bottom of the tank. Check and change the compressor oil as needed.

continued on page 31

AIR SYSTEM DIAGRAM

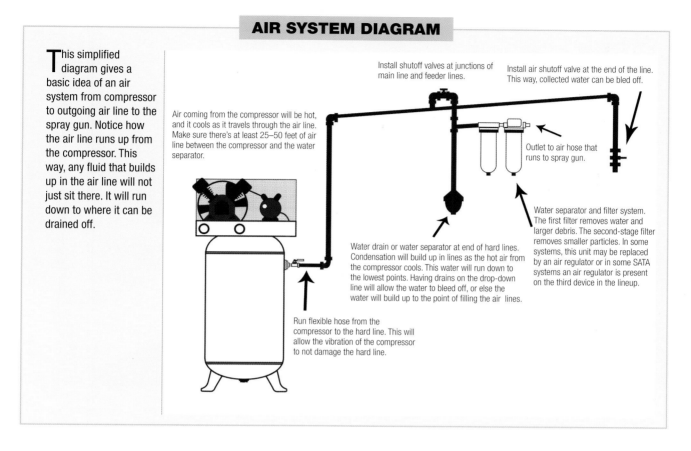

This simplified diagram gives a basic idea of an air system from compressor to outgoing air line to the spray gun. Notice how the air line runs up from the compressor. This way, any fluid that builds up in the air line will not just sit there. It will run down to where it can be drained off.

Air coming from the compressor will be hot, and it cools as it travels through the air line. Make sure there's at least 25–50 feet of air line between the compressor and the water separator.

Install shutoff valves at junctions of main line and feeder lines.

Install air shutoff valve at the end of the line. This way, collected water can be bled off.

Outlet to air hose that runs to spray gun.

Water separator and filter system. The first filter removes water and larger debris. The second-stage filter removes smaller particles. In some systems, this unit may be replaced by an air regulator or in some SATA systems an air regulator is present on the third device in the lineup.

Water drain or water separator at end of hard lines. Condensation will build up in lines as the hot air from the compressor cools. This water will run down to the lowest points. Having drains on the drop-down line will allow the water to bleed off, or else the water will build up to the point of filling the air lines.

Run flexible hose from the compressor to the hard line. This will allow the vibration of the compressor to not damage the hard line.

TOOLS FOR PAINTING, BODYWORK, AND PREP

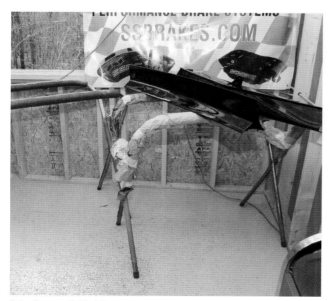

Astro Pneumatic Tool Company portable work stands (#557003) have many uses, including panel stands for painting and part holders for fabrication and prep. Lay a board across them for a large work surface or to create a table for setting up small parts when painting.

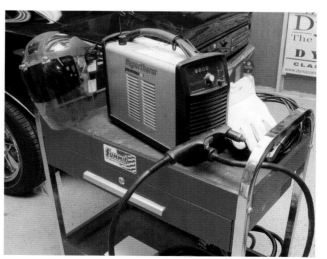

Here are two of my favorite tools in the shop. My Hypertherm Powermax45 Plasma Cutting System is very portable, easy to use, and easy to store when not in use. The cords are long, and the torch reaches just about anywhere on a car or truck without moving the unit. A Hypertherm tinted face shield and Hypertherm gloves are hanging on the unit. Never use a plasma system without wearing eye protection. The system is sitting on a Summit Racing Shop Cart (#SUM-900089), my second favorite tool in the shop and easily my most versatile piece of equipment. I use it for everything from holding bodywork supplies and tools to an airbrush station to a plasma or welding cart and more.

If you are doing any metal fabrication a TIG or MIG welder is a must, and these days good quality welders are very affordable. This is my Miller Diversion 180 TIG Welder. It's another great tool that doesn't take up much space in the shop and is easy to store when not in use. It has a hand control and an optional foot control (look under my right foot). The cords on the welder are pretty long and make it easy to move around the car when welding. Under the car is a Steiner Industries Velvet Shield welding blanket. It's protecting the painted floor of the shop from any dripping hot metal.

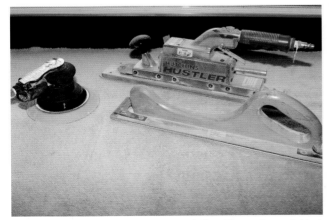

Having air tools for bodywork saves so much time. The most essential tool is a DA sander. Having an air board or straight-line sander will also shave hours off the average time for bodywork on an automotive project. From left to right are a Summit Racing DA sander (SUM-DA089) and a Hutchins Model 2000 Hustler straight-line sander. For finish bodywork sanding on flat surfaces, a Hutchins 5502 Speed File Sanding Board works great.

Some of the most used air tools in my shop are the right-angle die grinders. At times there will be two grinders going at once. My CP Compact 90° angle die grinder (CP9106Q-B) is a multipurpose tool. It can be used as a grinder/sander by placing a 2˝ or 3˝ backing pad with arbor on it. The sanding pads for the grinder come in two styles, aluminum oxide (sanding) and fibered ceramic (scuffing), and a variety of grits from very coarse to super fine. You can also insert a cutoff wheel arbor and use it with cutoff wheels. Always wear face protection when using a die grinder. I also use a CP Heavy Duty Belt Sander ⅜˝ (CP9779). It's great at getting into tight places where other tools won't fit. In fact, it fits into places I can't even hand sand.

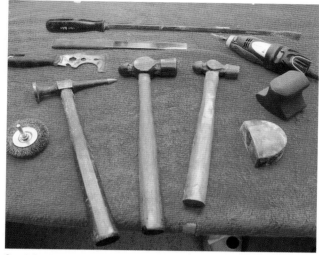

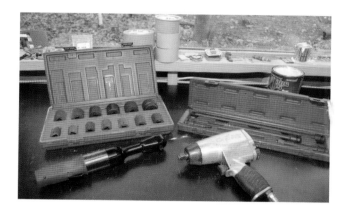

Style-Line's Soft-Sanders are flexible sanding blocks that come in six different shapes in three different densities that vary in firmness yet are flexible enough to bend around shapes and corners and compress into places that are hard to sand. They come in 5″, 8″, 11″, 16″, 20″, and 24″ lengths. They can be used wet or dry and have their own sandpaper, which features an adhesive backing.

Specialized hand tools are a must and very affordable. Starting at the top, a pry bar comes in very handy for getting panels into place. If you are doing any kind of fabrication work a Steck Seambuster (the blue-handled tool) will be your best friend. It can also be used for scraping and prying. A Dremel tool is great for getting into really tiny places. Wire brushes are also a must-have. Body hammers and dollies work great for flattening out bumpy metal, and ball peen hammers are great for shrinking metal, taking out dents, and just about anything else.

Impact tools are a must in shops, but they are also very afforable for the DIY garage. In our shop we have a Summit Racing Pro impact wrench (SUM-GN25820), Sunnex Tools impact sockets (SXT-2650), Sunnex impact extensions (SXT-2500), and the brutal cool Chicago Pneumatic ⅜″ quiet impact ratchet (CP7830Q).

These next two pieces of equipment get a real workout in my shop. The Summit Racing pit mat (SUM-G1028) is the best $17.97 you could ever spend for your shop. The Omega Lift (#91000) is awesome. It rolls extremely smoothly, is incredibly stable no matter where you sit on it, and adjusts from a creeper position to a rolling work seat.

Getting the vehicle off the ground and keeping it securely in place once its lifted is not something people think about until it needs to be done. Project vehicles take a pounding as they are worked on. One of worst things that can happen in a project is for a car to fall off a jack or jackstands. It's a safety issue. Here, the Firebird is securely supported by eight Craftsman 3-ton high lift jackstands (SHC-950159) as a Summit Racing low profile floor jack (SUM-G1020)—the best floor jack I've ever used—lifts the new floorpan in place. The difference between a cheap jack and a good one is how easy you can control it when it's lowered. Twist the handle on a cheap jack, and many of them tend to come down too quick. Good quality jacks are fine-tuned to allow you to lower the car as slowly or as much as you want.

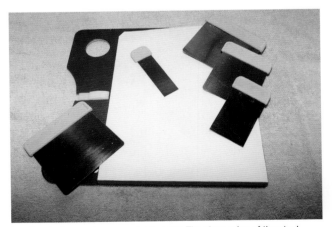

I prefer steel spreaders over plastic ones. The clean edge of the steel spreader gives a much smoother flow out of filler. But steel spreaders must be cleaned immediately after use; the filler should not be allowed to dry on them. I also like Eastwood body filler mix boards (#31273) for mixing filler rather than mixing on pieces of cardboard as the cardboard can soak up the epoxy in the filler.

Buffing equipment is another one of those tools you don't think about it until you need them. From left to right: Meguiar's dual-action polisher #G110 with a Meguiar's #W8207 foam pad, the FLEX XC 3401 rotary polisher with a Meguiar's #WWHC7 wool pad, a Meguiar's sanding backing pad (#E-7200), and brushes used for cleaning and conditioning the pads.

The SATA Fresh Air System is the best choice when using catalyzed paints. It's lightweight and easy to set up. A two-outlet manifold attaches to a wall-mounted air pressure regulator; then, simply hook up the spray gun hose to one and the air system air hose to the other. The hose runs to a belt unit with a carbon filter that blows air through a hose and into the hood. The face shield has replaceable tear-off sheets. When painting a car, the painter can spend a good deal of time—sometimes hours—in the booth, and without a fresh air hood, you can feel pretty awful afterward. A fresh air system is perfect for painters who do not have good air flow in their paint area.

Continued from page 26

SAFETY EQUIPMENT
Respirators

Never paint without some kind of respirator. A standard respirator is what most painters wear when spraying non-catalyzed paints (paints that do not require a hardener). Yet, if the paint area does not have good air flow, an air-supplied respirator or fresh air system is the best choice. But an air-supplied respirator is the best and only choice for spraying catalyzed paint applications. These days, fresh air systems are very affordable and simple to set up.

Always wear eye protection when painting or using paint chemicals. Paint does not have to splash on your face to be absorbed through the eyes; the return blast of air against a surface can deflect paint chemicals into the eye. And never, ever grind metal without wearing eye or even total face protection like a face shield.

When using a plasma system, it's mandatory to wear a tinted face shield like a Hypertherm face shield (#127103). The shade on the Hypertherm Face Shield flips up, can be removed, and is used for grinding too. Always wear gloves when using plasma, like the Hypertherm leather cutting gloves (#127169) seen earlier in this chapter.

After 20 years of using a traditional welding helmet, I finally used an auto-darkening helmet and I was hooked. I use a Miller Digital Elite Fury (#256158). Miller Welding's Digital Elite Series are lightweight, super easy to adjust, and the settings on this helmet are awesome. I wear Miller's Arc Amour (#249178) TIG gloves.

Always wear disposable gloves when painting or when using paint, prep, or cleaning chemicals. These chemicals will easily and quickly absorb into your skin. My favorite gloves are SAS Safety (#66518) Raven powder-free disposable nitrile gloves. They are solvent resistant and have a textured surface, which makes it easier to grip and pick up things.

Chapter 3
Restoring a Hot Rod: Prep, Bodywork, and Priming

It all looks so easy on TV. They start with a rusty hulk, and by the end of the show, it's a pristine show car. And somehow, this all happens in just two weeks! That is not the reality. The car in the main focus of this chapter is a 1967 Pontiac Firebird. We had a two-person crew working on it full time, part-time help on it a few nights a week, and friends who came by and helped in the interim. After all that, it was still a brutal challenge to get it done in three and a half months. Shops who do this for a living know the reality of what it takes to do a quality restoration, and some projects can take a year to get the job done properly.

The techniques here can be used to repair dents in old sheet metal as well as imperfections in new metal. The main thing to remember in any restoration is to start with a fresh surface. Know for certain what you are working over. Don't put hours of labor into a surface that may have issues down the road.

GETTING STARTED

One advantage in our Firebird project is we knew much of the history of the car, as it's been my boyfriend's car for over 30 years. It had been involved in two accidents: one rear-end collision that tweaked the rear section of the car, and a serious hard hit to the front end that totaled the car almost 20 years ago. My boyfriend had bought back the car from the insurance company and replaced the front sub-frame and sheet metal, but the car had never made it back on the road. It sat for 15 years outdoors, rusting away. Could it be saved?

MATERIALS & EQUIPMENT

Equipment
Hypertherm Powermax45 plasma cutting system
SATA 100B spray gun
Hutchins Model 2000 Hustler straight-line sander
Chicago pneumatic right-angle die grinder
Chicago pneumatic
Summit Racing DA sander SUM-DA089
Summit Racing shop cart SUM-900089
Steiner Industries Velvet Shield welding blanket #31646
Astro Pneumatic Tool Company portable work stands #557003
Craftsman jack stands
Miller Diversion 180 TIG welder
Millermatic 211 MIG
Hutchins 5502 Speed File sanding board
Soft Sander sanding pads
Steck Seambuster
Albion B26T825 multicomponent cartridge gun
Steel spreaders
Gerson 8111P disposable dual-cartridge respirator
Hammers

Materials
PPG Deltron K38 primer surfacer
PPG Deltron K36 primer surfacer
PPG K201 catalyst

PPG DT 885 reducer
PPG DP90LV epoxy primer
PPG DP401LV hardener
SATA rapid preparation system cups/lids
Evercoat Quantum 1 Single Step Repair
Evercoat Metal 2 metal-reinforced filler
Evercoat #6022 heavy-bodied seam sealer
Evercoat #6023 control-flow seam sealer
Soft Sander 80, 100, 120, 150, 180, 220, and 320 grit sandpaper
Summit® Quick-Change sanding discs, 2″ and 3″ aluminum oxide (sanding) and fibered ceramic (scuffing)
POR 15 rust prevent paint
3M 80 grit 01816 Purple Clean Sanding Hookit Disc, 6″
3M 120 grit 01818 Purple Clean Sanding Hookit Disc, 6″
3M 150 grit 01817 Purple Clean Sanding Hookit Disc, 6″
3M 320 grit 01812 Purple Clean Sanding Hookit Disc, 6″
3M 400 grit 01811 Purple Clean Sanding Hookit Disc, 6″
American Tape orange mask and aqua mask ¾″, 1″, and 3″
RBL Pre-Treatment Cut Through Wipes
3M 64660 Scotch-Brite™ Durable Flex hand pad
3M 7447 Scotch-Brite abrasive hand pads
Gerson Blend Prep tack cloth #020008C
#8 Tek screws
SAS Safety 66518 Raven powder-free disposable nitrile gloves
Masking paper

THE NUMBER 1 RULE OF RESTORATION

What is the single biggest mistake most people make when restoring a car or motorcycle? Rushing through the project. Why is this?

- In your hurry, details will be overlooked, like not replacing a panel that should have been replaced. These mistakes come back to haunt the project. Things that would have added a day or less to the project do not get done. Trying to fix these things down the road can double or triple the time it would have taken. And in some cases, the problem cannot be fixed without setting the project back even further. And if the problem is ignored, what might have been a first place award-winning hot rod or motorcycle will come up short. And you will do anything to go back to that moment and do it correctly the first time.

- Rushing through and improperly installing a welded-on panel. Or not taking the time to properly fit the panel.

- In a multiple panel replacement, not tacking and Tek screwing the panels together on the car and properly adjusting the fitment of the panels in relation to each other before welding them on.

- Not properly preparing the metal for body and paint.

- Rushing the drying process for the filler and paint materials.

- Many more reasons, too numerous to be listed here.

- And lastly, adding untold stress to a job that could have been enjoyable. These projects can become very stressful when you are taking your time, as unexpected issues tend to pop up. Giving yourself a hard deadline makes a hard job even harder.

For our Firebird, all the frontend sheet metal was removed and will be replaced with new metal. That includes the hood, fenders, fender extensions, valance, and cowl. The front fenders were rusted through in places. Rather than take the time to cut away the rusted areas, weld in patch panels, and then spend hours doing bodywork, it made more sense to simply replace them with new parts. New replacement sheetmetal parts from Dynacorn were affordable and required little prep, and it was a great feeling not to worry about rust popping up down the road. We also needed to replace the left quarter panel, taillight panel, left door, trunk pan, and floor pan.

For stripping the car, we decided the best option was to sandblast the car. Vintage Cars of Indian Land (South Carolina) are experts at old car restoration. They usually sandblast all the bodies they work on. This leaves a nice clean surface with a great tooth to which filler can stick. Unless you are set up for blasting and have a good deal of experience, it's better to have a professional sandblast the car. We did consider renting a sandblaster, but then sand ends up all over the place and it's a mess. Refer to chapter 4 for more information on sandblasting.

The smartest and best decision was to replace the roof. Some shops will cut panels and replace only the strip along the front and rear edges of the roof. But then

This is what we are starting with. From a distance, it doesn't look too bad. The body appears pretty straight, no large rusty holes. But it's what you don't see. Look carefully. Can you tell what needs to be replaced? The problem areas? What lurks under that old paint? Take the time to find out. Try and guess which panels we will be replacing?

A RESTORATION TRUTH

These pictures are the bitter truth of restoration. There are so many little details that can get overwhelming—like small bits of decay that hide under weather stripping—and take days to replace. We found only a few bits of rot in the drip channels around the trunk, but doing it the right way meant completely replacing the channels, and that was not an easy task.

Be honest with your project, with what needs to be done. There were times when I simply just wanted to get it done and over with. But I am so glad that I faced the reality of what the project needed and then did what it took to get the job done. Don't fool yourself into taking shortcuts or not replacing panels that need to be replaced. When working on a project, think of the long term effects of taking a shortcut. It's never fun when a customer calls a year or two later and bubbles are popping up under the paint.

Shortcuts are even more painful when you know how easily the trouble could have been avoided. For instance, I did not want to replace the roof on this car. I had never done a roof and was nervous about it. But it ended up being far easier and took much less time than just patching it. And once the roof was off we found serious decay. If this rust had not been fixed, the inner framework would have been compromised, and it would have been too late to save the car. Take the extra time.

How much rust is too much rust to be simply repaired or patched? It's OK to cut and patch a few small rust holes, but when whole areas are compromised by rust, it's best to just replace the panel rather than try to patch it. This door is a perfect example. The bottom edge of the door is completely rusted through. Patching or just replacing the door skin won't work. It needed a new door as the inner structure was compromised. Before sandblasting, this rusty area could not be seen.

We removed all the glass and trim to prep the car for sandblasting. Gary Blakely of Quackt Glass came by and removed the front and rear glass. Here, he uses a cable knife to cut and separate the glass from the black strip of sealing urethane that attaches the glass to the window frames. Removing the glass for a restoration is a must.

The Firebird is back from sandblasting, and a few surprises were revealed once 46 years of paint and filler were blasted away. First and foremost was the roof. There were little holes along the edges of the front and rear window frames where water got trapped behind the window trim. Those areas started to rust and holes began to form. In the Firebird's earlier life, someone had applied plastic filler over the holes during a windshield replacement and the filler had cracked. Water seeped into the cracks.

that whole seam needs to be welded and then smoothed with bodywork. By the time it's done, the bodywork area may extend 8 inches or more from the edges of the roof. It made much more sense to simply install a new roof.

In addition to the roof, we made other unpleasant discoveries. The passenger side rear quarter had a good deal of decay along the bottom edges. The whole structure was compromised. Both of the outer wheelhouses were lined with rot along the edges of the wheel openings and needed to be replaced, as did the drip channels around the trunk opening. And there were rust holes along the bottom edge of the passenger door. We ended up replacing all but one panel on the car, welding on eight panels. The extra work added at least two weeks to the job.

PANEL REPLACEMENT AND BODYWORK

While many panels were replaced, the focus here will be on the quarter panels. The installation for panel replacement is different for each part. But the one thing they have in common is that the body dimensions and openings should be measured from various angles before the car is cut apart. Draw diagrams and carefully document the measurements. For example, when I replaced the floor pan, there were 12 different measurements I took as well as reinforcing the interior with rebar before any cutting or panel removal. For more information on sheet metal replacement and fabrication, check out the resources page at the end of the book.

After the vehicle has been sandblasted or stripped, any sand or media must be removed from the surface. For the Firebird, this meant vacuuming up any sand on the car, then blowing every crack, crevice, and hole to remove every bit of sand left on or in the car. Using an air gun and safety glasses, the entire car was blown out. This is also a good time to go over the car and check for things like debris in places like the rockers. Several pounds of sand from the sandblasting also ended up in the rockers. We estimated about 25 pounds of sand was removed from the car after sandblasting, and all of it must be removed. Much was removed as we were replacing panels. We'd hammer on the car and sand would fall out from places. The shop-vac was kept close by to quickly vacuum it up. By the time we were ready for paint, any sand that might have come loose and gotten in the paint had been removed.

Next, using a wire brush on a drill, any bits of old body filler or paint that was not removed by blasting must be wire-wheeled off the car. Now the metal must be protected from rusting. There are a number of

RESTORING A HOT ROD

REFERENCE PHOTOS

Take detailed photos of the car from every angle, and don't forget to take close-up photos as well as overall shots. These photos will be critically important as the project is progressing. You also want photos that show how panels fit together, how the gaps look, and every bit of the vehicle—even under the vehicle if you're doing floor or trunk pan work. Take photos from angles you don't think you need. It's better to have them if you need them than to have a question about that area and not have the photos.

HANDY HINT

Vehicles that are stored for years outdoors usually become storehouses for the local mouse and squirrel populations. The rocker panels on our Firebird were literally filled with nuts and other debris. The process to remove the nuts was to blow out the rockers using the access holes on each end. Point an air gun through the hole on one end and blow the debris to the other end of the rocker. Then with a long nozzle on the end of a shop vacuum, clear out the end of the rocker. We'd then repeat the process on the other end, blow the debris back, then vacuum the other end, and then repeat until most of the nuts and junk were removed. The white arrow shows the access hole on the back end of the rocker.

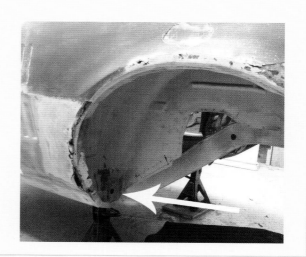

products that can be used. (Refer to chapter 1, Paint and Materials, for more information.) For this project we used RBL Pre Treatment Cut Through Wipes. You just wipe down the surface with the RLB cloth and it leaves a film that protects the surface until it's time for paint.

The next step is to pick a place in the shop where the vehicle will remain while it's being worked on.

The front sub-frame and the rear end will be removed, so the car needed to be in a place where it could be worked on without being moved. The interior of the car was measured and reinforced with rebar. Keep in mind, before any part was cut and removed, a complete set of measurements and photos were taken. Next, the floor pan was replaced with a one-piece Dynacorn full floor pan. Then the trunk floor and taillight panel were plasma-cut and a new Dynacorn full trunk pan was fitted and Tek-screwed into place.

Now came the hard part: cutting away the roof and quarter panels. This way, we were able to keep the measurement somewhat close. By keeping one quarter in place, the inner structure of the car did not sag as much. Before a quarter panel is cut off, you need to have a reference for lining up the new quarter. The door will be that reference.

Removing the spot weld ribbon is a tedious job. There are many spot welds, and some of them are in hard-to-reach areas, so you need to be innovative and

The rear quarter panel was cut away with a Hypertherm Powermax45 Plasma Cutting System. I start by using a marker to draw the cut line on the quarter, making sure to draw around the B pillar of the car and the reinforcing plate so they will not be cut into. Note how I am cutting *around* the B pillar. Then the rest of the quarter is rough cut, leaving 1″–2″ of quarter panel attached to the car. This strip or ribbon of spot welds can be removed by grinding, drilling, or plasma gouging. I used a combination of plasma gouging and grinding to remove the spot welds. This kind of work is tedious and not to be rushed through.

MULTIPANEL REPLACEMENT MUST DO!

Replacing body panels on a vehicle is like putting together a puzzle. Everything has to fit together. Never simply attach a panel, weld it on, then move on the next. The panel locations are determined by the way they fit against each other. For our Firebird, the floor pan was the only part welded in before the other panels were installed. We next replaced the trunk pan, then the left quarter, then the right quarter, then the taillight panel, then the roof. Each of these pieces were fitted and trimmed as needed, then Tek-screwed into place. We found that as we installed each panel, some of the other panels needed to be refitted. In fact, we ended up moving the trunk pan back ¼ inch. Only once everything was fit together properly and the measurements were very close to what they had been did we start welding the parts onto the car. *Do not rush through the fitting process.*

THE CHECKLIST

There are so many things to keep track of when doing a restoration. We kept a checklist all the way through this project. At the beginning and end of the day, the checklist was updated. The checklist ended up being several pages long. As we would finish one part of the job, a new checklist would be started at the beginning of each phase. This way it was easier to track and remember all the minute details.

think your way through the job. Also you must take care to only grind or cut through the first layer of metal.

Once the spot welds had been burned/melted or ground or drilled, we used a Steck Seambuster and a hammer to slice through any remaining bits of metal that were holding the ribbon in place. Just insert the Seambuster between the two layers of metal and drive it with the hammer. Any leftover metal on the remaining lower layer was ground off with a die grinder and an 80 grit abrasive pad.

With our Firebird, we attached and fitted all the rest of the panels and then started welding. The quarter panel plug welds were welded with a Millermatic 211 MIG.

Use care when welding panels in place. Tack the panel first, then recheck the measurements and fit. Then weld a plug in one place, move to a different part of the panel, and weld one there. Don't just go the down the line and weld. The metal will distort if heated too much.

After the plug welds were done, we welded the sail panel areas with a Miller Diversion 180 TIG machine. This welding was done in ½ inch stitches, allowing the metal to cool between welding each stitch. This is not the time to hurry. A few impulsive moments here can mean many hours of bodywork, as once that metal warps from the heat, nothing can change it back flat other than more hours of bodywork. Once the panels were welded in place, it was time for bodywork.

continued on page 40

Here, I'm using a feathering technique with a Hypertherm PowerMax45 Plasma system to burn away the first layer of metal around the spot weld. Before using a plasma torch for this step, it's best to practice on an old piece of car with spot welds until you feel comfortable with the technique. It requires a combination of adjusting the heat control and learning the feathering technique to remove spot welds with a plasma torch, but it saves hours of labor in a restoration like this. A spot weld drill, grinder, or cut off wheel can also be used to remove the spot welds. Here, I'm burning away the frame rail spot welds on the leftover spot weld ribbon for the trunk floor.

Look what we found under the old quarter skin: rust. The inner frame of the car is its foundation, so take the time to clean it and protect it. We ground the rust away using 80 grit abrasive pads on a grinder, then wire wheeled it, blew it off with an air gun, and wiped it clean with lacquer thinner.

Next, I brushed on a light coat of POR15 rust preventer paint. I poured a small amount of POR15 into a small container and dipped the brush into that. Do not leave the can of POR15 open as you paint and do not dip the brush into the can. Be sure to wipe away any paint that has collected on the top of the can before you put the lid back on. If there is paint in that area, it pretty much glues the lid to the can once it's dry. *Make sure not to apply paint on the areas that will be welded!* Do not brush this product on heavy. It tends to run easily. Just brush on a light coat, and it will flow out. It dries quickly, and once it's dry, it's on to stay. So make sure to clean the brush immediately after painting.

BONDING PANELS

One of the best ways to attach plates and panels is to use a panel bond adhesive. For example, the middle top section of the quarter panel is under a good deal of structural stress. To help reduce the flexing on the metal, the factory installed a reinforcing plate. This plate was panel bonded from the factory. It was removed from the old quarter and reinstalled on the new one. Care must be taken when removing plates like this so they are not damaged.

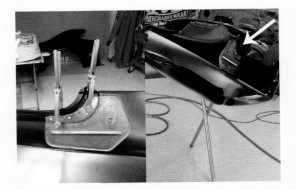

Here's the process for using panel bond:

- Wash with an all-purpose solvent cleaner.
- Remove the damaged panel and grind or sand all areas to be bonded to remove old adhesive, paint, primer, and other contaminants.
- Remove dust using compressed air and reclean with an all-purpose solvent cleaner.
- Straighten damaged metal, dry-fit the parts, and use a marker to indicate the exact location of any small parts or plates.
- Have clamps nearby and adjust them to fit the parts.
- Equalize the cartridge and gun out a bead of adhesive the length of the static mix tip to check for proper mix.
- Apply a bead of adhesive to all bare metal surfaces of both pieces to be bonded.
- Brush the adhesive to a thin coat to cover all exposed bare metal surfaces.
- Apply a bead of the adhesive to the frame or new panel.
- Clamp the new panel in its proper position.
- Do not remove the clamps for 1.5–2 hours.
- Remove all excess adhesive from the seams.

HOW TO SAND FILLER

When working with filler, only work on one area at a time. And then stay close by after the filler is applied. Don't wander off and start on something else while it dries; you'll want to keep checking on the hardness of the filler. The filler cure time will reach a sweet spot, when it's not rock hard but soft enough to sand easily without clogging up the sandpaper. Grab a piece of 80 grit, and when it starts to harden, give it a sand with the paper. If it clogs the paper, wait a few moments and try again. Rough sand and shape the filler this way. If you don't use a DA or are working in an area where a DA isn't suitable—for example, a round area like a motorcycle frame—this method is a lifesaver. Most of the material can be removed quickly in this way. It will harden as you're sanding. By the time it's starting to feel rock hard, most of the shaping work is done. Never apply filler all over the vehicle or parts at one time or you'll wear yourself out sanding rock hard filler.

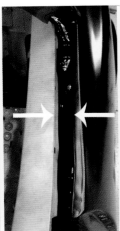

We prepped the quarter panel for installation by drilling ¼" holes for the plug welds along the weld areas and transferring any plates or pieces that need to be attached to the new quarter. Then, I put the quarter panel in place, using welding clamps and Tek screws along the weld areas to attach it. At this point, check the fit and how it lines up with the other parts. Check the door gap and other places as seen in these three pictures. Also check the fit around the taillight panel and make sure it's lined up and also fitting tight against the rear deck. One critical place is the measurement between the quarter and the rear inside panel where the rear quart window slides down. Make sure that measurement is the same as it was with the old panel.

HANDY HINT

Don't buy cheap body filler. Not all body fillers are created equal. Many times, people skimp in this area, and that is a mistake. Your paint is only as good as what's underneath it. If you have a favorite body filler that works for you, that's great. If you are new to bodywork, then use a very good quality product. Do not buy the cheapest filler at the parts store.

I used an 80 grit abrasive pad on a right-angle grinder and ground down the high spots on the welds as well as roughed up the surrounding area to give the filler a tooth to stick to. I used a Summit Racing DA and 80 grit to rough up the area around the welds. Now, the fill area for this sail panel weld will extend well past the weld. Don't skimp here or else you'll have to go back and repeatedly extend the sanded area.

The sail panel area needs a special filler. This area gets a good deal of stress, so I'm using a metal reinforced filler: Evercoat's Metal 2 Metal. Add 12 drops of catalyst to a golf ball–sized puddle of hardener and mix it well with a spreader.

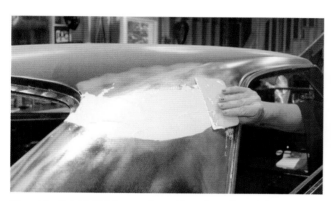

Spread the Metal 2 Metal across the welds on the sail panel. Make sure to get the filler in any little hollows; otherwise, air pockets will form and you will have to go back, open them up, and fill them again.

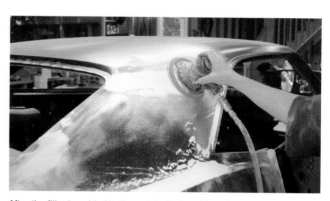

After the filler has dried to the point of being able to be sanded—but not rock hard—I rough in the area with a DA and 80 grit.

Next, I run 80 grit Soft-Sander paper on a blue 16˝ Soft-Sander block. I'll sand up and down then back and forth, evening out the surface until it's pretty much flat. The soft blocks form against the surface, helping to keep the contour.

I used an air gun to blow sanding dust out of any pinholes. This step is very easy to overlook but is very important. Blow off the filled areas every time you are finished sanding.

Next, I filled this area again with Evercoat's Quantum 1 Single Step Repair. Quantum 1 comes in two styles of containers. One is a cartridge style dispenser. The cartridge fits into an Albion B26T825 multicomponent cartridge gun. This system makes it easy to mix the two components in the proper ratio. Just pull the trigger and the correct amounts are released from the cartridges; mix them up and apply. Quantum 1 also comes in cans and the catalyst in tubes. The mix ratio is 10:1. For a 4″ puddle, spread a line of catalyst across the puddle. For a 6″-wide puddle, spread two lines. Mix up the components. I repeated the fill and sand process on the sail panels with the Quantum 1 filler. It sands finer than the metal filler. I used a metal spreader to apply the filler. If you are using a metal spreader, make sure to immediately wipe it off after using it. Do not allow the filler to harden on the spreader.

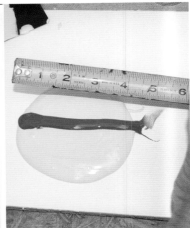

Continued from page 36

Dedicate an area near the car for mixing plastic filler. Or better yet, use a rolling cart. We used Summit Racing's (#SUM-900089) Shop Cart so we could mix the filler right next to the area where it was being used.

Less time getting to the car means more working time until it hardens. Have everything ready—spreaders laid out, sanders, and blocks—as you don't want to look for things as the filler is hardening.

Next, I moved on to the other problem areas on the quarter panels. It's easy to see these areas as the panel is scuff sanded. For example, the top area at the middle of the quarters is usually a problem spot. Several parts of the quarter come together here, and they require filling and sanding. I sanded the surface using a DA and 120 grit.

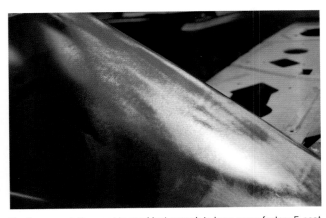

Don't oversand. You want to sand just enough to have some factory E-coat left on the surface. This way, the high spots are sanded and the low spots still have paint on them. Here, a few ridges next the rear window are visible. These need to be filled.

I spread Quantum 1 filler across the surface of this area. But note how I stay away from the seam where the quarter panel meets the rear deck. Do not fill this seam with filler or primer. If any filler gets in this seam, use a knife or tool to scrape it out. This seam will be filled with seam sealer later in the process, but for now, keep it clean and open.

CLEAN THE BARE METAL

This is a step we do that in some cases is not necessary, but we do it anyway. Some metal protecting products need to be cleaned off the metal before any work is done on it. Some products are paint friendly and can remain on the surface. We always remove any protective films or chemicals before we apply filler or paint. If you applied a rust preventive on the bare metal of your project and are not certain if you can paint directly over it, wipe it off with lacquer thinner or acetone.

I used a DA and 80 grit to rough out the filler.

OVERSANDING

Don't oversand your filler. One of the biggest and easiest bodywork mistakes is sanding away too much filler. Filler is softer than metal, so the sanding pad will glide over the metal high spots and sand down into the filler, creating low spots. The trick is to sand away just enough. When you see the filler getting thin over the high spot, stop sanding before the filler is completely sanded off the metal high spot.

Next, I used a 5″ Soft-Sander yellow pad and 80 grit to fine sand the filler. Each color Soft-Sander pad has a different contour. The blue pad is very flat; the yellow pad has a slight roundness, which makes it perfect for sanding this area. Now that it's been sanded, the high spots are easy to see as they are peeking up through the filler. Don't oversand.

The rest of the quarter panel is sanded and areas that are difficult to sand with sandpaper are scuffed. Here I'm using a 3M 7447 Scotch-Brite abrasive pad to scuff the recessed areas of the chevrons.

I worked my way around the panel, finding areas that need bodywork. The front part of the edge of the quarter panel by the quarter window was a little too sharp. It needed to be more rounded like the rest of the edge. I smoothed some Quantum 1 filler on it, and then I start to shape it. First the flat side of the edge is sanded flat with a blue 5″ Soft-Sander block and 120 grit. The block is moved up and down, then side to side.

Then, I curved a piece of 120 grit sandpaper around the edge and gently sanded to round the front edge so it matches the rest of the edge. The car is blown off to remove any sanding dust and wiped with a Gerson Blend Prep tack cloth to remove anything left on the surface.

I primed the sides and sail panels of the quarters with PPG K38 using the SATA 100B spray gun. It is a high-build urethane primer mixed 4:1 with K201 catalyst. I mix right in the SATA RPS disposable cup, which has measurements on the side for different mixing ratios. It also has a built-in filter, so there's no need to strain the material. We primed these panels first as it was going to take a few rounds of filler and sanding to get the sail panels perfectly smooth. We did not want to load up primer on areas of the car where it was not needed. So we first focused our attention and materials on the areas that needed the most work. After the priming was done, we misted a light coat of black primer to serve a guide coat.

A PAINTING REGRET —WISHING FOR POLYESTER PRIMER

In chapter 1, I explained polyester primer and had meant to use it on the Firebird, but I decided to go with a thicker urethane primer instead. Looking back, I should have used the polyester primer. It is designed for this exact kind of work. Even the experts can make mistakes, and this is the one mistake I made in this restoration. Anytime you are doing this much bodywork, consider using a good brand of polyester primer surfacer. PPG makes several that would have great with the Deltron system I am using here, Vibrance VP-2100 or Shop Line's JP 205.

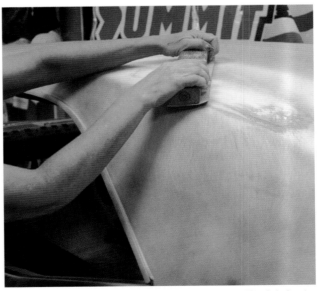

The primer and guide coat were allowed to dry overnight. The Soft-Sander blocks come in 5″, 8″, 11″, 16″, 20″, and 24″ long. I'm using an 11″ blue Soft-Sander block to smooth the top of the sail panel area. The low spots show up as they still have guide coat in them. After I'm done sanding, I'll rough up the low spots so the filler will stick. The area will be blown off and tacked to remove sanding residue. Any low spots will be filled with Quantum 1 and sanded.

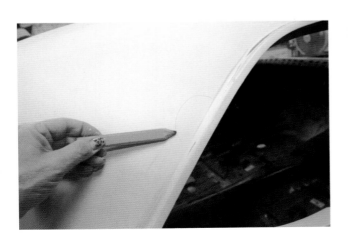

After a few rounds of primer, it gets harder to find the low spots as they become quite shallow. I used a pencil and drew a circle around the low spot that needed to be filled.

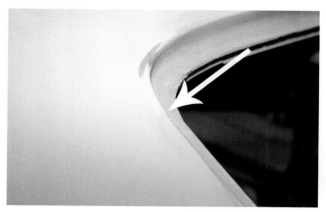

Pay close attention to any areas that are close to where the chrome trim will be, such as the end of the weld where the sail meets the roof. Make sure the bodywork goes all the way around the edge of metal, neatly smoothing the entire length of the weld. Don't stop short.

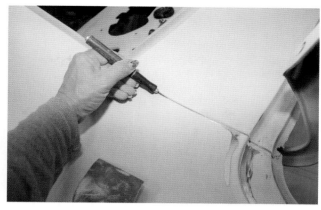

I'm using an X-Acto knife to clear and scrape out any primer that has flooded into this seam.

For the bodywork and priming on the sail panels, it took eight rounds of applying filler, sanding it, priming, and sanding it again. Keep in mind there was a weld that ran the width of the panel, plus spot welds that ran down the drip rail. We left plenty of dry time between rounds to ensure less shrinking of material over time. Problems happen when the dry times are rushed and layers of material are piled up without enough cure time. The next steps were seam sealing, mounting the doors and front end, and priming the rest of the car.

SEAM SEALING

Seam sealing is one of those small details that don't get much attention, but if it's poorly or improperly done, the area will crack and get the wrong kind of attention. Seam sealer is a caulk that is applied in the area between two panels. Never allow body filler or primer to bridge across the separation between panels as it will crack over time.

Then I used the edge of a piece of 120 grit to sand the seam and give a slight rounded contour to the edges. Then the seam will be blown out with an air gun.

Here is a neat little trick. Run tape along the seam to help control the sealer. The tape will keep the sealer from extending too far over the edge of the seam, and it will not require much sanding. Also, as the bodywork was finished in this area, we did not want to sand into the bodywork when we sanded the excess sealer. A small bead of Evercoat 6032 Control Flow seam sealer was run into the seam. This two-part product cures very quickly. Test touch after 5 minutes, and if it's hard, pull the tape. Do not leave the tape on and allow the seam sealer to fully harden. I will sand the hard edges of the sealer with 150 grit after the sealer has dried, taking care to sand the edges flat and feather them into the surface.

Seam sealing can get messy pretty quick. And depending on the kind and brand you use, it can dry very quickly, so you may need to work fast. Have everything in place before you start. Unlike in these photos, I suggest wearing disposable gloves. For any seam sealing after this, I wore Raven Nitrile gloves and they worked great.

Most of the seam sealing that is done on a restoration project starts like this. First thoroughly scuff or sand the seam. Here a 3M 7447 Scotch-Brite abrasive hand pad is used. Then the seam is blown out with an air gun and wiped down with PPG DX330 precleaner. I'm using Evercoat 6032 Control Flow Seam Sealer 2-part sealer. It comes in a two-cartridge dispenser that loads into an Albion B26T825 multicomponent cartridge gun. Equalize the cartridges (hold the gun over a trash can and apply pressure until both streams of material are coming out evenly), then it's ready to use. Apply steady pressure to the caulking gun at all times during application. The sealer is mixed as it passes through the application tube. A thin line of sealer is applied to the seam, from the edge of the trunk opening all the way down to the bottom of the panels. Then make sure to remove the mixing tube and replace the plug back on the end of the cartridge tip once finished.

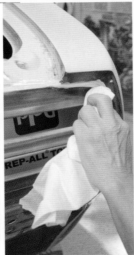

I use my finger to wipe the sealer and press it down into the seam. I keep a wipe towel close by to wipe away any excess. Then I wipe my finger down the seam again, smoothing the sealer.

After the sealer is dry, I sand off most of the excess with a Summit Racing 2″ Fibered Ceramic scuffing disc on a right angle grinder then finish-sand the seam with 120 grit. These seams are now ready for priming.

Once the bodywork at the rear of the car was pretty much complete, it was time to assemble the rest of the sheet metal on the car. Do not just quickly hang or mock up the sheet metal on the car. Mount the panels as if you are doing the final assembly. Line everything up, using shims to adjust each mounting point. In addition to body lines, make sure the surfaces of the panels are level with each other. Expect this preassembly to take a day or more to properly assemble all the panels on the car. *This is a critical requirement, because if the parts are not exactly where they need to be during the bodywork phase, they will not match up for final assembly.*

Left: We mounted and adjusted the doors first so they could be lined up with the body lines on the quarter panel. We had to do a little bodywork along the door gap to get it perfect. The door/quarter panel gaps and body lines came out very good. But this result took hours of adjusting and realigning the doors.

Below: Next, we hung and adjusted the front fenders and mounted the front fender extensions and front valance. Again, we spent hours to get everything where it needed to be.

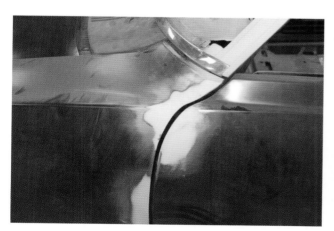

A little bodywork was needed along the door/fender gaps. Make sure this gap is large enough to open and close the door without the door catching on the fender. Open and shut the door and look closely at this area. Make sure to leave enough room for the paint that will be going on this area.

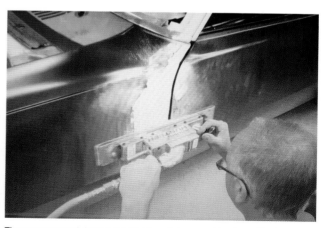

There was a good deal of sanding to get done, and having a Hutchins 2000 Hustler straight-line sander made it easy to level out the flat areas. Terry is moving the sander up and down along the seam, evening out the surface.

SMALL DETAILS

The difference between a regular restoration and an award-winning, pristine work of rolling art is the small details. The little impressions that run along the back of the new taillight panel are one example. They are covered by the bumper and won't really show. But at some angles they might be seen. We took the time to fill and sand these little spots and fine-tune every little seam and line on the car. It made a big difference! By the time the clearcoat was done, the Firebird had that amazing dipped-in-liquid-glass effect. Taking the time with these kinds of things is the difference between an average car and a head turner.

We used a DA with 120 grit on the flat areas and hand-sanded with 120 on the corners of the new sheet metal to scuff it up for bodywork and priming. After any bodywork was done, the car was blown off and the

Another batch of PPG's K38 primer surfacer is mixed up, and we applied four coats to the entire car using a SATA 100 B spray gun.

Left: Then, we guide coated the car with some PPG DP90LV primer. See chapter 10 for more information on using this product. **Right:** I sanded the tops of the fenders with a 20˝ blue Soft-Sander pad and 120 grit. I move the pad up and down, back and forth, and then diagonally across the surface to get it flat.

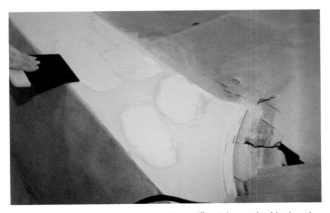

Left: The low spots start to show up, and they are circled with a pencil. **Right:** I applied Quantum 1 filler to the low spots using a 5˝ metal spreader. I try to get the filler as thin as possible around the edges of the areas. The metal spreader is great for this. These areas are roughed in with 120 then final sanded with 150.

UNDERSTANDING SANDPAPER GRITS

Knowing which sandpaper grits to use and the order in which to use them can get confusing. Most painters will have a general consensus on this, but everyone has his or her own preferences. For myself, when doing bodywork, I follow these guidelines:

- I start out with 80 grit, followed by 120 grit for the beginning bodywork.

- As I refine the bodywork, I'll go up in paper grit, 150 to 180 to 220.

- For flattening a surface, the courser grits work better for me. They carve more effectively, scraping away the high spots, whereas the finer grits tend to remove less of the high spots, passing over the bumps.

- Once the surface has the desired shape, then it can be fine-tuned with the higher grit paper. For example, after the first or second round of primer, if the surface has very few high or low spots, then I use 180 or 220.

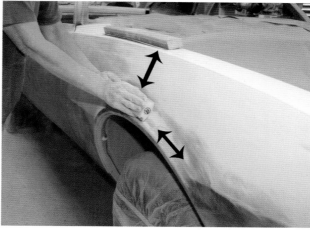

The green Soft-Sander block has the perfect shape to fit the contour around the wheel well. I moved the block back and forth a few passes, then up and down. Always change the direction when sanding primer or bodywork. If the block keeps moving in one area and one direction, grooves will be formed. Always check to see if impressions are forming on the surface from sanding in areas like this.

A Hutchins Speed Board with 120 grit was used on the door and fender sides. I'm sanding along the fender/door gap on both sides at once. This way the top of the surfaces will be even with each other. The flat board is moved up and down, side to side, and diagonally. The high spots are quickly becoming visible. You can tell the surface of the door is a little higher than the surface of the fender as the primer is sanding off the door first. We had to readjust the fender mounting to bring the fender out a little.

It's always good to check how the bodywork will line up with the trim before the paint is done. Here, the windshield trim is mocked up and a little filling work needs to be done. Use care when doing bodywork around trim. It's better to have a little less than too much. Always remember, the paint and clear will build up the thickness, and if the trim digs into the paint, it will crack and chip.

The top area of the left sail panel needed a little more work. I did some skim coating of Quantum 1 and some fine sanding with 150 and 180. Quantum 1 is called a single-step filler because it flows so well, leaving few pinholes. It eliminates the need for finishing putty.

I'm using an 11″ purple Soft-Sander on this round contour below the sail panel. On areas like this, where a flat surface flows into a round contour, make sure to sand up from the contour onto the flat surface and back down into the contour as well as back and forth in the contour; otherwise, a groove might form.

Left: Only one more round of primer will be done, so it's time to apply seam sealer to the drip rails. I was doing quite a bit of bodywork in that area and was concerned about building up too much primer over the seam sealer, as I did not want the primer to crack over time. I ran a bead of Evercoat 6032 control flow, wiping away the excess and neatly shaping the sealer to the contour of the drip rail. Leave a good coat of sealer here, don't make it too thin.
Right: David blew the sanding dust off the car, then ran a Gerson Blend Prep tack cloth over it to remove any residue left on the surface.

HOW TO GET STRAIGHT BODY LINES

The main body line on the doors needed a little more work, so here's a great trick I learned from legendary painter Tom Prewitt Jr. This technique can be used on most body lines to get a crisp, straight line. Run ¾″ masking tape down the body line. Then, using a long flat board and a medium grit paper like 120 or 150, sand up the line from different directions working the bottom section of the door. As I did not want to sand into the surrounding panels, I protected them with 2″ orange mask tape.

Once that side is done, remove the tape and place it on the opposite side of the body line. Repeat the sanding on that side. Make sure to keep the pressure even on the sanding pad. The flexible sanding pads work great for this.

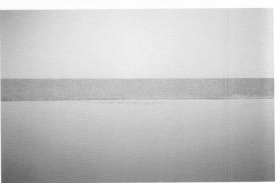

This photo shows the low spots along the line where it was uneven. These places are very shallow and several good coats of primer will fill them very effectively. These low spots will be scuffed with a 3M 64660 Scotch-Brite pad.

The entire car was primered one last time with PPG K36 urethane primer. This primer is mixed 5:1:1 with K201 catalyst and DT885 reducer. It was about 80ºF in the shop and we used a reducer that was best suited for that temperature. If it had been cooler, a colder temp reducer such as DT870 would have been used. Three coats were applied with a fourth coat on areas that had additional bodywork done. Guidecoat was then applied to the car.

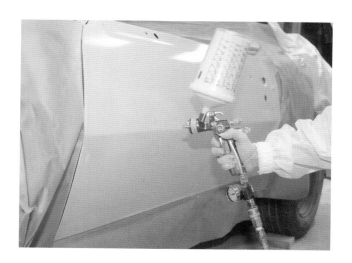

Above: The entire car was dry sanded with 320 grit. I used sanding pads wherever I could, especially on the flat areas.

Left: The fenders and quarters were masked off and the doors were primered one last time with four coats of K36, guidecoated, and allowed to dry overnight.

engine compartment and wheels were masked. Then the body was tacked to remove any debris on the surface.

I taped off seams on the firewall and seam sealed with Evercoat #6032 Control Flow. I also seam sealed areas like the bottom rear of the quarter panels and along the bottom of the taillight panel. In areas like that, where you do not want the sealer to flow, use a full-bodied sealer like Evercoat's #6022 heavy-bodied seam sealer. Carefully check over the vehicle; any changes or rework can be still be done at this point. If you have not yet done so, create a checklist and go over it. Check to make sure any holes needed have been drilled, clear out any holes that might have body filler in them, make sure the seams are sanded and neat, and check the lower areas on the car—as these are easy to overlook—for

Next, I wet sanded the body with 400 grit and a spray bottle of water. Then, I removed the fenders and front end parts. I used a 3M 64660 Scotch-Brite pad to scuff around all the edges of the fenders and doors. A number of other parts that are not seen in this chapter required bodywork and priming, such as the hood, trunk lid, spoiler, and some small parts. It took a few days to finish sand all the parts and car. Then, it was prepped for basecoat.

Chapter 4
How to Select and Prepare New Body Parts

This chapter will help you to purchase and prepare new body parts or sheet metal for your project. New, very costly, and poor decisions in this area raise the overall cost of a paint job. Buying new parts for your project is no guarantee that you will not need to do any bodywork. Any metal or plastic will require preparation and some bodywork—even if the metal or plastic comes with no paint or with primer. What happens is the metal is stretched and little ripples can form on the surface as the metal is stamped. And plastic can sometimes have slight distortions from the heat, or there might be imperfections from the mold.

PICKING OUT NEW PARTS

One of the most important things to do before ordering replacement sheet metal is to find out everything that's wrong with your project. It may look like a few small rusty areas at first, but more often than not, you'll find that the half-dollar-sized rust bubble on the door or quarter panel is just the tip of the iceberg. Old repairs with putty or fiberglass can hide a nest of "rust termites" that have eaten good metal for years. Only when all the old paint, seam sealer, and previous handiwork have been removed should you start deciding what can be patched and what will need full replacement panels. And if you plan on any upgrades to the power plant, suspension, and brakes you need to be hypercritical about structural integrity. Unibodies like Mustangs, Firebirds, Camaros, and Novas can flex through patched structural panels (floor, trunk, rockers, and roof) and ruin an expensive paint job with one good stomp of an accelerator pedal. Once the old metal is naked, it can't lie about any rust, previous collisions, and repairs done to it. Spend the extra time and expense to strip the car, removing all paint and body filler by media, soda, or sand blasting. You never know what's under the surface until the panels are stripped down to the bare metal.

One would think brand new sheet metal would not need any attention other than a wipe down to be ready for priming. Not hardly, especially concerning parts that come new in bare metal. Carefully check over any new parts, looking for defects that may easily be missed. Small dings, lines of shallow ridges and bumps, poorly welded mounting tabs, poor welds, uneven fender edges, missing spot welds. . . Be familiar with your old parts so you know what to look for. Chances are these days you will be purchasing the new parts online and not get a chance to see the parts until they arrive. So how can you find the best sheet metal?

- Do the research. Go online and research the companies and their products. Look at the company's social networking pages. Read what people are saying on forums.

- Look closely at an unrestored model of the car or truck you are doing. Sometimes there are inherent flaws in the old dies from the OEM. Flaws you see on the new parts might have also been present on the original vehicle. Sometimes new sheet metal will have the same flaws; sometimes it won't.

- Ask around. In the months before doing your project, go to car shows and check out any vehicles

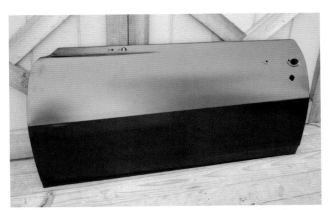

This is a new Dynacorn door for the Firebird. It has a black E-coating, which makes it easy to check for flaws. Sighting down the body line on the door, it's easy to see how straight the line is.

like yours. Look closely at how the parts fit together. Take photos of the door gaps, the gap between the windshield trim and the top of the front fenders, and similar spaces. How does the trim fit up against the parts? Talk to the owners about their project. What did they go through? What did they use? Any advice and information is good to have. And do this before you order parts.

Always remember, time, gravity, and road wear have stressed the body of your project vehicle. Sure your old parts fit, but they have also sagged along with the car. Plus once you start cutting that car apart, the stress is relieved and stuff starts to move. Things no longer line up. Chance are it will take some work to get those parts to fit properly. Door/fender gaps will need to be adjusted. Places on the weld on parts like the rear quarters, roof, and trunk floor will need trimmed. What is your best tool for these situations? Patience. Don't give yourself a make it or break it deadline for your project. It adds stress that will hurt the project by taking the fun out of it. Do it the right way, and give the project plenty of time. If you are a small shop, then remember: it's always easier spend an extra day or two doing it right the first time than to get further on in the project and realize you made a big mistake and it will be a huge hassle to fix at that point.

METAL THAT COMES PRIMED

Most replacement panels have an electrically bonded (E-coated) primer on them. Most are either black or silver and fall into EDP (electro-deposited primer) or "weld-thru" primer that have positive-charged coatings applied to negative-charged parts that are then baked to set the coating. Whether sprayed on or dipped from a vat, the electric charges get the coating deep into the surface of the steel and in every nook and cranny. Most E-coat can be welded without having to first grind it off, although some welders prefer to grind the coating away from the weld area. It's a good idea to verify with

There are welds along these seams where the quarter panel was welded on. These welds need to be smoothed. I ground off the E-coat using a Summit Racing 3˝ 80 grit abrasive disc. This will rough up the metal surface. The plastic filler will need this rough surface in order to adhere properly. Note how the area below the Chevron impression has been ground. Areas like this often need a little smoothing, as imperfections may be caused by the stamping process. Make sure to check over trim details like this on your parts.

Keep the grinder moving smoothly over the part. Don't press the trigger down all the way on the tool or use it full speed. Use a medium speed on the grinder and just scuff it over the surface. Don't dig into the surface and gouge it up. If the grinder stays too long in one place, it may create low spots or unevenness in the surface.

your paint manufacturer if leaving the primer on is an option or if the steel must be stripped completely and their seam sealer, primer, and paints applied. Some paints have "lifetime warranty" if their instructions are followed. But E-coat must be sanded or scuffed before any bodywork or paint is done.

Another great thing about getting parts in black E-coat is that surface flaws are easier to detect. For example, during a 2 a.m. session of mounting the taillight panel on the Firebird, the tops of the quarters received a little damage in the form of an outward dent. But it was easy to see (right).

And it was easy to fix. We placed a heel dolly under the dent. A few firm, but not too hard taps with a body hammer knocked the dent in. When repairing high spots like this, it's better to err on the side of caution, that is, have the metal lower around the dent rather than higher. You can always fill it more. Its easier than having to go back and knock down any high spots after you've started applying filler.

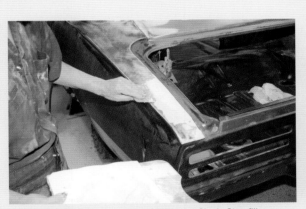

We filled the area using Evercoat Quantum 1 Single Step filler.

The dent appears to be gone, but now there is a slight low spot.

Using a Summit Racing's DA sander and 80 grit paper, we worked the filler down. It's not taken all the way down. We just roughed it in, creating a smooth surface.

The filler was fine sanded with a Soft Sander block and their 80 grit paper. Note how much filler was left on the surface—all from what appeared to be a rather small dent. Small dents are actually much larger than they appear. The area around the dent may appear to be flat, but it is not. When the metal is dented in, the area around the dent flexes in the opposite direction. A dent that is 2 inches across may be surrounded by another 2 to 3 inches of slightly flexed metal. People new to bodywork are always wondering why they have to keep extending filler to get the surface smooth. Its faster to simply extend the repair area at the start of the repair rather than during.

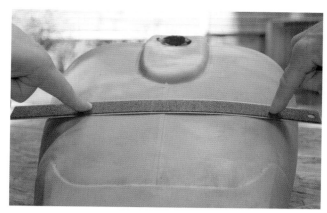

Here is a new motorcycle tank. A seam runs down the center. On most bikes of this model, this area is covered by a dash. The owner of this bike did not want to run a dash, so this seam will need to have filler applied over the seam. This photo gives an idea of how much filling the area will require. The body filler will pretty much cover the top surface of the tank.

This new model fender has ridges that run down the center. Sometimes these ridges are formed due to the stamping or forming process. Other times, the part is made in two pieces then welded together. When a part is ordered online, flaws like these are not readily visible.

Here's one of the fenders after priming and sanding. Now it's very easy to see the high spots of the ridges. These ridges were fairly shallow, and several rounds of primer did the job of smoothing the surface.

HANDY HINT

Make sure the parts have been pre-fitted to the car, truck, or bike. There's no sense in painting a part that needs an adjustment in order to fit properly. If you do not have the vehicle on hand and are only doing a paint job on that part, make sure you have it in writing that the customer is responsible for that part of the job. You don't want them showing up at the shop later and saying, "This fender doesn't fit my car."

BARE METAL PARTS

Here are some mean little truths about bare metal parts.

- They are usually coated with some kind of rust-preventing oil. This coating must be completely removed. I wipe the coating with lacquer thinner several times to remove this coating. Both sides of the part—the top and bottom surfaces—must be free of any oils or silicone.
- A good deal of aftermarket motorcycle sheet metal comes as bare metal. Some of these parts have imperfections from the stamping or forming process and will require bodywork in order to be smooth.

SHOULD NEW PARTS BE SANDBLASTED?

I leave sandblasting to the professionals. It's very messy, and parts can be ruined if they are not sandblasted properly. The force of the sandblasting creates heat, and when heat is applied to metal body parts, it can distort the surface. If you're doing the sandblasting yourself, keep the nozzle at an angle and lightly "dance" the flow; try not to concentrate it in one spot or you may warp the metal. The replacement parts I use when doing automotive work come with E-coat, so there's no need for sandblasting. Motorcycle parts are another matter.

Myself, I always have bare metal motorcycle parts sandblasted. Most of the time, those parts are covered

Take a look at these fiberglass saddlebags. Note the seams running down the front of the bags? They should not be there. That area has no trim line. Those bags will need a good deal of bodywork in order to be painted and have a smooth surface. Always be aware of how the body parts should look before you start working on them. That way, if there's an issue, you may be able to return them. Those seams would have added many unnecessary hours to this job.

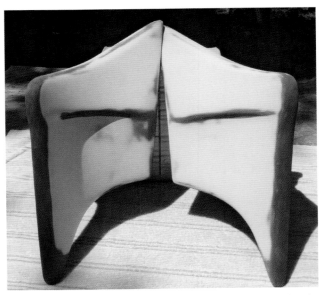

Here are the covers after the surface was smoothed with filler. The filler is not very thick; it's more of a skim coat. These were pretty nice sidecovers. But this material is not easy to form and get a perfectly smooth surface. Chances are when you get a plastic part some work is going to be needed. It's just a matter of how much work it will take to get the surface smooth and ready for paint.

This plastic sidecover looks pretty good. But notice the slight line on the left side of the front?

with specks of rust and oil. Make sure all openings on gas tanks and oil tanks are stuffed with paper towels and sealed with duct tape so sand doesn't get inside. Then wash the metal down with lacquer thinner and sandblast the parts. One thing to remember: do not to touch the sheet metal parts with your bare hands after sandblasting. The oils and moisture that are caught in the ridges of your fingerprints will leave rusty fingerprints on the freshly blasted metal.

RAW PLASTIC AND FIBERGLASS PARTS

When dealing with plastic and fiberglass parts, look for cracks, uneven areas, distorted or stretched areas, and poorly ground edges. Run your hand over the surface, checking for waviness. Also check for thickness. Not all aftermarket parts are created equal. If the material is too thin, especially near mounting holes, the part may tend to crack over time. If the part is too thick, you may encounter fitment issues when it comes to mounting the part, especially if it's replacing an OEM part.

Many body panels and kit cars are plastic or fiberglass. If possible, look carefully at the product before you purchase it. Hoods can be especially wavy and require a good deal of bodywork to be made flat. Rushed judgment in picking out plastic body parts can result in many hours of bodywork. Don't grab the first good deal that comes along. If a body kit or parts are extremely cheap, chances are you will end up with many hours of filling and sanding.

For more information on preparing and painting plastic parts refer to chapter 7.

Chapter 5
Paint That Trunk!

Whether you're completely restoring a hot rod or simply refreshing your daily ride, most people never give much thought to the trunk until it's absolutely necessary. The trunk is one of the most overlooked areas of a restoration project. The quarter panels seem to get all the glory. But always remember, it's the details that count. And a clean, professional finish in the trunk will give your project that extra edge. It's also easier than you might think. Here's a quick easy way to get a trunk finish that looks great.

WORKING WITH A NEW TRUNK PAN

The first step is to prepare the surface. If the trunk pan has been replaced, then it's a simple matter of sanding and priming the E-coat of the new pan. Why not simply paint over the E-coat? It all depends on what kind of result you want. The E-coat could be scuffed and then painted with the trunk paint, but you might want to grind the welds and make the surface smooth and flat. That was the route we took with our Firebird. We ground the welds flat using a right-angle grinder and 80 grit grinding discs from Summit Racing. Then we smoothed the welds using Evercoat Quantum 1 and sanded it just like we did for bodywork on the exterior of the vehicle.

Once the surface was flat, I primed the trunk with PPG K36 urethane primer. Once dry, I sanded it smooth with Soft-Sanders 320 grit paper, readying it for the trunk spatter paint.

WORKING WITH AN OLD TRUNK PAN

If your trunk surface is looking pretty rough, then you'll have to spend more time on prep. First, clean the surface thoroughly with strong wax and grease remover like PPG's DX330. Dampen a cleaning cloth with the DX330, wipe it across the surface, and then use a dry cloth to wipe it dry. Repeat this step using fresh wipes until the wipe comes away clean. Then sand away any rust using course grit, like 220. Remove any flaking paint. Refer to chapter 3 for more information for preparing old surfaces for paint.

It's not only what's on the outside. Time spent detailing areas like the trunk is a worthwhile investment in your ride.

THE FUN PART

Some parts of restoration are more fun than others; trunk spatter paint is pretty fun because it's just so simple. You don't have to worry about getting dust in the paint. And the only rule for spraying it is to be consistent.

Any holes in the interior and exterior need to be covered with tape. This should be done even if you are painting the trunk before painting the car. Trunk spatter paint is very textured and is a pain to remove from a primered surface ready for basecoat. Any outward facing surfaces, like the taillights on this Firebird, must have tape applied directly to the surface. Then another piece of tape is run across the actual hole. If you are taping on a freshly painted surface, try using a tape made for using on that kind of surface. 3M precision masking tape was designed for use on new paint. It doesn't leave an imprint in the paint like crepe (traditional) masking tape tends to do. Make sure to securely seal the opening with the tape.

Left: The big as well as small openings between the trunk and interior of the car must be taped over. I used the 2″-wide aqua mask from American Tape. It made short work of the task. Don't forget the openings in the rear deck and the opening behind the quarter panels. **Right:** Now the rest of the car is masked off. We start by running the 3M precision tape around the edge of the trunk opening channel. Then, we tape masking paper to that, and plastic is used to completely cover the car and is taped to the paper. Note how the drain plug holes are taped from underneath the car. Make sure to get under the trunk and tape over any openings on the underside. Don't forget the shock mount holes.

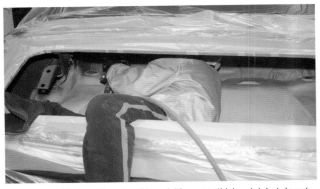

Left: Zolatone is a water-based trunk spatter paint that comes ready to spray. It does not need to be reduced or thinned. It's a very thick paint, but do not shake it. Simply stir the mixture until all the thick material on the bottom of the can is mixed into thinner material on top. Do not strain it into the gun. Just pour it in the cup and you're ready to spray. Make sure to use a gun with a big fluid tip size, 2.0 –2.4. I sprayed it at 30 psi. **Right:** Unfortunately, if you don't have very long arms, the only way to get good coverage in the front areas and top surfaces of the trunk is to climb in. And that was what I did. This way I was able to get in position to spray those areas.

Left: Here I am spraying the wheelhouse and the trunk lid hinge mount. First spray one thin coat and allow the flash. I will follow with a second heavier coat that will give good coverage and have an even pattern. **Right:** I brought a light into the trunk in order to help see what I'm spraying. It's very difficult to see the top surface of the trunk. It's in shadow and if you cannot see it, it's hard to know if you are getting good coverage. You need to make sure these surfaces are protected with paint, especially if you're doing a restoration and the car has been sandblasted or media blasted. Any bare metal must be painted, and it's too easy to overlook these hard to see areas. Rust can grow and spread and ruin all your hard work.

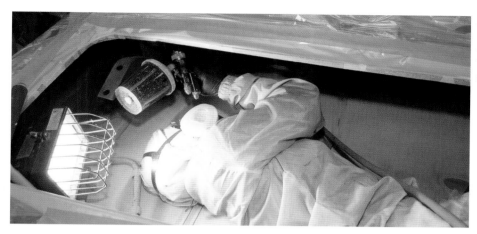

Another hard-to-spray area is the just inboard of the trunk hinge mount. Make sure to get good coverage there. Turn down the pattern of your gun so that it's narrow and carefully spray.

Now, the goal is just to get a consistent even pattern across the trunk. I'm using a 50% overlap.

SPATTER PAINT

Spatter paint works great for camouflaging small imperfections. And it comes in various color combinations like gray and black or gray and aqua. I sprayed the gray and black.

CREATE YOUR OWN SPATTER PAINT

You can create your own spatter paint. Simply spray a coat of a dark gray sealer like PPG's DP90LV. Then remove the spray cap from the gun. Not having the cap on the gun will keep the paint from atomizing. The paint will spatter out. Then just spatter spray your desired color combination. You could have black and purple or gray and blue. Keep your paint mixture on the thick side. And definitely test your colors and the technique on some cardboard or masking paper before you apply it to the trunk surface.

And here's what it looks like after it's dry! Very professional looking! This was the first time I ever sprayed spatter paint in the trunk, and it was as easy as I had hoped it would be.

Chapter 6
Small Repairs: Fixing Dents and Chips

Left: This hood has a dent. But dents are not just dented in. When the metal flexes inward, the area around the dent flexes in the opposite direction. This sort of ridge around the dent is very hard to see, but it's there. **Right:** Sand the dent and the area around the dent to remove any loose or chipped paint and prepare the surface for filler. The body filler applied to the surface of the dent will need a rough surface in order to stick. We used a right-angle die grinder with a Summit Racing #80 grit abrasive disc to sand down and feather edge the broken paint edges. Next, we sanded the top surface around the dent with a Soft-Sander flat blue block and 150 grit paper. Note how large the repair area is getting.

Fixing a dent is a two-part process. First, the dent must be repaired. Then, the paint has to be matched and repainted. Fixing the dent is the easy part. Matching and blending the paint is a little more challenging. Chapter 8 shows how to match colors. Chapter 11 shows the process for blending in repairs.

FIXING A DENT

First, clean the area thoroughly with a precleaner like PPG's DX330. Wipe it on using a clean wipe cloth, then immediately wipe it off. Repeat this process several times until the surface is squeaky clean. Make sure to clean the entire panel, not just the dent area. The entire hood here was cleaned.

One thing to be aware of: the repair area will always be much larger than the damaged area. The reason for this is that the repair has to transition smoothly into the surface. Say the dent is 2 inches across. The area around the dent will be slightly flexed up, which adds another 1–2 inches around the dent. Then there needs to be a transition range for the filler that can add another 1–2 inches. The repaired area could end up being 6 or more inches across.

After the surface is clean, mask off the area around the dent. The mask helps to keep the sanding from going too far past the damaged area and will protect the rest of the panel from primer overspray.

WHAT IS FEATHEREDGING?

Featheredging is sanding down broken paint edges until there is a smooth, almost flat transition between them. For example, the left side of the picture shows an area of broken, chipped paint that was cut away, leaving a sharp rough edge. On the upper right, all the broken and loose paint was removed and the rough edge was sanded smooth. The bottom right is another place where the rough edges of a paint chip were featheredge sanded.

DENT REMOVAL PROBLEMS

Not all dents are in places where there is access to the backside of the panel. Sometimes a reinforcing structure might cover the back of the dented area. Body shops deal with these situations in a number of ways. One is to drill holes and use a dent puller/slide hammer to pop out the dent. Another is to weld studs along the dent, attach the slide hammer to that, and pop out the dent. Both of these methods involve welding, as one creates holes in the panel and the other may cause the welded studs to break off the metal, leaving a hole.

For the backyard bodyman with limited tools, the method detailed here is the easiest choice. If you cannot pop or flatten the dent with a hammer and dolly, and do not have the equipment for pulling dents, then filling the dent with filler might be your best option. If you do end up with holes in the panel, make sure to weld them or use a product like Evercoat's Fiber Tech reinforced repair compound filler. Never try to fill holes on metal or any kind of substrate with body filler. It will eventually crack and chip out.

Next, flatten the dented metal with a body hammer and a heel dolly. The dolly is placed over the dent. Lightly hammer the dent from the bottom. The top surface may need a little light hammering to flatten any raised metal. If you are working on a newer model car or truck, maybe 1990s or newer, please keep in mind that the metal in these vehicles is very thin. The metal may want to spring back, so use care when hammering out a dent.

Left: Next it's time to mix up some filler. We used Quantum 1 Single Step filler and applied it using a metal spreader. The metal spreader helps to spread a nice, smooth layer. **Right:** Using 80 grit paper on a Summit Racing DA sander, sand the filler. Note how there seems to be a low spot in the middle. It's hard to see, so a black arrow points to the low area.

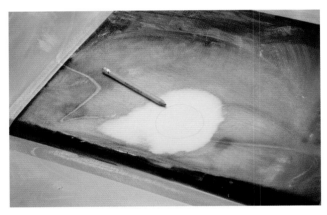

Left: Next, sand the area with a finer grit sandpaper, such as 120 grit on a blue Soft-Sander block. Watch how far you go with the sandpaper when sanding. It's easy to get carried away, and next thing you know, the rough sanded area extends far beyond the where the filler is. **Right:** Here's a good look at the sanded surface. I've circled the low spot with a pencil, and a pencil points to the edge of the low spot. This area will need another layer of filler. The area is blown off with an air gun to remove the sanding dust from any pinholes.

Left: Mix up and apply more filler. This second layer is only applied over the low spot. **Right:** Block sand the filler with 120 grit followed by 150 grit. The surface is now flat and smooth. Go over it lightly with 180 grit. It's now ready for priming.

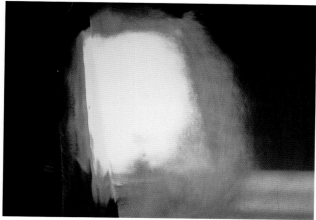

Left: Blow off the area again. Next, mix a small amount of PPG K36 urethane primer 5:1:1 with K201 hardener and DT870 reducer. We used a SATA RPS 0.6 l cup to mix the primer and apply it with a SATAjet 100 BF spray gun. One medium wet coat was sprayed and allowed to flash; then, the process was repeated two more times. **Right:** After the primer has dried properly, emove the masking and dry sand the area with 220 followed by dry sanding with 320. The area is now ready for basecoat paint.

FIXING CHIPS

Those pesky little chips in paint . . . what is the easiest way to fix them? Well, fixing chips is a tedious task. And it's not just chips. Many times what happens is paint on an area around a mounting point will bubble, crack, and chip away over time. That is what happened with the parts in the next step-by-step photo examples.

The custom paint on these parts had been very thick, and the parts had been bolted on the motorcycle before they were completely dry. The fender mounting point had squeezed the paint down and caused it to rise up around the mounting holes. Over the next 10 years the paint started to crack at these areas. Also the bike took the normal amount of wear and tear and the paint had some rock chips in places.

HANDY HINT

The trick to successful chip or dent repair is to be sure to seal the edges of the old paint layers with filler. This suggestion holds true even after the edges are feather sanded. If any edges of the old paint are not covered with filler, there is a good chance the solvents from the primer and basecoats will soak into them, irritating them. This moisture may cause little wrinkles to appear along those paint edges. This one simple little trick works for me every time. Please note that if you are using waterborne primer and basecoat, this step is not so critical as waterborne solvents do not soak in and react with the old paint edges.

On the top half of the photo, you can see where the lifted paint has been cut away with a #11 X-Acto knife. The bottom half of the photo shows the area that was featheredge sanded with 120 grit paper, making sure to remove any lifted or damaged material.

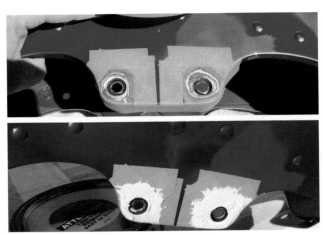

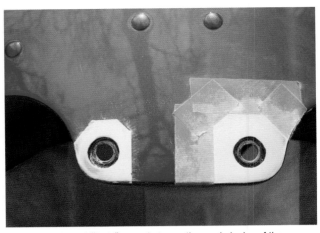

Left: In the top half of this photo, note how the area around the damage was masked off, leaving a ⅛″ to ¼″ space between the sanded edge of the damaged area and the tape. In the bottom half of photo, a small amount of Quantum 1 Single Step Repair was mixed up and spread over the taped-off areas. **Right:** Once the filler is dry, dry sand it with 120 grit then with 150 grit. *Do not sand away the filler covering the edges of the paint layers.* If the filler is no longer covering the paint layers, then apply more filler. *The edges of the paint layers must be sealed by the filler if not using waterbourne paints!* The tape is then peeled off.

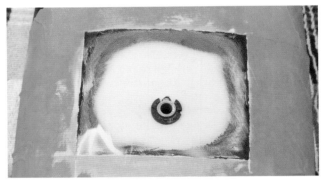

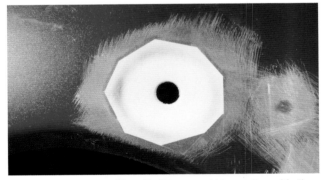

Left: This photo is from a different chip repair, but it shows the next step in the process. Next, wet sand the filler with 400 paper, which smooths and feathers the edges of the filler along the lines where it was taped. Again, be sure to leave a good layer of filler over the old paint edges. They must be covered with filler. The area is then taped and masked off again. Leave about a ¼″ space between the edge of the tape and the edge of the sanded filler. **Right:** Prime the repaired areas with PPG K36 urethane primer mixed 5:1:1 with K201 hardener and DT 885 reducer. Let it dry overnight and remove the tape.

Left: Wet sand the primer with 400 grit paper wrapped around a blue Soft-Sander block. This was a chipped area at the back of the rear fender. Now it's ready for color match and basecoat. **Right:** Here's the finished product. Once the color match and blend were completed, the fender was clearcoated. It looks brand new and is ready for another 10 years or more.

Chapter 7
Plastic and Fiberglass: Prepping, Repairing, and Painting

Working with plastic is very different than working with metal, yet in some ways, it's very similar. Plastic, fiberglass, and composite materials are not hard to work on—if the correct materials and proper techniques are used. These days with new technology products it's easier than ever to repair and repaint nonmetal substrates. In fact, one product in this chapter was not even available when I first started writing this book.

Fiber-reinforced products like Evercoat's Fiber Tech are changing the way painters work on nonmetal surfaces. Fiber Tech is a repair filler formulated with a combination of Kevlar and high-tech short- and long-strand fibers. We used to have to identify the exact kind of plastic being worked on. Fiber Tech works on nine different kinds of composite materials, including fiberglass, fiberglass composite, and SMC and ABS plastics. It's great for double-sided repairs like the following example, and on most repairs, backing mat is not needed.

REPAIRING FIBERGLASS AND PLASTIC COMPOSITES

We're repairing the quarter panel from a Corvette. It has a shattered crack in the material, but this repair can

MATERIALS & EQUIPMENT

Equipment
SATA Minijet 3000B
CP compact 90° angle die grinder CP9106Q-B
CP palm sander RP3611
Soft-Sander sanding blocks
Astro Pneumatic Tool Company portable work stands (#557003)
protective goggles, gloves, dust mask, and a long-sleeved shirt

Materials
80, 120, 180, and 220 grit sandpaper
Evercoat's Fiber Tech #633
Evercoat Quantum 1 Single Step Repair
Evercoat Plastic Repair 5 #6105
Evercoat Maxim Panel Prep #881
Fiber reinforced tape
Evercoat multipurpose repair panel #828
PPG's DX330 precleaner
PPG SU4901 Clean and Scuff pad
PPG SU4902 plastic adhesion wipe
PPG SU4903 advance plastic bond
PPG SXA103 or DX103 multiprep antistatic final clean
Clean white rags or cloths
Masking tape

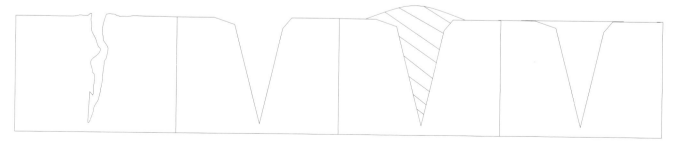

This very simple graphic shows the basic steps to repairing plastic and fiberglass composites. First, a crack or hole in the material is identified. Next, the damaged material is removed and the area is beveled. Then, the area is filled and sanded.

also be used for fixing a hole in a fiberglass panel. First, we washed the panel with soap and water to remove waterborne contaminates. Try not to get water in the interior of the exposed material. If it does, allow the material to dry out. We followed the washing with a solvent based cleaner like PPG's DX330 to remove any wax and grease. If a large area of fiberglass is exposed, avoid soaking the exposed fiberglass with solvent cleaner as it's slow to evaporate once it soaks into the fiberglass. If small cracks radiate from the damage, then drill a small hole at the end of the crack to help keep it from cracking farther.

PROTECT YOUR HEALTH!

Always wear protective goggles, gloves, dust mask, and a long-sleeved shirt when working with fiberglass. Any time you are grinding or sanding, eye and breathing protection should be worn, but it's critical when working with fiberglass or any kind of fiber-reinforced filler.

1

Here's a close up of the crack we are repairing. The crack goes all the way through the material and can clearly be seen on the backside on the right half of the photo. We thoroughly cleaned the top and backside of the panel and put IP orange mask 2˝ tape around the repair area, leaving plenty of room around the damage. You can also apply the repair material without running tape around the repair.

2

3

Left: Next, we beveled out the crack at a 45-degree angle using a CP Compact 90° angle die grinder (CP9106Q-B) with a 3˝ Summit Racing 80 grit abrasive disc. **Right:** We removed any loose material and sanded the surface around the crack with 150 grit on a blue Soft Sander block. The back side is prepared in the same way. Any dust is blown out of the cracks with an air gun.

4

Fiber Tech comes in pouches and cans. Stir the contents of the can, making sure its mixed well and avoid separation of resins and solids. If you are using a pouch, knead the pouch before opening it to ensure the material is mixed. Be sure to also knead the tube of creme hardener. Then squeeze the material out of the pouch onto a mixing pallet and use a spreader to cleanly break off the flow of material from the spout. Spread out a 4″-diameter puddle and place a ribbon of hardener the length of the puddle next to it or across it. The products mix at a 50:1 rate. Mix the two components until they are one color. Use firm downward pressure to remove any air pockets.

HANDY HINT: ALWAYS STIR AND MIX

The resins in most kinds of automotive fillers have a tendency to separate over time as the product sits in its container. Always stir or mix the product before it's used. For example, you might open a can of filler and see a small amount of liquid sitting on the solid material of the filler. That liquid is resin and it needs to be mixed back into the solids of the product before use. This is also true of crème hardeners; knead the tube before opening and using them.

5

6

Left: We started on the back side and applied Fiber Tech with a spreader, using firm even pressure make sure to get in the crack. Start small, working in a thin layer so you can see that the material is getting down into the crack. We applied another layer so the material is slightly above the surface of the panel. **Right:** We allowed about 5–10 minutes for drying then filled the top side of the panel. On the left, you can see how a small amount of the filler is pushed down into the beveled crack. On the right, a thicker layer is applied over it. This creates a double-sided repair for maximum strength. We removed the masking tape before the material is hard.

7

8

Left: We used a CP palm sander (RP3611) with 80 grit paper to take down most of the material and sand the filler level with the surface. **Right:** Then we removed the tape and sanded the repair with 150 grit so the edges of the repair were feather sanded and smoothly transitioned into the surface. The crack is now repaired.

PLASTIC AND FIBERGLASS

The repaired area is now ready for further bodywork and smoothing with a product like Evercoat's Vette panel repair, which is a polyester filler designed to prevent repair mapping and bond line swelling when applied over a fiber-reinforced filler. A filler like Quantum 1 could also be used. The next repair shows this step being done.

FILLING A HOLE IN RIGID PLASTIC

The next repair is very similar to the last one, in that Fiber Tech was used for both. This fender extension is made of ABS plastic, which is very rigid. The customer did not want the antenna holes in the extension, so they must be filled. As in the last repair, the Fiber Tech was applied to both sides of the repair area and the reinforcing matt was not needed as the long and short strands in Fiber Tech gave plenty of support for the repair. Reinforcing matt can always be used when the repair is in an area that receives stress or if more support is needed. But these holes are pretty small. For a larger hole, adding some matt to the back of the repair would be a good idea.

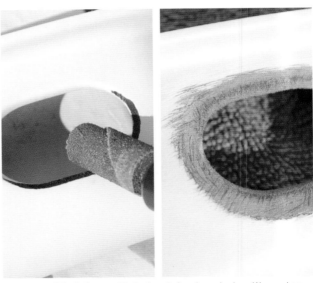

The edges of the holes need to be beveled and roughed up. We used an 80 grit sandpaper roll on a CP compact 90° die grinder. It can also be done by hand. The roughed up surface will give the filler a tooth to grab on to. This procedure is repeated on the back of the panel. On the right is the hole ready for filling.

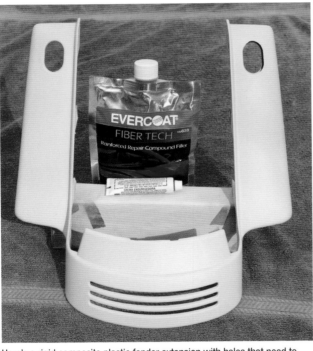

Here's a rigid composite plastic fender extension with holes that need to be filled. If this is not done properly, over time an outline of the holes may appear in the paint, and at the worst, the repair may crack around the holes.

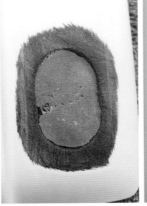

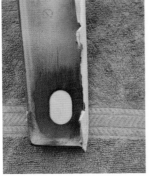 

The back of the piece will be filled first. We taped IP 2˝ over the holes on the top side. Next, we mixed Fiber Tech and applied it on the back side of the part.

After 5 minutes, we removed the tape and the part was allowed to dry for another 5 minutes. On the left is what the top side looked like. On the right, you can see the top side of the repair is sanded with 80 grit. It's now ready to be filled.

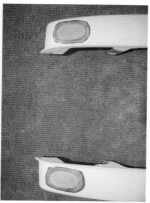

Left: We taped off the area around the hole. We mixed another batch of Fiber Tech and applied it on the top sides of both holes. We removed the tape 5 minutes later. On the right, after 10 minutes, the filler is hard and sanded almost level with 80 grit. Then it's finish sanded with 150 grit until the fill is flush with the surface. **Right:** On the right, the holes are taped off again, leaving a little more than a ¼" between the repair and the tape. We mixed Evercoat's Quantum 1 Single Step Repair with hardener and applied it over the repair area. On the left, once the filler has hardened for 10 minutes, it's sanded with 120 grit.

Left: We removed the tape and sanded the repair area with 180 grit on a block until it transitioned smoothly with the surface. Now it's ready for urethane primer. **Right:** Here is the finished piece after priming, sanding, sealer application, basecoating, and clearcoat. It looks like the holes were never there, and this repair will last as long as the part. It will not crack or shrink.

HOW TO PREPARE PLASTIC FOR PAINTING

Prepping plastic composite parts for paint has also been made much easier due to new technology products. The painter only needs to follow a few simple steps and the part is ready for priming or sealer and basecoat.

In this chapter, we are using PPG's One Choice Plastic Prep System. Whatever brand of paint system you use, get the P sheet, as products other than One Choice may have different application techniques and requirements. And follow the instructions to the last detail.

PREPARING UNPAINTED/UNPRIMED PLASTIC SUBSTRATES

Here's one of the saddlebags we'll be prepping. It's bare plastic with no kind of coating on it. The One Choice System is a three-step process with a product for each step.

Left: First, the parts need to be cleaned and scuffed. We thoroughly scuffed and cleaned the part with the scuff side of the SU4901 Clean and Scuff Pad. Then, we rinsed it with water and blew and wiped it dry. The entire surface must be deglossed. Pay special attention to corners and recesses, making sure to get into any nooks and crannies. The surface must be completely dry before proceeding. **Right:** Next, we used SU4902 plastic adhesion wipes. This advanced film former promotes excellent adhesion and removes static charge from unprimed plastic substrates. We applied a light even coat over the entire area, wiping in one direction to minimize product overlap. Allow 3–5 minutes flash time.

SU4903 advance plastic bond comes in both an aerosol and a quart. You can use either. We're using a quart can. We shook the can for a minute then strained it into a SATA minijet 3000B with a 1.2 fluid tip and sprayed one light coat. We allowed the parts to flash, and after 5 minutes, the parts were flashed to a dull finish and ready for sealer. Do not apply a heavy wet coat. If we were working on a large part, we would have used a full-sized spray gun.

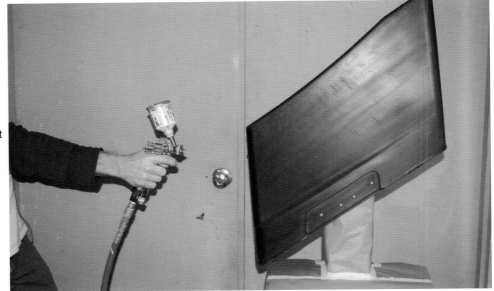

PREPARING PAINTED OR PRIMED PLASTIC SUBSTRATES

This process is very similar to the previous process. In this example, we are prepping the plastic shell and fascia around a 1967 Firebird steering column. The plastic was very old and worn. We cleaned and scuffed it the same way with the SU4901 Clean and Scuff Pad. Then rinsed and dried it.

The plastic was then sanded with 400 grit. Any shiny places or spots had to be sanded or scuffed. If it's shiny, the paint will not stick to it. Next, it was wiped clean and dried.

REPAIRING A BUMPER COVER

Yes, it's a pain to remove the bumper cover, and unless the damage is very minimal, it's best to remove the cover. Plus, having the cover on a bench, saw horse, or panel stand puts it at a better, more comfortable angle to work on, protects the surrounding panels from damage during the repair, and saves time by not having to mask off the car when it comes time to paint.

Bumper covers are held on by a variety of hidden screws, bolts, fasteners, and self-locking tabs. Every car manufacturer is different, so you may have to do a little hunting around to find them. Look for them under the

We final cleaned the part with a clean white cloth and SXA103 or DX103 multiprep anti-static final clean, wiping in one direction. Then, we immediately wiped it clean using a separate clean white cloth. We allowed 3–5 minutes for proper flash time before proceeding to sealer or topcoat.

should be identified on the back of the bumper cover by a three letter code.

- PPO, PP, TEO, and TPO are thermoplastics and make up about 80% of bumper materials. One thing to remember about thermoplastic bumpers is that the molding process introduces a small amount of wax-based mold release into the plastic, which repels adhesives and paint. The surface requires an extra step during prep to remove this. Each time the cover is sanded, it has to be cleaned with a special panel prep solvent. Thermoplastic material melts and smears easily with grinders and sanders, so if the surface starts looking stringy or gets hot, allow the repair area to cool down from time to time when prep sanding.
- TPUR and PUR are thermoset material. They only make up about 15% of bumpers. Their surface powders when sanded, and they are easier to repair.

DOUBLE-SIDED BUMPER COVER REPAIR

In this section, we'll be explaining how to use Evercoat's Plastic Repair 5 to repair a torn or badly cracked bumper cover. Plastic Repair 5 can be used on most thermoplastic and thermoset bumper materials. The process is very similar to the two previous repairs presented in this chapter. The surface is cleaned, scuffed, filled, and sanded.

1. Begin by washing both sides, front and back, with soap and water, and dry them with a clean cloth.
2. Clean both sides with a product like Evercoat Panel Prep #881 to remove any contaminates. Spray panel prep onto a clean rag, and wipe the surfaces. Avoid spraying it directly on the repair area.
3. Bevel the front side of the repair to about a 45° angle with a rotary file or sandpaper roll on a die grinder.
4. Sand the surface immediately around the repair with 80 grit in a palm/DA sander or by hand with a block. To help support the bumper during the sanding process, use a wooden paint stick under the repair area.
5. Next, sand the back side of the bumper cover with 80 grit.
6. To ensure maximum repair strength on an edge or in a high stress area drill ⅛" holes along each side of the tear. This process creates a rivet effect. If any

hood or trunk, along the wheel wells and underneath the car. Some of them might be round plastic fasteners and some of them will have a Phillips screw head in the middle. Once they are all removed, the bumper cover should pull off with a few tugs. If it doesn't come off, you might have missed a fastener, so look again where the cover seems to be sticking.

Some plastic or bumper repair products are designed for specific types of plastic, whereas some others are made for several different kinds. Do the research on whatever product you are using. It helps to be able to know the material the bumper is made of. The material loose plastic remains, use a DA sander and 80 grit to sand it off.

7. Now, reclean both sides with #881 Panel Prep. This will remove any mold release that may have come to the surface during the sanding process. Allow 5–10 minutes before proceeding.

8. While not always needed, fiber-reinforced tape can be used to strengthen the repair. This is another option when the damage is very extensive or goes to the edge of a bumper. Cut some tape to size if it will be used and set it aside.

9. Next, if the repair area is very large or is in a high stress place, a repair panel like Evercoat's Multi Purpose Repair Panel #828 can be used in addition to the reinforcing tape. Cut this patch to size also and put it aside.

10. Place a piece of 2″ masking tape on the front side of the repair, and flip the cover back over.

11. Plastic Repair 5 has two components that come in a two cartridge dispenser. It requires a dispensing gun that pressurizes both cartridges at the same time. Evercoat also makes a line of two-component Maxim repair products that are packaged side by side in a single tube cartridge and can be used with a regular caulking gun. The process explained here can be done with either Plastic Repair 5 or Maxim #898. This step is the same for either product. Load the cartridge into the dispensing gun, remove the cap plug from the end of the tube, and push a small amount of material out of the cartridges to ensure even flow of both products. Then screw the mixing tube onto the end of the cartridge tip. Run out a test bead of material the length of the mixing tip on a random surface.

12. Now apply a bead of material on the backside of the bumper, weaving it back and forth from side to side. Then use a plastic spreader to spread the material across the surface, pressing it into the repair area. Slightly build up the material, adding more repair material if needed.

13. Next, if you are using reinforcing tape, place it over the wet repair material and use a spreader to smooth it down and work it into the plastic repair product. If the tear or crack goes around an edge, wrap the material around the edge.

14. If you are using Multi Purpose Repair Panel #828, place the patch on the back side over the tape and the repair product. Seal the edges of the patch to envelope the repair material. Gentle press on the patch, working the material to the center of the repair area. This will work the material up through the holes and into the repair.

15. If the crack is on an edge, place a plastic spreader on each side of the repair and clamp them together. This step will help keep the repair flat across the tear. After a few minutes, remove the tape from the top side of the repair. Allow 4–6 minutes for the material to harden; remove the spreaders.

16. Lightly sand the top surface of the repair to remove the excess material and reclean it with panel prep. Allow 5–10 minutes for flash time, and apply a bead of Plastic Repair 5 on the top surface of the repair. Press it into the tear or crack with a spreader, and build up a smooth layer of Plastic Repair 5 until the level is slightly above the surface of the bumper material. This will help to eliminate low spots and ensure that the repair is done in one application. While the material is still wet, use the spreader to help create a feather-edge transition around the edges of the material. This step will make sanding the repair easier.

17. Allow 20–30 minutes of drying, then contour sand using a DA or sanding block with 180 grit until the repair is smooth and level. Plastic Repair 5 can also be used as a skim coat if a little more filling is needed. Let the skim coat sit for 1 hour before contour sanding with 180. Then the repair is ready for primer or sealer.

SINGLE-SIDED REPAIR ON A BUMPER COVER

For small repairs, like little cracks and scrapes, a single-sided repair may work well. The initial prep process is similar to the double-sided repair, but the repair work is only on the top surface of the bumper cover. Clean the damaged area with panel prep, sand it down and feather it, remove the loose material, and clean it again with panel prep. Apply Plastic Repair 5 or Maxim 898 to the damaged area, allow it to dry, then sand it smooth.

If there's ever a question about whether a particular product can be used on a certain type of plastic, call the company's tech line. That's what it there for. They are there to answer questions about their products. It's not that difficult to repair and paint plastic. Just do the research, get the correct products for the job, and take the time to do the job right.

Chapter 8
Color Matching

To describe how color ingredients work together to create colors could be a book in itself. In fact, PPG teaches color adjusting classes that cover several days. But this chapter covers the basics and should help in many color matching situations. A number of options are available when it comes to matching paint colors. The simplest is to use a vehicle's make, year, and model and have your local paint jobber mix up the stock, original color. But in some cases this doesn't work.

- For some reason, the color doesn't match.
- You need to match a custom color, and you don't know the color code or paint brand.
- The paint you need to match is old and faded.

So how to custom match a color? Some paint companies have a paint color analyzer. PPG's RapidMatch X-5 spectrophotometer device is capable of scanning a painted surface from five reflective angles to precisely measure its color. You simply bring a part of the color to be matched to your paint jobber and they use the device to analyze the color. But this only works for OEM car colors. There will be times when you have to match up and custom mix a color yourself. So here are several examples of custom matching and mixing a color.

LEARNING TO ANALYZE COLORS

Let's say you've had a color mixed up at your paint jobber but it doesn't match. The first thing you need to do figure out why. What exactly about the color is different?

- Is it too dark or too light?
- Is the tone of the color off? For example, a red that is too much on the side of orange.
- For metallic or pearl colors, is the grain of the metallic or pearl too coarse or too fine?
- Is it an OEM color or a tri-coat custom color? (Refer to chapter 12.)
- Does the color "flop" incorrectly?

WHAT IS FLOP?

A metallic or pearl color can appear different when viewed from different angles. The same color can also appear different depending on if it's in direct sunlight, shade, or indoor light. This is due to the way light reflects off the metallic or pearl particles in the paint mix, which depends on how these flakes are angled in the paint layer. One way paint companies manipulate flop is to add a flop adjuster. PPG has several products that are used to adjust flop. They are added to metallics or pearls to change the flop and make the metallic spear larger. The more adjuster that is added to the mixture, the brighter a color will appear when viewed from an angle.

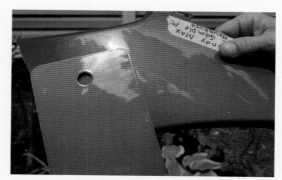

Looking at a color from a straight on angle in direct sunlight, the color looks nice and bright. The color sample appears to be a perfect match to the original color.

But when viewed in the shade from a slight angle, the sample flops dark—darker than the color. It's not a big difference, but it's enough of a difference to be noticed as not matching.

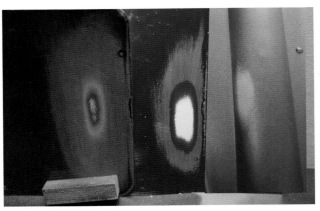

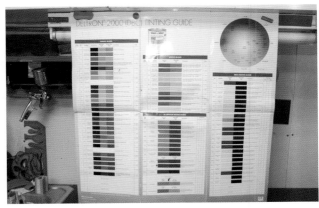

The first thing to do is to determine if the color is a tri-coat. A tri-coat is a basecoat layered with a candy or pearl color. This task can be hard to accomplish if there is no damage to the part you are trying to match, because you need to see the layers of the paint. Here, I've sanded through the layers on three samples. The right sample shows a metallic color over primer; you can see only two coats of metallic, no matter which base is under it. The middle sample shows a pearl color over a white base; that's a tri-coat, as the blue pearl requires a white base. The left sample shows a candy over a metallic base over primer; you can see the black primer, ring of the silver metallic, followed by the five layers of candy blue, which appears as a soft blue fade.

Anytime you are mixing, matching, or creating paint colors, the best place to start is the tinting chart of whichever paint brand you are using. This is the PPG tinting chart—my best friend in the paint shop. On the left are the mixing bases. They are shown as the mass tone of the base, mixed 50/50 with white and 50/50 with a silver metallic. Many of these are transparent bases used in metallic colors. The descriptions of the bases to the right of the color chips have more information on how each base is used. The top middle of the chart shows the highly concentrated yellows, reds, and oranges in solid colors. The bottom middle of the chart shows the metallic bases, shown in their mass tone and mixed 50/50 with green. The right side of the chart shows many of the pearl colors sprayed over white and also mixed with black.

You don't need art school experience to know color; you just need to know how to correctly figure the specific factors in paint colors. If you only have ever bought premixed paint, it's harder to figure out how the color's ingredients work together to create a paint mixture. Knowing information about basic paint color components will help a painter to know how to create and manipulate paint colors. Here's the starting point.

MATCHING A SOLID COLOR

There are several quick ways to match a solid color. The quickest way is to find a color that is close. Most paint companies have fleet charts. These can range from a simple assortment of a few hundred basic color chips to decks with over 3,000 colors. I use a PPG color selector chart as a starting place when trying to match solid or metallic colors. It is seen here on the left. I also refer to PPG's custom colors, like their Hot Licks Collection of solid colors (on the right), as well as solid colors from the Vibrance Deck.

If you find a color that's close, you can go online to find the color's formula. For this example, I'm using the formula for Hot Red. This is the online page from the PPG Refinish website. This red has three ingredients: a highly concentrated scarlet red, an orange tint from the center of the tint chart, and a touch of white mixed in. Mix up a test batch of the color, then refer to the chart and add a little more of whichever tint is needed. Fine-tune it until it's the color you want. This next section shows how to fine tune a color.

One of the most unlikely ingredients in many bright colors, like yellows and reds, is black. Experienced painters know just how true this is. Black calms down bright toners. Sometimes they can be too bold, overpowering even. Whenever a color is too strong, add a little black. Sometimes just a few drops will do the trick. Don't be afraid to experiment. Look at your color match and think, where does this color need to go? Does it need more green, more red, brown? By experimenting, you'll see how you can manipulate the various toners to create the desired color.

MATCHING A METALLIC COLOR

There are three types of colored toners.

- Solid or opaque toners
- Transparent toners
- High strength, very concentrated toners

Transparent toners are pretty much how they sound, very transparent, and they mix well with metallics as their transparency allows the full strength of the metallic to show. Opaque toners can also be mixed with metallics, but because they are not as transparent, the effect of the metallic is slightly muted. The high strength toners are only mixed with solid, non-metallic colors.

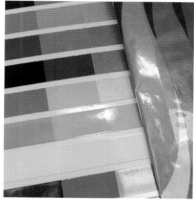

Ah, this is where the real fun starts. In chapter 21, I show how I reproduced a 1979 Trans Am Graphic, but before I could paint it, I had to match the colors of the old decals and graphics. There were five colors that needed to be matched. The first step was to find the main components of the colors by matching one of the two lightest colors, giving me the "master" color. The other four colors were variations of those ingredients. Holding the decal against the chart, I compared the second lightest decal color (color #4) and found two of the toners on the PPG chart were pretty close. But which one should I use? In this photo, the left side shows the two gold/yellow toners under indoor shop lighting. The right side shows the toners in the sunshine. One works better indoors, and one is closer outdoors.

Always judge colors from different angles. A color may be a perfect match from one angle, but look completely different from another angle. For example, both the orange candy on the left and the orange pearl on the right look very bright when viewed straight on.

But look at them from an angle, and the orange candy color goes dark while the pearl stays bright. This is because the metallic base of the candy reflects light differently than the pearl.

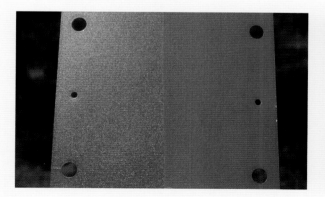

COLOR FACTS

Two colors can appear completely different from each other in one light but look almost the same in another. It all depends on the way the light hits the surface. Here, we have two color samples, one darker than the other. The main toner in the mix is a highly transparent toner. The darker color has small amounts of brown and black mixed in to make it darker than the other. On the left, it's easy to tell the two colors apart. But on the right, these same samples look very much alike because of the way the sun is hitting them. This can be avoided by using an opaque toner instead of a transparent toner. Then the color difference would be consistent from any angle.

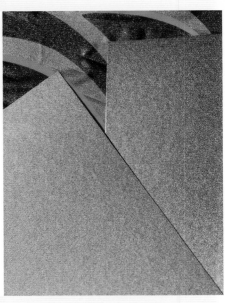

Indoors the bottom gold matches better and outdoors the upper gold matches better. Remember earlier what was said about different kinds of light changing the way a color appears? A color must match in direct sunlight, shade, and indoors. It makes no sense to have a color match great on a sunny day and appear completely different on a cloudy day. And to have a color match in all three kinds of light is not that easy. Sometimes, you have to find a happy medium and get as close as you can.

The next step is to find the correct metallic. Different metallics do different things. Some flop darker than others. Metallic usually come in fine, medium, coarse, very coarse, and sparkle, which is the biggest flake you'll get without going to a big metal flake. Looking at the chart: DMD1687, a medium satin metallic that does *not* flop dark, seemed to be a perfect

match. The grain of the metallic was the same as the decal. Next, I had to find the other colors that would be added to the mixture in different amounts to obtain each color. Some of the colors appeared to have a great deal of brown in them. Looking at the chart, DMD623 is a transparent red oxide. It gives a red gold tone in metallics and a beige tint in solids. In short, it's a very

The gold toner on the top is DMD641, a transparent toner. The gold toner on the bottom is DMD642, an opaque toner. This photo shows just how differently they each reflect light. On the left side they are angled so the sun achieves maximum reflection on the surface of the chart. On the right, the chart is angled so that the sun hits the surface but doesn't reflect as much. Notice how much brighter the gold on the top (641) is when the sun hits it. The transparency of the 641 allows the metallic to really shine. If I used 641, the transparent toner, as the main toner for my master mix, from the right angle, the brightness of the metallic would overpower the differences in the five colors of the graphic. The graphic would be one big gold flash on the hood of the Trans Am. So I need to use the opaque toner, the DMD642, the toner on the bottom. It allows the metallic to sparkle, but it mutes it enough so the differences in the graphic colors can be seen from any angle.

PAINT FACTS

Each paint company is different and products are always changing, but keep in mind, many tints or toners require some kind of paint binder to be mixed with them to help the paint dry. PPG calls theirs DBX1689 Basecoat Converter. How do you tell which tints require binders? With PPG's Deltron paints, any three-digit tint or toner number, like DMD 614, needs to have converter mixed in, usually at a 1 to 1 ratio. Four-digit numbers do not require converter. You can find out this information in the tech sheet for a product or in a paint's formula.

brown toner and perfect for the brown that is needed for the graphic colors. The last toner to be added is black. A little black will mute down the warm tones of the 642 and 623 and darken the darker colors.

MATCHING A CANDY COLOR

Matching tri-coat colors can be a little tricky because so many factors affect the end result color.

- What metallic base was used?
- How many layers of candy color were used?
- How concentrated or strong was the candy mix?
- At what gun speed was the candy sprayed?

- What is the pattern overlap of the candy color?

Hopefully you can find out the brand of paint and the colors that were used. But if you don't have that information, here's a quick guide to matching a tri-coat. It's easy enough to figure out the candy color. But the real starting place is finding out what base was used. If the vehicle is damaged, you can sand around the damage and see the layers of paint. This way you can get an idea if a gold, silver, or colored metallic was used for the base. And don't forget about the flop factor. If you cannot see what color the base is, then you need to start comparing the color to the colors on a candy paint chart.

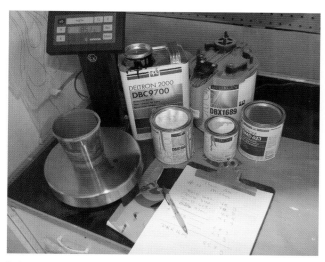
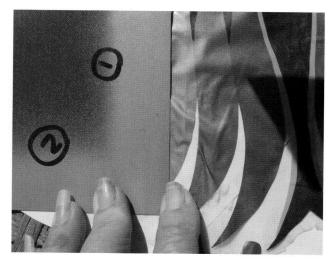

Left: Now to mix the master color. I have all the components of the mixture ready, plus I am writing down the amounts in grams of each component as they're poured into the mixing cup. I'm starting out with a 50/50 mix of the 1687 metallic and the 642 opaque yellow; small amounts of the 623 red oxide and the 9700 black are added. **Right:** The colors are mixed, and I compare some of the mixture on a paint stick to the decal. It looks pretty close, so I spray some on a sprayout card and compare it to the decal. On the color card I note that it's Sample #1. It looks a bit green, a little too cool, and it needs to be warmer. I add a little more 642 yellow and a few more drops of 623 red. I make sure to note these amounts on the paper.

Sample #2 is too warm, too yellow. It needs to be cooled down slightly. I'll try adding a little black to take the yellow down a notch.

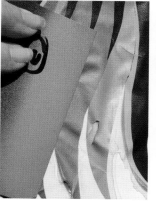

Sample #3 is just right. It matches in sunshine (on the left), and it matches under indoor lighting (on the right).

Left: The first of the five colors to be painted for the Trans Am graphic will be the darkest color. Now that I have a formula for the master mix, which is Color #4, I mix up a quart and use this as the base mix for the dark brown color. To turn this into a dark brown, more of two of the main ingredients are added: the 623 red oxide (brown) and the 9700 black. The trick is figuring out how much of each to add to create a perfect match. This mixture looks to be pretty close, maybe a little light. **Right:** Wow, looking at it from a slightly different angle reveals it's actually quite a bit lighter—too light. I'll try adding more black.

Now it's too dark, too much black. I need to add a little of the master mix to lighten it up (just a little bit). I make sure to document everything I add.

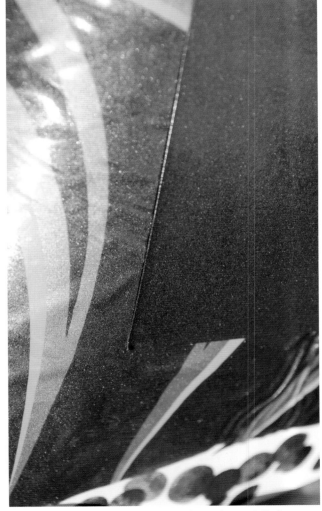

It actually took 11 mixtures to find the right match. I ended up with two pages of notes, documenting all the different mixtures as toners were added. What are the main tools a painter needs when matching a color? Sunshine, a good paint scale, a toner chart, and lots of patience.

OK, it's a pretty good match and about as close as I can get. It's the same tone, same sparkle, same brown.

COLOR FACT

If you're trying to match an OEM tri-coat, get as much information about the vehicle as you can. Start with make, model, and year. Was it a special order or limited release color? Sometimes you can get the formulas for some OEM tri-coat colors. For example, many of the Harley Davidson tri-coat colors have PPG paint codes. Or you can look them up online by using a search engine and typing in the name of the color and any other information you have about the color. Online research is a big help when trying to figure out a custom OEM color.

DON'T FORGET

Don't forget about the flop factor. Just because you've figured out the color of the metallic base doesn't mean you matched it. You might need to adjust the degree of flop. Make sure to check your color match from all angles.

I'm trying to match this orange candy. I sanded into the layers of the part, and it seems that the metallic base is a gold or yellow/orange metallic. Now I compare the color to the PPG Vibrance Candy Colors. Some colors are close, but none of them match. The base and candy will both need to be custom mixes.

I've looked up the mixtures for a few of the Vibrance gold bases to see what toners are used in them. One base had transparent yellow, some black, transparent orange, and some black mixed with course aluminum silver. Others used a Vibrance product called Starfire, an orange aluminum base that has a medium-sized grain. It's very intense in color but appears dark on the tint chart.

HANDY HINT

One trick to lighten the flop in metallics is to add some pearl to the mix. Pearl is a finer grain than metallics. The fine sparkle of the pearl gets lost in the sparkle of the aluminum base, but because pearl particles reflect light differently than metallics, the base will appear brighter when viewed from an angle. I used this trick in trying to match the orange candy.

Left: I've prepared several different bases. One is DMD1687, the medium satin aluminum I used before. I've mixed in a little PLRX3 gold pearl to brighten the flop. The other base is Starfire. Three samples are made of each base color. **Right:** Next, I mix up some orange candy using DBC500 mixed with DMX211 orange concentrate. I have to figure out how many layers were applied and how concentrated the actual candy color is. Looking at the candy color I'm trying to match, it seems to have a little red in it, so I add a little DMX212 red (yellow shade). I try different mixtures of orange and red candy, trying them out on the six samples I made. After four mixtures, I come up with a mixture that matches the orange candy. The Starfire base flops too dark. But the aluminum/gold pearl base has the right amount of flop. Mix #4 candy over this base is a pretty good match. On the left, it matches in a direct view. On the right, it matches at an angled view.

ANOTHER CANDY MATCH

It matches from a sharp angle in the sun and flops the same. **Below:** It even matches in the shade when viewed from a sharp angle—the tone of blue is exactly the same.

Judging a color match from multiple angles. The candy blue matches in the sunlight from a straight on angle.

Left: Now the real test—it's easy enough to match a small sample piece, but will the colors sprayed onto a large fairing match up? The candy has to be sprayed evenly, using the same gun speed, the same pattern overlap, and the same concentration as the sample. In the sun, the fairing I painted appears to be a good match to the fender I'm trying to match. **Right:** Again, it even matches up pretty well in the shade. For this paint job, I actually had to match four colors and one textured silver effect.

A PAINT TRUTH

One thing I did not talk about was how frustrating color matching can be. You can spend a whole morning or day trying to match a color. It will look great, then it will dry dark and not match. Or you think it's a great match and someone with a fresh pair of eyes who hasn't been looking at color samples all day will walk up and comment how the color doesn't match. I'll start working on a color match, and bang, the sun will go behind the clouds and not come out again. You can use Sun Guns and daylight lights, but the real sun will give you the best results. To get those best results try to match colors when the sun is pretty much overhead. Not too early in the day and not too late. If you start getting frustrated, put that project aside until the next day and try again. Sometimes it takes a fresh pair of eyes and a ton of patience to get the best result for a color match. Better to get it right than spend the time and materials only to finish the job and realize that everyone notices how the colors don't match. I see many bad color matches that ended up on vehicles. Good color matches can take time.

One last color match: candy red pearl with a dark red pearl graphic and off white pearl pinstripe. This was a toughie as I had to use flop adjuster in the base and also in the candy pearl color, which was layered over the base. I got the red candy pearl and the dark red pretty close. The pinstripe is a little light. It took many samples to get all three colors matched up. Eight days were spent doing the color match for this job alone.

Chapter 9
Understanding and Finding the Most Effective Color and Design

Color and design can make or break a custom vehicle. Most of the time when people look at a vehicle with great paint, they simply appreciate the way it looks. They don't think about what exactly makes it so good, or rather, *why* it so effectively captures their interest. I've gone to many, many car and bike shows; sometimes I'll look at a vehicle and wonder, "What were they thinking?" Gorgeous car, lame paint—like a

dead, dull yellow paired with dark, dark blue. Others paint poor designs that do not work with the lines of the vehicle.

When color and design come together in the proper combination, a professional paint job can work to a vehicle's best advantage. This chapter is designed to help you understand how color and design work together to bring out the best features of a vehicle.

HOW COLOR WORKS

Note the way the orange bike stands apart from the others. They are all beautifully painted custom bikes. I should know—I painted them! There is an amazing amount of detail in all four of the bikes behind the first one, and the orange one actually sports the least amount of artwork. The intense glow of the orange pearl base paint grabs your attention more than the other bikes in the photo. Color makes the difference.

SOLID COLORS

Solid color is a paint that contains a pigment and no other color additives like metallic or pearl. You cannot see through a solid color. While some solid colors are less opaque than others, they are not transparent like a candy color. If used on the right vehicle or in the right color combination, solid colors can be the perfect choice. Some solid colors do not need an undercoat like white. But some colors, like yellow, work best if a white undercoat is used as yellow is a transparent color and does not appear very solid. A white undercoat can make a color like yellow or red really jump. In fact many seemingly solid colors are quite transparent. How can you tell which ones are transparent? One quick and easy way is to reduce a color and look at it on a paint stick. Can you see through the color? Another way is to spray some of the color on a color card with dark and light toned sections. Can you still see the dark and light sections after a coat or two? One coat will give you an idea of how well the color will cover.

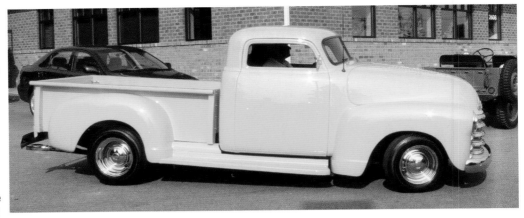

Here is another great example of a solid color bringing out the best features of a hot rod.

BEWARE OF RED

Beware of red! Red is a tricky color to use. It is one of the most eye-catching and easy colors to use. But these advantages make it a very popular color. Use it sparingly on your projects, and then only if you truly feel it is the best color to suit the project and/or if your customer is determined to use it.

PEARL COLORS

This hot rod was a big hit at the 2004 SEMA Show. Note how it has only a small pinstripe? The color is the feature, and the color is so intense that if any artwork were added, it would only take away from the color. Pearl is a great choice for hot rods as the tone of the pearl changes from various angles depending on how the light hits that surface. Note the way the light plays over the surface, some areas lighting up as if they were glowing, contrasting against the areas that are in shadow. The color is, in itself, the artwork.

CANDY COLORS

This hot rod truck is a perfect example of candy apple red. Candy colors are transparent tones that are usually applied over a metallic base. The metallic base can be almost any color. I tend to use candy or dye concentrates and mix them with clearcoat, using that as my candy paint. This way I can control the intensity of my candy paint. This truck also shows the result of very thorough prepaint preparation as the paint is so straight.

Here is an example of a candy color used over artwork. The metallic basecoat was done and then the artwork was done over that. Next a few coats of candy blue were applied over the entire truck.

FACTORY COLOR, FANTASTIC RESULTS

Don't ignore the factory color charts! This sweet 1951 Merc is painted with a stock 1995 Ford color called Ultra Violet Poly. Al Baglione is the owner of this beautiful creature.

FLAKE PAINT

Left: Flake colors are big flakes of reflective material that are mixed with clearcoat. They are best applied over a metallic basecoat that is slightly darker than the desired finish color. Flake paint comes in many colors. Many painters apply candy colors over flake paint, richening the color and giving it more depth. Depending on the brand there are several sizes of flakes, usually medium- and larger-sized flake. The parts on the left were painted with a gunmetal colored flake. Then the flames were taped off and sprayed a red flake, with a coat of candy red sprayed over the flake to give it a little more depth. **Right:** Lowrider paint jobs use a great deal of flake. Most of the time, the painters start with a basecoat of large flake, then tape off the graphics, using candy colors, allowing the flake to shine through. This paint is by Craig Fraser.

METALLIC PAINT

Most paint companies offer many different grades of metallic or aluminum to add to your toners. PPG offers nine different grades of coarseness. From fine satin to medium to coarse to sparkle. These metallics can be manipulated to create many different effects.

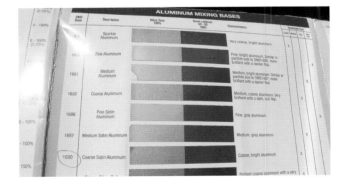

COLOR-CHANGING COLORS

Left: Color changing paint is a pearl-style paint that changes color as it viewed from different angles. It is available in many color combinations. A purple to teal to blue is seen here. **Right:** This Harley VRod is painted with a red to gold color-changing paint. Be careful in the use of color-changing paint as it can have an overwhelming effect. In some projects color-changing paint works great as a graphic color.

COLOR COMBINATIONS

It's too easy for custom painters and their customers to fall into rigid rules about which color pairs best with another color. And remember, a single color can fall into many different tones depending on what toners are mixed in; think of how some reds burn like fire while others are so dark they're nearly black, like the darkest cherries. A lemony yellow is very different from a school bus yellow. Color choices are a time for brutal honesty. If you have a poor sense of color and cannot tell the difference from lime green to a darker Kelly green, ask someone for their opinion.

Painters and artists need to understand the following six characteristics of the color wheel.

Hue

This is the actual color. Based on the color wheel, there are about 12 hues. From top clockwise: red, red-violet, violet, blue-violet, blue, blue-green, green, yellow-green, yellow, yellow-orange, orange, red-orange.

Lightness or Tone

This represents the shade of the color. It constitutes the amount of black and white added to the particular hue. For example, pink is the shade of red due to the result of more white. And crimson is a darker shade of red due to more black.

Similar Colors

These are colors adjacent to each other. Examples are red and red-orange, or yellow-green and yellow. Or

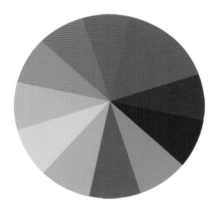

A color wheel is a very handy tool in figuring out color. Compare the color combinations in the previous photos with the color arrangement on the wheel. There are six characteristics in the color wheel the painter or artist needs to understand.

colors with one color in between on the color wheel, like blue and green, or red and orange.

Contrasting Colors

This is when there are three colors between one another on the color wheel. Examples include blue and yellow, red and blue, and orange and violet.

Complementary Colors

When colors are opposite each other in the color wheel, they are considered complementary. Examples include red and green, or yellow and violet.

Color Combinations Based on the Same Hue

These are colors of the same hue but of different shades and vividness. This street rod color combination is a perfect example. Both colors are the same hue, a red on the purple side. Only the top is a lighter shade with a darker shade on the bottom.

Color Combinations Based on Similar Hues

As explained above, these colors are adjacent to each other on the color wheel. They have common characteristics in color, yet a slight difference between these colors can be felt. Here a red base color has been paired up with an orange flame. A blue pinstripe helps them play off each other.

Color Combinations Based on Contrasting Hues

Was this guy at the Tulip Fest? Two-tone street rod, orange topped with purple, separated by a teal graphic striped with lime green. An additional graphic, dark orange striped in light purple, runs beneath it. Note the soft black airbrushed shadows under the graphics, which give the graphics dimension, "lifting" them off the surface. The contrast of the orange and purple is very bold. If bold and bright are what you want for your vehicle, then contrasting colors are the best choice.

Here are three examples of contrasting colors. I saw these bikes pull up and they caught my eye right off. Something as simple as color combinations can make all the difference in how effective a paint job is. You can have the most detailed design but without the right colors, it will simply sit there dead.

ASSORTED COLOR COMBINATIONS

Pairing colors with black can create a striking contrast and be very effective for bringing out the best features of your custom ride. Vehicles painted with black have a more edgy, intense effect as opposed to the shimmery feel of street rods or bikes with lots of chrome.

The solid red basecoat paint accents the sweet curves of this Ford truck. The black grill offsets the red and gives it attitude.

On the top half is a car I saw from a long distance and it drew me right over to it. Bumblebees did not come to mind. Just clean and evil attitude. Keeping the yellow on the lower half of the car and trimming off the upper half with black accents the lower portion of the vehicle and makes this already long car look even longer. Sleeks it right out. On the bottom of the photo, purple and black complement one another very effectively. Not as dramatic as pink and black. It is a sleeker look, more subtle.

Cream and candy russet gives this old street rod a classic effect and is harmonious with the warm tone of the russet. The champagne bronze would also complement the russet. Would the cinnamon russet work as well with silver? No. The silver is a cool color and would look awkward with the hotter tone of the russet.

Left: This silvery white pearl contrasts dramatically against this candy tangerine. I don't know for certain how this paint was applied, but it appears as if the silver white pearl was sprayed on first, then the upper half of the car was taped off and candy tangerine was sprayed over it. A quick and easy technique. The brightness of pearl white base gives the tangerine an electric glow. **Right:** This icy pearl silver and light blue pearl combo is pure cool elegance.

COLOR DEBATES

Is it blue or is it purple? Sometimes colors walk a fine line between one color and the color next to it on the color wheel. Red and orange, purple and blue; out of 20 people who might look at this truck, half will say purple and the other half will say blue. Pairing the right color can help viewers see the main shade in its (and your) intended light.

COLOR MYTHS

Is there such a thing as colors that do not belong together—colors that should not be used in certain designs? When you mention lime green to someone, most of the time they don't think it's a good choice for custom paint. But as you look through this chapter, you'll see a lot of lime green as well as many other colors that may not seem to be good choices for killer custom paint. But pair the right colors together in the right design, and you'll get some amazing results. Some colors get bad raps, green most of all. But without green, custom paint would be pretty dull.

The Green Myth

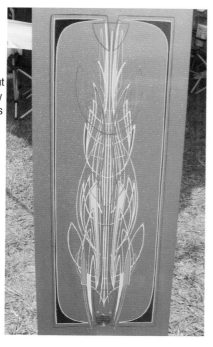

How about an olive greenish gold basecoat with pink, powder blue, and lime green? It does sound like these colors would not go together. But looking at this photo, they look awesome. Jim Norris is a legendary pinstriper from North Carolina, and he made this very finely striped panel.

Lime green gold candy? It sure works here on this rigid chopper. But I knew I needed some purple to go with it. My purple flames give the lime gold something to contrast against.

The Pink Myth

Pink is another color with a bad rap. Can pink be used without it seeming feminine? Take a look at these examples.

Here's a truck with a flame graphic that works as a border between the two colors. The result here is an incredibly clean look. The white works great with the orange. It is interesting that the flame is done in pink. Yet, in no way does this truck appear feminine. Note the lime green pinstriping around the flame.

Pink can be used as a main color. This is more of a soft pink, a bit "grayer" or more muted. The color was pretty much dead until the flame was added. The reason it was dead was that it needed something to contrast against. The yellow/orange hot rod flames provided that contrast. Note the way the flames are arranged on the car. The way the flames on the hood transition to the flames on the sides, and how the big swoop shape come down to a neat arrangement of three flames make it very balanced yet random. Paint by Crazy Horse.

Can pink have attitude? It can when it is paired with black. Edgy elegance. The pink candy basecoat seen here is very rich and deep.

FINDING THE MOST EFFECTIVE DESIGN

One of the questions I hear the most is, "How do you come up with your designs?" I also hear, "I have no idea what kind of design I want for my ride." So how *do* you find the right design?

Sometimes a person knows exactly what he or she wants, but is it the best design for their project? This is one part of the custom build process that should not be rushed. Take your time and thoroughly research the design; look in magazines and online to see if there are vehicles like yours with a similar design. See if you like it. Or better yet, try it out on paper by tracing an enlarged photo of your project to make several "blanks" of your project. Next, simply sketch any designs directly on the copies. It's a rough method, but with a little practice you can get an idea of how to create the best design for your project.

HOW A DESIGN WORKS

Is a custom car or bike without artwork as custom as one with artwork? It is purely a matter of personal preference. This Ford Hi-Boy looks very cool painted this fiery tone of red. But would it look better with artwork like flames or graphics?

Here's a Hi-Boy with black flames and a wicked killer rainbow fade basecoat. Now these cars are exactly the same length but the flamed car looks longer. Note the trim line along the bottom of the car. On the flamed Hi-Boy it has been painted black and disappears. That plus the flames narrows the body of the car and accentuates the length of the car. The fade also helps this lengthening effect. The brightness on the front of the car, makes the surface look bigger, farther away from the dark colors on the rear of the car. Flames by Wade Hughes.

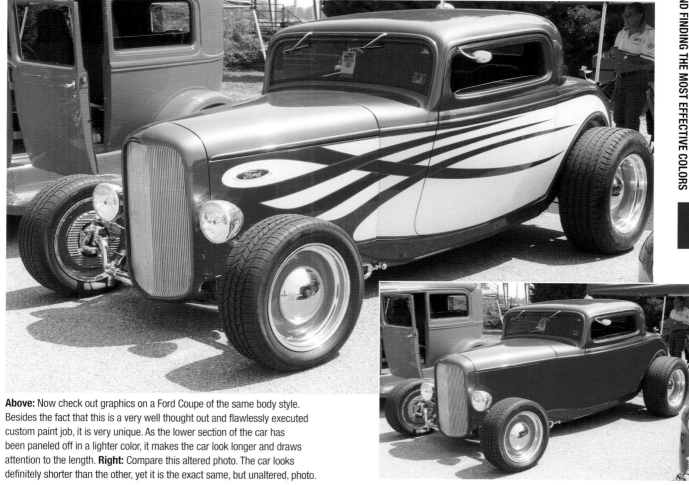

Above: Now check out graphics on a Ford Coupe of the same body style. Besides the fact that this is a very well thought out and flawlessly executed custom paint job, it is very unique. As the lower section of the car has been paneled off in a lighter color, it makes the car look longer and draws attention to the length. **Right:** Compare this altered photo. The car looks definitely shorter than the other, yet it is the exact same, but unaltered, photo.

TRYING ON A DESIGN

This '32 Ford is pretty sweet, but the owner, Raymond Mays, wanted me to spice it up. The overall shape of the car appears pretty square in this photo. This a PhotoShop drawing I made after talking to Raymond. He wanted real fire flame, but just enough to complement the car. He did not want people to see the flames first then notice the car. Compare the shape of the car in this photo to the previous one. The yellow on the front of the car seems to actually shrink it down, giving the 32s form and a more graceful shape. The car even appears longer. Prepaint drawings are very helpful and sometimes essential for finding the most effective paint design for a vehicle.

Here is the '32 Ford after I finished painting the flames. It's the same car, but it sure looks different.

DESIGN AND COLOR

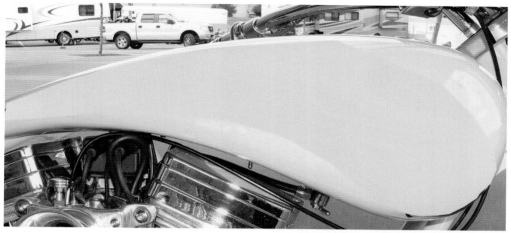

I like the bikes I paint to have a long, lean look. When the customer wanted yellow for this bike, I knew it would be a challenge to find the right color for the artwork. Yellow is a glow color and makes a vehicle look bigger, but in all directions, not just the length.

I came up with this black and white gear design that slashes across the tank. The black and white has a touch of blue and the colors are very cool yet work great with the yellow. Black and yellow work great together. The angle of the design makes the most of the downward curve of the front of the tank. It slims down the tank, and the gears make the paint very interesting. There is a lot to look at. The paint goes from boring and bland to sleek and intricate.

WHAT IS AN EFFECTIVE DESIGN?

In the top of the photo, the new improved paint can be seen. A customer sent me this tank with his old paint job still on it. The old paint did not work the tank to its best advantage. It was too round. The colors were too subtle. No drama. No interest. They say black is slenderizing. It sure seems so here. What is true for fashion is sometimes true for custom paint. The artwork cuts the tank in half, giving the illusion of more length. The black frames the red, creating contrast, and in turn making the red look brighter. The liner design is limited to the middle of the tank. It is more than just a straight line, but it is still not overly complex. There is only one real curved line. The rest is all straight lines. Paint by Crazy Horse.

DESIGNS AND TRIM LINES

Look closely at how the colors are split along the body and trim lines in many of the two-tone paint jobs in this chapter. This method is commonly used in automotive graphic paint design.

This photo shows a great color combination of two solid colors split along the body line by a simple yet very effective graphic.

PAINTER VERSUS CUSTOMER PREFERENCES

Pink and blue? Normally this color combination would not be something I would put together. But somehow, on this truck it works. Keep an open mind when it comes to colors.

This brings up another subject: painter preferences. Just because I, as the painter, love a certain color combination, does not mean the customer likes it. Painters should try not to force their color desires on customers if the customer has something else in mind. What the painter prefers may be quite different from what the customer likes. This is why customers and their painters need to be able to communicate freely.

Chapter 10
Solvent-Based Painting

Can an award winning detailed paint job be done in by the DIYer in a home shop? It sure can. This 1965 Impala has won numerous best paint awards, and it was done in a home shop.

Chapter 1 explained how solvent-based paint works. This chapter follows the process as solvent-based two-stage paint is applied to the Firebird we restored in chapter 3.

Back in chapter 3 we finished the bodywork and priming on the '67 Firebird. Now it's time to paint it. The first thing we needed to do was come up with a color. Once we had a color, we would know which tone of sealer we would need to use. PPG has a chart that shows the different sealer tones. Some basecoat color formulas will even recommend which undercoat tone to use for maximum hiding.

We had to work with several main requirements for the basecoat color for the Firebird.

- It needed to be easy to spray. We had a tight deadline, and there was little room for errors.

- We wanted a color that would be easy to match and blend in case we needed to make repairs.
- We did not want a high build-up of coats.

These factors ruled out using a tri-coat color. A tri-coat color involves coats of paint color that are semi or fully transparent, like a candy or pearl color. A tri-coat

MATERIALS & EQUIPMENT

Equipment
SATA 4000 HVLP spray gun
SATA 4000 RP spray gun
SATAjet 3000B mini spray gun
Astro Pneumatic Tool Company portable work stands #557003
Summit Racing shop cart SUM-900089
Craftsman jack stands
Meguiar's sanding backing pad E-7200
Gerson 8111P disposable dual cartridge respirator
Eye hooks, S hooks, and chain for hanging parts

Materials
PPG Deltron DP90LV epoxy primer
PPG DP401LV hardener
PPG Deltron DBC9700
PPG PLR89 violet pearl
PPG DC2000 ultra velocity clear
PPG DCH 2015 hardener
PPG DT 885 reducer
PPG DX330 precleaner
SATA Rapid Preparation System cups/lids 0.9 l and 0.3 l
Soft-Sander 800 grit sandpaper
American Tape orange mask and aqua mask ¾″, 1″, and 3″
Gerson Blend Prep tack cloth #020008C
SAS Safety 66518 Raven powder-free disposable nitrile gloves
Masking paper

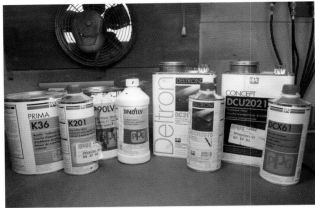

Don't use a hardener or reducer designed for one kind of paint with something it does not go with. On the left are two kinds of urethane clear but they both have their own hardener. These hardeners are not interchangeable. On the right are two kinds of primer, and they also each have a hardener specifically designed for each primer. They also are not interchangeable. Doing things like using a hardener not specified to go with that paint product or mixing up types of hardener and reducer is how painting nightmares start. Sometimes painters will be ready to start painting and not have exactly the right ingredient to go with their paint, so they grab something they think might work. This is always a bad idea!

color will change with each coat of paint that is applied. Tri-coat colors are usually very deep and rich looking. And many show cars are painted with tri-coats. It can be a bit of a challenge to paint a car in pieces with a candy or pearl unless the painter is experienced with this method.

While I have many years of experience, the deadline with this car left nothing to chance. So I wanted to play it safe and make it easy. But could we come up with an eye-catching, show-winning color that could give great coverage in three coats?

It helps to have experience with a brand of paint when you are picking what kind of color to use. But what if you have little experience? Then it helps to use a respected brand name of paint. Go to your local auto body paint supplier and talk to the owner and staff. They can help lead you in the right direction. Look at their paint charts.

Chapter 8 talks about mixing custom colors. If you have a color in mind, then test it out before you spend hundreds on paint materials and apply them to your project only to find out the color is not exactly what you thought it would be. Buy a pint of the color you are interested in, the reducer to go with it, and small cans of the urethane clearcoat and hardener. Then go home and spray some samples. Be sure to spend the time and money to clear those samples as colors will look different once they are cleared. And reread the first section of chapter 1, Understanding How Paint Works.

What's the best advice I can give a new painter about solvent-based paint? Follow the rules. Get the sheets for the specific products being used and follow the specifications down to the last detail. Don't mix paint brands.

One of the biggest challenges in mixing up paint is knowing how much paint will be needed to do the job. Too many times painters have calculated how much paint will be needed only to get into the booth and run out of material halfway through that last coat of paint.

For the Firebird, I kept track of how much primer it took to do four coats on the whole car. This gave me an idea of the amount of paint the job would take. Granted

| | | Mix Ratio by Volume | Mix Ratio by Cumulative Weight | | | | | | | |
| | | | Grams | | | | Parts | | | |
Group	Component	Mix Ratio	¼ Pint	½ Pint	Pint	Quart	¼ Pint	½ Pint	Pint	Quart
G1	DP48LV	2	90	180	360	720	102	203	406	812
	DP401LV	1	122	243	486	971	137	274	548	1095
	D87xx / DT18xx	1	157	314	628	1256	177	354	708	1416
G2	DP48LV	1.6	72	144	288	576	81	162	325	650
	DP50LV	.4	89	177	354	708	100	200	399	798
	DP401LV	1	120	240	480	959	136	271	541	1082
	D87xx / DT18xx	1	156	311	622	1244	176	351	702	1403
G3	DP48LV	1.5	92	185	270	540	76	152	304	609
	DP50LV	.5	88	176	353	706	99	199	398	796
	DP401LV	1	120	239	478	957	134	269	539	1079
	D87xx / DT18xx	1	155	310	621	1242	175	350	700	1401
G4	DP48LV	.5	23	45	90	180	26	51	102	203
	DP50LV	1.5	84	169	338	676	95	190	381	762
	DP401LV	1	116	232	463	927	130	261	522	1045
	D87xx / DT18xx	1	152	303	606	1212	171	342	684	1367
G5	DP50LV	2	83	166	331	662	93	186	373	746
	DP401LV	1	114	228	456	913	129	258	515	1030
	D87xx / DT18xx	1	150	300	599	1198	169	338	676	1351
G6	DP50LV	1	42	83	166	331	46	93	186	373
	DP90LV	1	82	164	328	656	92	185	370	740
	DP401LV	1	114	227	454	907	128	256	512	1023
	D87xx / DT18xx	1	149	298	596	1192	168	336	672	1344
G7	DP90LV	2	81	162	325	650	92	183	366	733
	DP401LV	1	112	225	450	901	127	254	508	1016
	D87xx / DT18xx	1	148	296	593	1186	167	334	669	1338

The PPG undercoat chart shows the different tones of undercoat that may be used under basecoat color to help achieve total coverage. Many paint formulas or colors will recommend what tone of undercoat to use to achieve maximum hiding or good coverage, that is, the paint completely covers and there are no light or dark spots. The entire surface is all the same tone.

primer sprays differently than basecoat, but it will help you to estimate what will be needed. And always mix up extra. If you think you will need one gallon, mix up or order another quart. Most of the time, you will end up getting into that quart. For the Firebird, I mixed up a gallon of Firebird Purple basecoat plus two more quarts. At the end of the paint job, there was a quart left.

For this book we wanted to duplicate the conditions the average DIYer would be experiencing. That meant no professional paint booth. So we hung up a plastic barrier in our shop. Summit Racing sells a line of Zip Wall plastic barrier accessories, like spring loaded poles and zippers, to create an enclosed plastic barrier.

WHY USE AN UNDERCOAT?

Why take the time and money to use a sealer or undercoat under the basecoat? The priming has been done, so is it really necessary? Not using a sealer is another one of the biggest mistakes a painter can make. Here's why. Sealer is very opaque, which means it covers very well. Most of the time when you sand primer, it will get sanded through in places and those sand-throughs may show up as a different tone. Plus there may be some deeper scratches from the sandpaper. Sealer evens out the any tone differences and helps smooth over the scratches.

Do not, however, try and use sealer as a scratch filler! Sealer helps to smooth over some scratches, but it is not a substitute for primer/surfacer. Don't take shortcuts in the preparation process. If you need to reprime some areas due to deep scratches, then take the time to apply more primer. Take extra care with this step especially if you are using metallic or pearl basecoats, because visible sand scratches in the surface will show up in the finished result. Again, don't try and use sealer or basecoat paint as a filler.

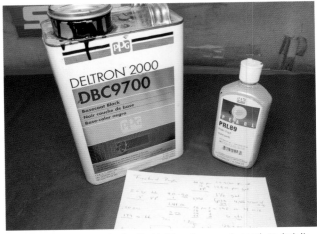

The paint color planned for the Firebird is a deep purple pearl, so dark it appears to be black on a cloudy day. But when the sun hits the car, the curves light up purple. The purple I'm looking for is not a black cherry kind of color, but a true purple. Not too blue or too red. PPG has a Violet pearl powder, PRL89. This will be mixed with DBC9700 Black. Now to find the right mix of black and violet.

Before the parts were put into place in the paint area, they were wiped with PPG DX330 precleaner and blown off with air to remove any debris or dust.

Next, it was time to prep the car and parts for paint. The hood, trunk lid, fenders, fender extensions, front valance, rear spoiler, and hood tachometer would all be painted off the car. We had two Astro Tool portable work stands to hold the fenders. Anything used for supporting parts was wrapped in masking paper and

Next, we needed to get all the paint materials needed for the job. First, we needed sealer to go under the basecoat and give us the best undercoat to work with our color. Our color is almost black and needed a very dark undercoat, a G7 according to the undercoat chart. A gallon of PPG's DP90LV epoxy primer was the way to go. The epoxy needed hardener, DP401LV. Next, we needed a gallon of DBC9700 black to be used over the undercoat but under the basecoat—it was a little extra insurance to help the purple black basecoat cover—plus another gallon and a half of black for use with the basecoat color along with a bottle of PLR89 violet pearl powder. We stocked up on reducer, 1 gallon of DT870 fast, 3 gallons of DT885 mid temp, and lastly 3 gallons of DC2000 ultra velocity clear with three quarts of DCH2015 hardener. We needed a gallon to use over the basecoat plus another gallon to use over the artwork for the final clear. And we wanted to make sure we had extra just in case it was needed.

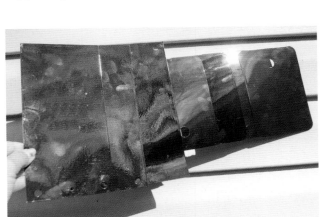

It took seven different mixes to come up with the right combination of color ingredients. Too little pearl and it would be too hard to see. Too much pearl and the purple would not have that "now you see it now you don't" effect we were after. Having a paint scale made it easy to document the mixture. I sprayed the colors samples on PPG sprayout cards and metal panels. The end panel on the right is the color we used. We named the color Firebird Purple.

We prepped the car for paint, wiping it down with DX330 precleaner and blowing it off with an air gun, with special attention paid to any cracks and crevices. Then, we masked off the door and window openings with masking paper and tape. The wheel wells and undersurface of the car are also masked off as these had been painted with Lizard Skin protective coating and we did not want overspray from the basecoat getting on them. Masking paper was run from the rocker/floorpan seam to the floor of the shop. The car was literally taped to the floor.

We carefully masked the windshield opening as we needed to paint the dash of the car. We picked a line halfway past where the dash pad would cover, so the paint area would go under the dash pad. Any seams on the firewall were taped off, then seam sealed with Evercoat Control Flow Sealer; then, the tape was removed. The lower part of the firewall had been painted with Lizard Skin Ceramic Coating, so we masked it off. Any openings to the interior of the car were masked off from the inside of the car by placing tape across the openings.

PAINTING DOORS

There are two ways you can paint doors: on the car and off the car. Painting the doors off the car will always give a more professional result as the door jams are completely exposed. But that means the doors must be remounted after the painting is done. For some situations, maybe due to time constraints or other issues, doors are painted while still attached to the body. This restricts access to the door jams and the paint in the jams might have serious orange peel and dry spray.

For our Firebird, we had a serious time crunch. The car needed to be at SEMA Show 2013 and there was no time to remove and then reinstall the doors. So they were painted on the car. After the show they were removed and the jams were repainted.

HORIZONTAL OR VERTICAL PAINTING?

There are pros and cons to as to which direction to mount parts. Mounting large flat surfaced parts like hoods and trunk lids vertically means they take up less space and less dust lands in the paint. The problem is that it's easier to flow paint on a flat surface. If the paint is applied too heavily, it will be more prone to run and sag. If you hang large flat parts, make sure plenty of light shines on the surface so you can carefully watch as the paint hits the surface and apply it correctly.

HANDY HINT

Marking the paint mixing cups is a habit I got into a few years ago, and I wish I had started sooner. I always mark the levels or amounts of the material I'm using on the cup before I add the materials. For example, in this cup, I'm mixing clearcoat at 4:1:1. I mark the levels of clearcoat, hardener, and reducer being used. This way if I have a question or problem, I know for certain exactly what I mixed up.

We hung the hood and trunk lid from the ceiling. Eye hooks were screwed into the joists of the ceiling and S hooks are placed into recesses on the backs of the two parts. Chains connect the eye hooks and S hooks. When hanging heavy parts always make sure the mounting points are secure. After mounting the top hooks, always test them to make sure they can support the weight of the part.

We arranged the parts in the paint area so that the painter can move around the parts without bumping into them.

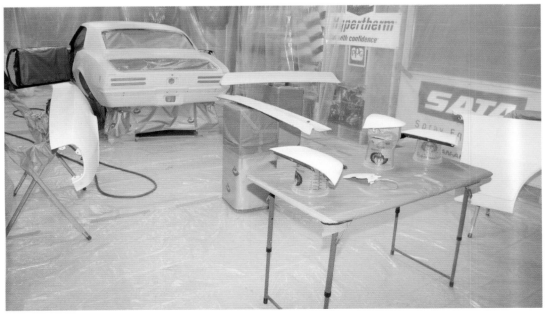

The problem with hanging a long part like this hood is that it takes up a good deal of vertical space. There's not much room above or below the part. The top and bottom edges of the hood must be painted very carefully. I had to get up on a step to paint the top and crouch down on the floor to spray the paint on the bottom of the hood to make sure the coverage would be consistent. The backs of the hood and trunk lid back had already been painted, so any holes on the top surface were taped off and the back sides were masked.

taped off. We taped together plastic crates and stacked them to hold parts like the spoiler and cowl. Note how wood blocks were placed under the parts to keep them off the surface. The blocks are positioned to support the part from underneath, this way the paint on the part would not stick to the block. Small parts, like the fender extensions and tachometer, were placed on a table with masked off paint mixing buckets under them.

Unless you are spraying in a down draft or cross draft booth, you will usually face a problem with overspray when spraying this many parts plus a car body. The overspray travels across the paint area in the

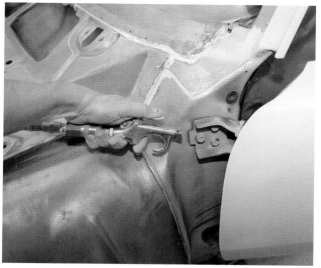

Once the parts had all been arranged in the paint area, we blew off the body and parts one last time and removed any remaining dust or debris by tacking with a Gerson Blend Prep Ultra tack cloth.

MIX THAT PAINT!

Take the time to mix the material in the can. Scrape every bit of stuff from the bottom of the can until all the material is thoroughly mixed. Here's what was in the bottom of this can of sealer. These solids help the sealer do its job—but only when they're mixed in. Solid material sitting on the bottom of the can is also a problem with basecoat mixtures. Don't give the paint a few quick stirs, stir the paint long enough to be sure it's mixed well.

direction of the air flow, landing on surfaces along the way. For me, it works best to start painting closest to the air outlet and work toward the air source. This way, the overspray lands on the newly applied paint and either melts in or lands as dry dust, which in some cases may be tacked off before the next coat is applied.

continued on page 102

Left: First the DP90LV epoxy sealer will be applied. The DP is mixed up 2:1:1 with DP401LV and DT885. Always use the reducer best suited for the temperature of the paint area. I mix a little extra reducer into the mix, about a half part. Using this as a sealer will help the paint to flow out a little more. I mix the DP in a SATA RPS 0.9 l cup, the largest size RPS cup. I started on the small parts. Here, I sprayed sealer on the spoiler. The backside and side edges were painted first. **Right:** I stared from the bottom and worked my way up with each pass.

I put epoxy on the hood next. Look closely and you can see the shape of the spray pattern coming from the spray gun. The arrow points to the top edge of the pattern. The white and orange line on the side shows the length of the pattern. The orange parts show the amount of overlap, about 75%.

The hood, trunk lid, fenders and small parts have all been sprayed, so I started spraying on the car. I started on the roof and worked my way down across the tops of the quarters and onto the doors.

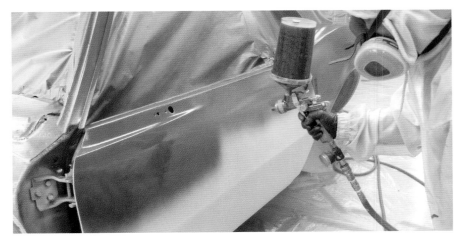

The body and parts have one coat of DP epoxy on them. The P sheet recommends waiting at least 15 minutes between spraying the DP epoxy and spraying the basecoat color. Its been at least that long since I started spraying the epoxy.

For the basecoat, I started by edging the sides of the parts with black. This is known as banding. It's very easy to overlook the edges of the parts and panels while you are spraying the top surfaces. It's better to make sure to hit the edges first at the start of each coat. This way you know they are getting coverage. But use care when spraying candy colors in this way; otherwise, you might end up with a dark line around each edge.

I'm using about a 60% overlap when spraying this black basecoat. PPG recommends using a 50% (minumum)–75% (maximum) overlap when spraying solvent basecoat. Make sure to have a sprayout card handy and spray that black also. It's very helpful to apply the paint on a sprayout card as you are spraying the coats on the car. This way, if you have a question about the color, you can take the card outside and compare it in the sun or in different kinds of light to your sample card or piece that was made earlier. It's much easier to check color on a card than try to remove parts from the paint area.

CREATE A SPRAY PLAN

Many painters don't think about this until the paint is flowing from the gun, but is there a best way to spray a car? Do you start at the front or back? Top or bottom? The time to create a spray plan is when you are painting the primer or sealer. A spray plan is not as essential when you're spraying a solid color basecoat, and while it's pretty important when you're spraying clear, it's extremely critical when spraying candy and some pearl colors. The more candy is sprayed, the darker the color becomes. You don't want one panel of the car to be darker than another. So figure out a plan of attack so each panel receives the same amount of color.

Everyone is different, but here's how I do it. I start on the roof and work my way down across one side, usually the left. Once the left side is painted, I move to the other side of the car and repeat the process. Then I'll paint across the back deck, around the drip channels of the trunk, and onto the taillight panel. I'll check under the bottom edges of the car and make sure they have coverage. Next it's onto the firewall and door jams.

Continued from page 99

Next, the DBC9700 Black gets mixed up. PPG recommends reducing DBC9700 25%–50%. I always go on the lower side, 25%. That means my mix will be 1 part black mixed with a ¼ part reducer. I sprayed one coat of this mix. I didn't spray it as thickly as the sealer, but I still mixed up a gallon and used most of it.

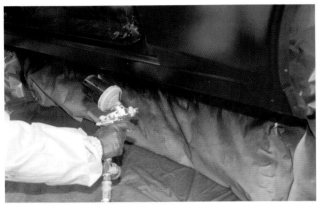

Make sure to get good coverage in hard-to-reach places like under the rockers. Because it was a very tight fit, I used a smaller spray gun and cup for the bottom areas of the car: a SATA Minijet 3000B with a SATA RPS 0.3 l mixing cup.

It's finally time for the color. The purple black mix is loaded into a SATA RPS 0.9 l cup and sprayed with a SATA 4000 HVLP spray gun with a 1.3 nozzle and tip set. The first thing to spray is the sprayout card. The color looked right on that, so we sprayed the first coat on the car body and the parts. This coat is followed by three more coats, all sprayed medium with a 65% overlap. The flash time in between coats is 10–15 minutes.

HANDY HINT

Here's a quick and easy way to keep paint from building up on the tops of the paint cans. Simply use an awl or pointed tool with a hammer and punch three or four holes along the recess on the top of the can. The paint will drip down through these holes and the recess won't fill up with paint.

TO TACK OR NOT TO TACK

The question of whether to tack in between coats of paint does not have a yes or no answer. In my experience, sometimes it's a good idea to tack, but sometimes it's not. When spraying sealer or primer, I wipe the parts with a tack cloth to remove the overspray. But when I spray pearl or candy coats, I try not to tack. In some situations I find tacking not only removes the overspray, but it also can affect the coat of paint by leaving marks in the surface or affecting the way the next coat reacts with the coats that I've already sprayed on. This is one of those, "it may work for me, but it's different in each situation" kind of things. If you have a question, then test the process on a hard-to-see area of the project. Tack it and then apply the coat on a small area. Take a good look at the result under a bright light, viewing it from different angles, before you make your decision to tack or not to tack.

So far five coats of paint have been sprayed. It is recommended to wait at least 15 minutes before spraying clearcoat. As there are five coats of paint that needed to gas out, I waited an hour before spraying the clear. Of course, a number of factors can determine exactly how long you should wait before applying urethane clear over basecoat.

- How thickly the paint was applied. Thin paint will gas out (release solvents) quicker than thick paint.
- The temperature of the paint area. The cooler it is, the slower the paint will gas out.
- The air flow through the paint area. The more air flow, the quicker the solvents will gas out.

But always refer to the P sheet and go by the manufacturer's recommendations. PPG advises not to wait more than 24 hours to apply urethane clear over basecoat; otherwise, the basecoat will need to be scuffed in order for the clear to stick.

For the clear, we used PPG's Concept DC2000 Ultra Velocity Clear. It's funny how I refused to try any other clearcoat than my trusted PPG DBU2021. But since I first tried DC2000, I'm finding it's quickly becoming my go-to clearcoat. It's proof to always keep an open mind about new products. I still like my 2021 for some things, but for everyday use, the DC2000 helps speed up production in the paint shop with its quick drying qualities. The DC2000 is mixed 4:1:1 with DCH2015 hardener and DT885 reducer.

I applied two wet coats to the Firebird body and the car. The DC2000 was sprayed wet on wet; that means no waiting between coats. First I sprayed two coats on a part, then I moved to another part and sprayed that one. After the parts were sprayed in this way, I then sprayed two coats on the body of the car.

DC2000 dries pretty quickly. Under the right circumstances, it can be sanded and recoated in 2–3 hours. But I waited 24 hours before sanding. The car and parts were wet sanded with 800 paper to prep them for artwork. Refer to chapter 26 to see the finished result of all this work.

SINGLE-STAGE PAINT VS. TWO-STAGE PAINT

In chapter 1, I discussed single-stage paint. If no artwork had been going on the Firebird, single-stage paint might have been an option for this car. The only difference when applying single stage is that it is applied like clearcoat, flowing it onto the surface in medium to heavy coats. Two-stage basecoat should never be applied like single-stage paint. Never try and flow out two-stage basecoat as layers that are too thick take a very, very long time to gas out.

You don't need a complex color or paint scheme to get noticed. Both of these hot rods boldly stand out in a crowd with their simple solid colors.

This Nova is another example of a single color as an artform. The medium blue really complements the lines of the car.

Here's a brighter example of a purple pearl. Its suits this '37 Plymouth perfectly. When the color is the main feature, it tends to draw your eye to all the little details on the body.

Solvent paint also works great for spraying mechanical parts on a car. These RUF calipers for a Porsche were painted with DP50LV, sprayed with a Porsche Yellow basecoat, and cleared with DC2000.

Chapter 11
The Truth About Waterborne Painting

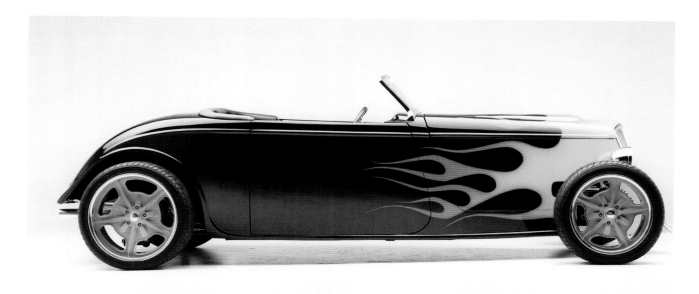

Guess what kind of paint (sealer is not waterborne) was used for this Factory Five 33 Hot Rod? PPG Envirobase® High Performance basecoat, a waterborne paint.

WHY WATER? WHY NOT?

Sometimes changes, even good ones, are not easy for people to deal with. Paint technology has changed dramatically over the last 30 years when the use of lacquer declined as acrylic basecoats and two-part urethane paint became the industry standard. Lacquer has very strong solvents; these solvents reach down deep in the layers of paint, bonding them together. But strong solvents made the paint problematic to work with, and it dried dull and had to be buffed. Over time, lacquer finishes cracked. Acrylic enamel basecoats and two-part primers, paint, and clearcoats solved many of these issues. The actual time spent painting was reduced, but the time spent preparing the surface for paint was slightly increased. The new paints covered better with less paint and were shiny when dry. They also were more flexible, chip-resistant, and stood up better to the abuses of the road.

When customers ask painters to use lacquer on their projects, the first thought that comes to mind is "Oh no." We are used to working with urethanes and acrylic enamel basecoats. It's easy to forget how, 30 years ago, painters were dragged kicking and screaming into using these products. And now it's happening again.

Paint technology continues to change, and over the last few years, waterborne automotive paint is replacing solvent-borne paint in the collision industry and is finding its way into the custom world. Waterborne paints can dry even faster than solvent-borne when applied properly. The thinner used in waterborne paint is less aggressive than traditional solvents, which allows for easy repair of damaged paint surfaces as the waterborne thinners don't irritate the broken layers of paint that have been repaired. Technicians appreciate the ease of working with the product. Chances are, if you take your vehicle to a collision shop to be repaired, the color will be repainted with a waterborne paint.

THE TECHNOLOGY OF WATER

Waterborne paint uses latex technology, yet it has characteristics of both urethanes and acrylic enamel. It is thinned with water that has been pH-balanced and deionized; it is mineral-free water with an anti-fungal preservative, not regular tap water. When initially applied, waterborne basecoat can be washed off with water or solvent. However, once it has dried, it will not reflow with water, solvent, or heat.

The waterborne system incorporates latex particles that cling together. These are the resins of the paint. Think of them as little fingers around a circular core. The fingers link together to create a gel that constitutes the paint. To untangle the fingers, you only need to gently shake the paint's container. Because of this anti-settling technology, you don't have to stir individual toners while they are in their original containers. Once the waterborne paint is reduced and sprayed, the water starts to evaporate from the paint. The latex particles form and bind together creating durability, chemical resistance, and alignment with OEM finishes.

Waterborne basecoat is designed to work in conjunction with select undercoats and topcoats. Always check the product sheet to see which products are recommended to go under and over it.

The shelf life of Envirobase High Performance basecoat is generally four years in its original unopened container. Once opened, shelf life can be affected by factors such as temperature, humidity, and more. Mixed waterborne color has a pot life of 90 days when stored in a closed plastic container. When using the optional activator, pot life is shortened to two hours.

SOLVENT VERSUS WATER
Solvents

In chapter 1, I went over the different kinds of solvents: front end, middle, and tail. An incorrect choice could lead to a wrong color, bad flow of paint, poor finish, and a multitude of even worse problems if a combination of incorrect flash windows or too many coats of paint are present. Solvents also affect the way a solvent-borne metallic color will look since the dry time can tweak the color (see below.) PPG's Envirobase High Performance basecoat has two thinners: T494 for primary use and T595 for high-heat, low-humidity areas.

Painting Conditions

Temperature, humidity, and air flow play key roles in how a metallic color looks when it comes to solvent-borne paint. Faster drying times yield a lighter color, while slower drying times yield darker colors. When applied properly, waterborne basecoat is less affected by these factors, helping to ensure consistent color alignment to the PPG standard.

Film Thickness

Waterborne paint is half as thick as the traditional solvent-based system. Hiding flaws or complete coverage can be achieved with a thinner film of material. Solvent basecoat usually requires 0.07–1.2 mm for coverage. Waterborne basecoat coverage can be achieved with 0.05 mm of material.

Better Coverage

Why does it cover better? The pigment in waterborne paint is more concentrated than in solvent. These high-opacity toners add to waterborne's efficiency by keeping the number of coats required to a minimum. This also makes it much easier to blend with waterborne than with solvent-borne paints.

No Cheating

Solvent paint shrinks over time. How many body shop techs see their repair work 30 days after it's done? Not many. Cars are usually delivered before the paint is fully cured. The car looks great the day it's picked up, but what will it look like a month later if the painter did not allow for full dry times?

Waterborne basecoat forces the painter to allow for proper flash-off. You can't stack layers without increasing overall dry time. Each layer should be dried completely before the next is applied. Because of this, you can paint on more layers than you would with solvent, although you would not need to; waterborne has great coverage.

Color Matching

Unlike solvent, you can't match the paint when the paint is wet. A waterborne color looks very different wet than when it's dry. The latex particles have a blue-green cast that can mislead you. The painter has to do a sprayout card, dry it and clear it, then spray the color on the vehicle. This process results in fewer issues with color matching, less material wasted, and less time dealing with poor color matches.

Repairs Made Easy

Collision technicians love the workability of the waterborne system since recoating over sensitive substrates is never a concern. Waterborne doesn't have the aggressive solvents of acrylic basecoat. It doesn't soak down into the sanded edges of a repair, irritating them or causing them to swell. The ability to tape or sand out imperfections quickly is also valuable; once it's dry, it's as dry as it will ever get. No long dry times.

Faster Finishing

As for dry times, if waterborne is prepped and sprayed correctly, it flashes off faster than solvent-based paint. When doing two-tone paint jobs or doing artwork over your basecoat, faster drying time means you can tape on it in about 5 minutes at a temperature of 70°F. Keep in mind that this can vary depending on humidity and air flow. The ability to tape or sand out imperfections quickly is also valuable.

It's Flexible

Waterborne is very flexible, which makes it great for painting plastic parts.

Spraying Application Differences

The waterborne spray pattern is slightly different from a solvent spray pattern. The solvent pattern is usually a long oval, whereas the waterborne pattern is a long rectangle. Also, waterborne paint requires a 75% overlap for the coverage coats and 85%–90% for control coats (more about control coats coming up), as compared to solvent products that usually require a 50%–75% overlap.

Storage

Envirobase High Performance basecoat and waterborne thinner should be stored in a cool, dry place away from sources of heat. During storage and transportation, temperature must be maintained at a minimum of 5°C or 41°F, and a maximum of 49°C or 120°F. Avoid exposure to frost or freezing conditions.

It's Green

Lastly, waterborne is environmentally friendly, whereas solvent-based systems are not. Using waterborne automotive paint is good for painters, too. Since waterborne contains lower VOC than solvent, it's easier to control the air quality inside a shop or spray facility. While standard safety equipment is still required, you can virtually eliminate the harsh odors associated with using solvent-borne paint throughout the shop.

THE TOOLS FOR WATERBORNE

Your brand of paint and your location (by state) will determine which gun to use for waterborne. A few years back, HVLP guns were the way to go with water, but these days HVLP is not always the waterborne choice.

Depending on the brand, nozzle size can vary from 1.1 mm to 1.5 mm. While SATA's WSB nozzle set is the choice for a paint company under normal conditions, other nozzles may work better in hot, dry conditions. The same is true for when a paint company recommends the 1.3 mm or 1.4 mm nozzles—a painter may need to go up in size to meet low humidity conditions.

SATA developed a nozzle for the HVLP called a 1.4 HC (hot climate). This nozzle has a slightly shorter, thicker fan to better focus the spray and to help wet the fan pattern for great results. For this project we used the SATA WSB, which works very well with PPG's Envirobase High Performance basecoat.

This is the SATA 4000 HVLP spray gun with its WSB (water-soluble basecoat) 1.25 mm nozzle set installed.

Even just a few years ago, most painters would likely have used the HVLP for waterborne basecoat and the RP for clear. But today, many painters choose the RP gun. RP technology offers a higher air cap pressure than the HVLP version, which is limited by law to 10 psi at the air cap. Deciding which nozzle size to run in the RP depends on which brand of waterborne paint you're using. Nozzle sizes range from 1.1, 1.2 and 1.2W for cool, wet climates, to 1.3 and 1.4 for hot, dry climates. The 1.2W is a special nozzle made for spreading the fan a bit wider. It puts out a very thin, even coat of waterborne basecoat.

With the HVLP using around 15 cfm and the RP using only 10.2, that can also be a deciding factor. If you are considering switching to water, be sure to consult your paint company or a SATA representative to decide which is best for you. For more information on spray guns, refer to chapter 2. For the best results when spraying waterborne, dedicate a gun to spraying only waterborne.

CLEANING THE GUN AFTER SPRAYING WATERBORNE

Cleaning a spray gun after spraying waterborne basecoat requires a water-based cleaner such as PPG's SWX100 OneChoice waterborne gun wash. It is inadvisable to clean the gun with lacquer thinner, since the lacquer solvent will not adequately break down the latex resins and will cause any waterborne residue to coagulate, ultimately clogging the fluid passage of the gun. Instead of lacquer thinner, use acetone as a final rinse after cleaning with the water-based gun cleaner; it will help

The SATA dry jet is perfect for helping dry the water out of the paint. It's more of an air diffuser than an air gun.

dissipate any remaining moisture. Finally, the gun needs to be thoroughly blown dry internally and externally to remove any moisture that could cause corrosion to some of the soft metals such as the brass and aluminum found in most spray guns.

While painters sometimes get away with not cleaning their guns immediately after using solvent base,

Paint booths now feature fans or blowers to move air in a way that helps dry the water out of waterborne paint. This booth has been retrofit with a drying blower and turbulent air system tower in each corner of the booth. These provide clean, filtered air, which helps promote a controlled flash off of waterborne basecoats and rapid curing of low-VOC topcoats.

you should never try this with waterborne. Take the time to clean that gun—and any others tools used with waterborne—immediately after painting; otherwise any residue won't come off easily.

Although air flow is important for all paint products, it is especially critical when spraying waterborne basecoat. Also, to shorten flash time in between coats, additional air movement across the panel will help draw the moisture out of the paint film. One way to accomplish this is to use a special air blower, or air diffuser, after each coat of waterborne basecoat is applied to make sure the water is completely dried out of the paint.

These air dryers are held at approximately a 45° angle to the car and blow air across the surface. The air movement forces the water from the paint. These are not traditional air guns. Regular air guns channel the air through a narrow nozzle and can't be used to dry paint—the flow is too strong and focused. Air dryers have a diffused pattern and distribute the air over a larger area. Read more about drying the paint layers later in the chapter.

DIVING IN: GETTING STARTED SPRAYING WATER

The first example here will show how waterborne sprays by spraying paint on sprayout cards. If you're spraying waterborne for the first time, using sprayout cards is an easy and economical way to get used to how a product sprays.

GUN DISTANCE AND OVERLAP

The distance from the surface will not vary much when spraying the waterborne product. The recommended distance for waterborne is 6–8 inches for coverage coats and 10–12 inches for the control coat. More about the control coat later.

HOLDING THE GUN TOO CLOSE TO THE SURFACE

Holding the gun too close to the surface (3–4 inches) restricts the separation of the atomized particles and the paint coats will be too wet. Other consequences include the following:

- Dry and cure times will slow.
- Water can be trapped, leading to die back and solvent popping.
- A darker flop angle may result.

HOLDING THE GUN THE PROPER DISTANCE FROM THE SURFACE

Holding the gun 6–8 inches from the surface will allow the correct amount of material to reach the surface and flow out.

- The material will dry and cure properly.
- An even film build will be provided.
- Proper adhesion will result.

WHAT IS A CONTROL COAT? AND WHY DO YOU NEED IT?

This step is necessary for all waterborne colors that contain metallic, pearl, or any special-effect pigments.

The control coat is a light-mist dry coat sprayed while holding the gun 10–12 inches from the surface. To obtain a proper control coat, reduce the gun inlet pressure by 40% and increase the overlap to 85%–90%. This allows the atomized paint to widely separate and lay down in a light mist coat.

The control coat is only necessary for metallics and pearls. It can accomplish the following:

- Help to eliminate mottling and striping, although extreme cases of mottling, striping or blotchiness can indicate a problem with the application of the coverage coats
- Adjust the metallic to match OEM colors
- Align the color to the PPG's Waterborne Variant Deck color chips

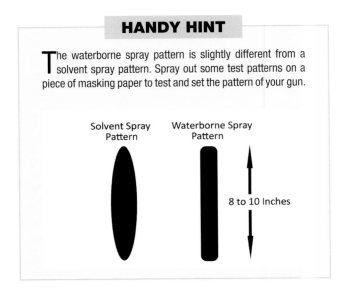

SPRAY GUN PATH, SPEED, AND OVERLAP

As with solvent-borne paint, hold the spray gun at a straight 90° angle to the surface. Make one pass, and move the gun down enough for 75% of your pattern to land directly on top of the first pass. Adjust your speed according to the material being sprayed. Your gun speed will vary depending on how much the material is reduced, the temperature of the booth, and the specific ingredients of the paint mixture. Always spray a few test passes just to adjust your speed. You want a nice, even dispersion of material.

When initially applied, the basecoat should have a uniform wet-dry appearance—not too wet, not too dry. It takes a little getting used to, but the main difference between the way solvent and water sprays is that solvent is usually sprayed wetter than water. Make a test pass, then speed up a bit so less material lands on the surface. Compare your results to the pictures in this chapter. This trick will help you get used to spraying waterborne. Chances are you will tend to spray too heavily at first since it takes some time and practice to break the solvent techniques that are automatic when you pick up a spray gun.

MIXING WATERBORNE

Each brand of paint has its own recommendations on how it should be reduced. For its Envirobase High Performance basecoat, PPG recommends an initial reduction of 10% for solid colors, 20% for metallics and pearls containing midcoats, and 30% for tinted midcoats. Always check the P sheet for the paint you are using. It will tell you exactly how best to reduce your paint.

VISCOSITY TESTING

Proper reduction of waterborne paint is critical. Always perform a viscosity test before you spray to check that the reduction of the paint is correct for the temperature and humidity where you are spraying. It's quick and easy to do a viscosity test. Simply fill a DIN4 viscosity cup with your reduced paint. It should take 23–28 seconds for the stream of paint to finish running out of the cup. Longer than that and the paint will need more reduction. Less than that and you will need to add more unreduced paint to the mix.

Use sprayout cards to get used to waterborne and see how it sprays. This way, you get an idea of how each layer of waterborne should cover. You don't want to spray it on too thickly. Try the following experiment a few times. Get some black or gray waterborne basecoat and practice. To achieve color alignment, most metallic colors will require two to four coverage coats followed by one to two control coats. Solid colors do not require a control coat. For the example below, we'll be spraying a metallic silver basecoat.

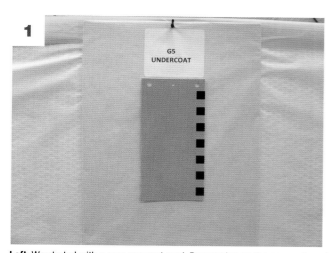

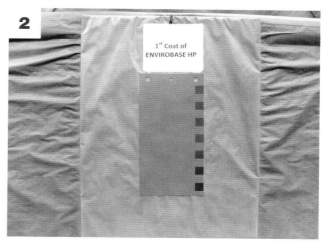

Left: We started with a new sprayout card. By spraying on the sprayout card, you can see exactly how each coat of waterborne should look on the surface. This will give you a good idea of the proper amount of coverage you need on each coat. **Right:** Here is the first coat of Envirobase High Performance basecoat sprayed on the card when it's still wet. Notice the even layout of color.

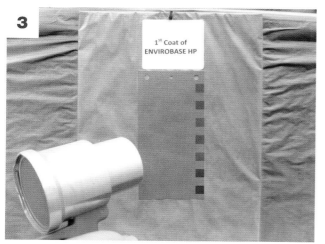

Left: Note the angle of the SATA dry jet during the drying of the first coat of Envirobase High Performance basecoat. **Right:** I applied the second coat of Envirobase High Performance basecoat and the contrast blocks on the right side are starting to disappear. Next, the dry jet will be used.

Left: After the second layer has dried, I applied a third layer. The black checks on the right side can no longer be seen. Most colors will require two to four coverage coats to achieve proper hiding. The water is then dried out of the surface with the SATA dry jet and it's ready for the control coat. Now, if we had been painting a solid color, the basecoat painting would be completed at this point and the sample would be ready for clearcoat. NOTE: When matching a low-opacity color, it is not necessary to achieve "full hiding" as long as a complementary spectral gray undercoat color is used. This will help achieve "perceived hiding" and proper color alignment to the OEM standard. **Right:** I masked off half the card and misted on the control coat. Keep your speed fast when applying the control coat. Spray one to two light, even coats. One coat may be enough for vertical surfaces. Two coats may be needed for horizontal surfaces if, after flashing off, the surface is not uniformly matte.

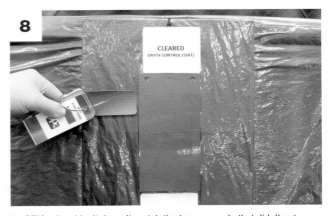

Left: Next, I applied clearcoat urethane to the sprayout card and compared it to the OEM color chip. It doesn't match the lower sample that didn't get any of the control coat. **Right:** But it does match the upper sample that had the control coat applied. Remember that waterborne will not look the way solvent-borne looks. It's almost impossible to judge waterborne until after the clearcoat has been applied.

COVERAGE AND CONTROL COATS

The control coat is a thin "orientation" coat. It is not designed to give coverage. Make sure to obtain proper coverage with your coverage coats.

HOW TO BLEND IN A REPAIR USING WATERBORNE

Making repairs is where waterborne shows its true value. While in some places the code requires use of waterborne, across the country, collision shops are converting to waterborne for one big reason: it speeds up the repair process significantly. Because it's so friendly to the repaired surface, it helps to ensure there will be no conflicts in the repair area.

continued on page 118

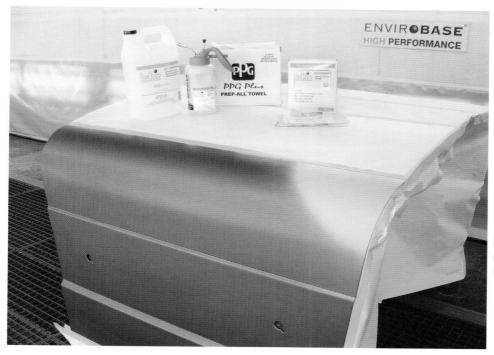

Here's the surface we'll be blending. The area has been repaired, primed and sanded. Most PPG two-component urethane primers, such as ECP15 2K® A-Chromatic Surfacer, or single-component waterborne primers, such as EPW115 Waterborne Speed Prime (designed for small repairs), work great with waterborne paint. The panel was then cleaned with PPG's SWX350 waterborne surface cleaner and tacked. Waterborne surface cleaner is used for removing most contaminates, including wax and grease, mold release agents, and sanding dust. SWX350 is compliant in the most stringent VOC markets with an ultra-low 0.21 VOC.

HANDY HINT

Frank Ruiz demonstrates how to properly prepare the surface with waterborne surface cleaner. He wipes it on with one cloth and then immediately wipes it away with another. When cleaning with a waterborne cleaner, make sure to wipe off any residue from the cleaner. Be very thorough. This is extremely important. Never rush through this step. If all of the residue is not wiped away, fisheyes may appear when the basecoat is applied. If you get fisheyes when spraying waterborne, it's most likely because not all the residue was removed from the panel.

Do not allow the cleaner to dry on the panel. Clean the vehicle one area at a time for best results. Waterborne surface cleaners can also be used with solvents, as they are great for removing organic contaminants like the oil from a fingerprint.

A wet bed, like PPG's T490, is a coat of clear basecoat (it has a bluish tint while it's wet, but it dries clear). This helps make a smoother surface for the blended color to lay into; otherwise, the metallic might lay at strange angles in the blend area, causing it to look scratchy. If the blend area is finished in P800 grit or finer, then the finish should be smooth enough to forgo the wet bed. Although it is optional, some technicians consider it a good insurance policy.

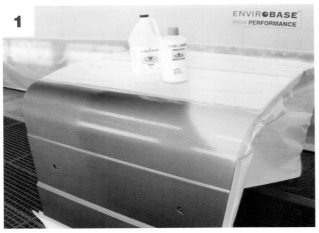

Left: I applied a "wet" bed using PPG's Envirobase High Performance T490 reduced with T494. Note the wet surface and the bluish tint. **Right:** The wet bed has flashed and is now dry and ready for the Envirobase High Performance basecoat. We'll do a viscosity test to ensure that the paint mix is properly reduced. The target is 23–28 seconds in a DIN4 viscosity cup.

We applied the first coat of Envirobase High Performance basecoat, dry to medium. Note the distance the painter is holding the gun. Note what the coat looks like. It's not completely covered. This is what a correctly applied first coat of waterborne should look like.

3

We are drying out the first coat of Envirobase High Performance basecoat. Note the angle and distance of the dryer. You can see that on the left side of the repair, the Envirobase High Performance basecoat has dried. But on the right side, the Envirobase High Performance basecoat still looks wet as the painter starts to dry that area.

4

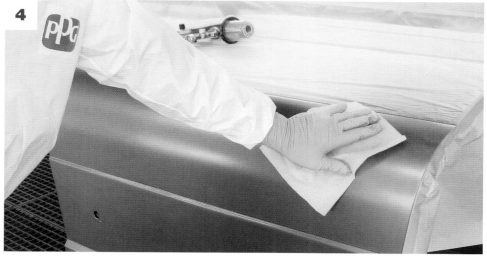

Next, we tacked off the first coat. Although the Envirobase High Performance basecoat is sprayed on the dry side, the metallic particles are not loose as they are with solvent-borne. They lie flat against the surface and are not disturbed by the tack cloth.

5

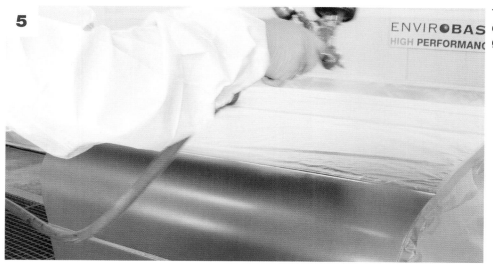

The second coat is applied again, dry to medium. Now the coverage is getting more complete.

The drying and tacking steps are repeated.

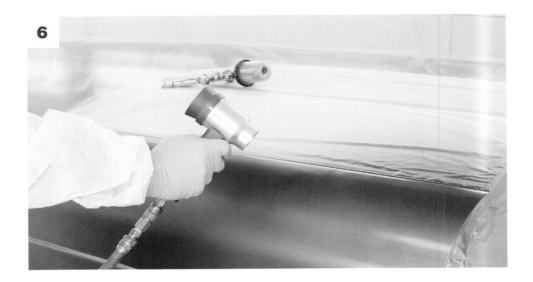

We applied the third coat. On the right side of the repair area you can see how it's more of a match than the left side of the repair area, as the gun has not yet passed over that side. In most cases, a third coat will give the area proper coverage when applied over the correct spectral gray undercoat.

The drying process was repeated, and you can see that the blend has been achieved. It's now ready for the control coat.

9

We applied the control coat. The gun was held farther away from the surface and the misting control coat was applied. *The control coat should go on very dry, with only a small amount of color going on the panel.*

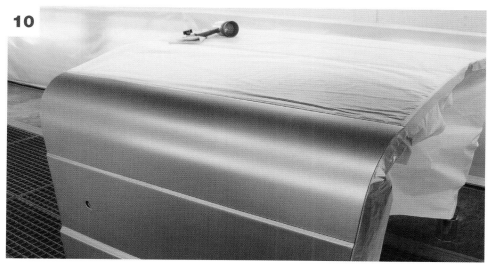

10

The control coat has done its job, and it's impossible to tell where the repair was made.

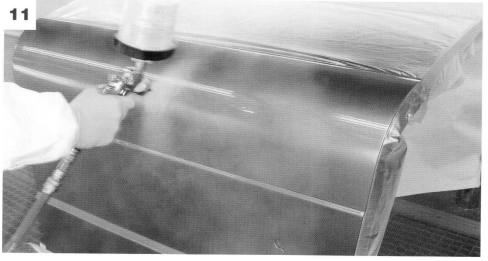

11

After the control coat has been dried out and the surface tacked, we applied the EC700 urethane clear coat. Most PPG urethane two-part clears will work over waterborne Envirobase High Performance basecoat (some perform better than others). EC700 is a one-visit production clear, meaning it can be applied in back-to-back coats with no flash time. It works well in one to three panel applications.

The clear is now dry and the match is perfect. The repair area cannot be seen.

12

Even in a different light, the result does not change.

13

Continued from page 112

BLOTCHY ISSUES

If you run into a problem with the surface being blotchy when spraying waterborne, the problem will not be the paint.

- Maybe it's not fully dry. Waterborne will appear blotchy while it's wet. Once it dries, it should be fine.

- Not enough paint was applied. Did the painter get complete coverage before the control coat?
- The spray gun is not spraying evenly enough. Clean out the air cap, nozzle, and needle.
- The control coat will not fix blotchiness. You have to solve the problem before the control coat is applied.

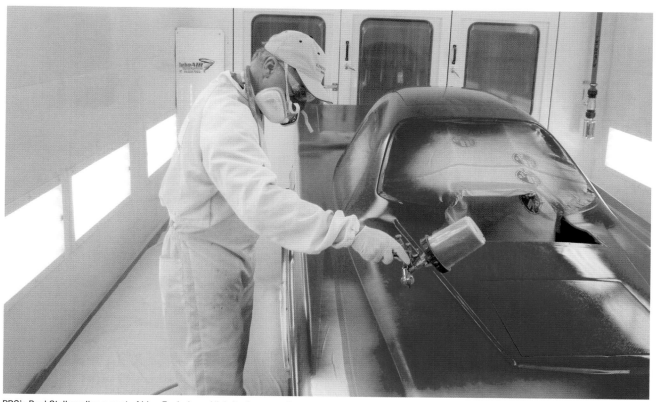

PPG's Paul Stoll applies a coat of blue Envirobase High Performance basecoat to a race car body. You can see how much of an overlap he gets on each pass. Very little paint extends beyond the width of the previous coat. Note how he's holding the gun about 6″ above the surface—the perfect distance for a coverage coat of waterborne.

Waterborne is great for doing custom work like this two-tone paint. It's ready to tape off as soon as the water has been dried out of the paint. Sometimes it's only a matter of a few minutes.

Above: This new Challenger is another two-tone done completely with waterborne paint.

Right: Charley Hutton of Hutton's Color Studio and Paul Stoll take a ride in a custom-painted golf cart. All the paint on this cart was done with Envirobase High Performance basecoat.

Chapter 12
Painting Candy and Pearl Tri-Coat Colors

Painting tri-coat colors is much like painting solid colors. The main thing to remember is that the coverage needs to be even. The best way to prepare for painting tri-coats is to practice on something. You can practice on spare parts or thick white paper. Or you can get a roll of white masking paper, some candy toner, and some basecoat clear and practice. The white background is unforgiving and shows every flaw. One of the hardest ways to spray candy is over white. Poor spray patterns show up better with candy than with pearl, so it's better to use candy for practicing.

SPRAY GUN SETUP

One of the biggest problems with spraying tri-coats is an inconsistent spray pattern. Please refer to chapter 1 for more information on spray guns and their setup. Spraying candy truly shows how well the gun is spraying. For painting pearl, I use an HVLP spray gun as I want a medium coat and want the paint to atomize very finely. For candy, I use an RP as I need the paint to flow on a little thicker.

The body of this Mercury has so much detail; it needed the right color to bring it out. The color appears to be a candy green, and it sure does the trick. In a world full of amazing show cars, this one stands out in a crowd.

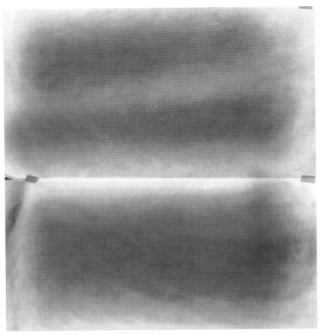

I hung white masking paper on the wall and mixed some candy toner with some reduced clear basecoat about 4:1:1 with reducer. The top shows a poor pattern: striped, very streaky. The bottom shows the proper pattern: even and consistent.

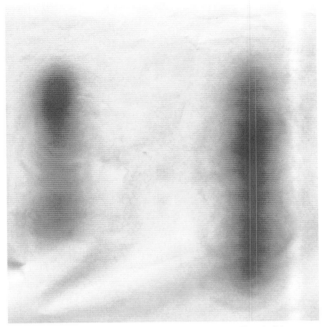

On the left is a candy spray pattern that is inconsistent. Next to it is one that's spraying correctly. Check the spray regulator cap on your paint gun or tip as debris stuck in it might be causing a poor pattern.

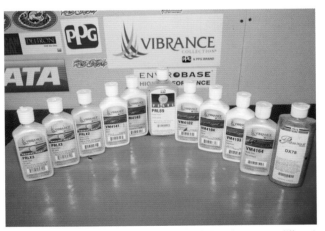

Here's my collection of pearl powders from PPG. They have many different colors and kinds and come in various sized grits.

MATERIALS & EQUIPMENT

Equipment
SATA 4000 HVLP spray gun
SATA 4000 RP spray gun
SATAjet 3000B mini spray gun
Summit Racing shop cart SUM-900089
Meguiar's sanding backing pad E-7200
Gerson 8111P disposable dual cartridge respirator
Uncle Bill's Sliver Gripper tweezers

Materials
PPG Deltron DP50LV epoxy primer
PPG DP401LV hardener
PPG Deltron DMD1684 white basecoat
PPG PLRX2 Silver Crystal Pearl
PPG DBC 500 color blender
DMX211 Radiance II orange candy toner
PPG DC2000 ultra-velocity clear
PPG DCH 2015 hardener
PPG DT 885 reducer
PPG DX330 precleaner
PPG DX320 precleaner
SATA Rapid Preparation System cups/lids 0.9 l and 0.3 l
Soft Sander 800 grit sandpaper
American Tape orange mask and aqua mask ¾″, 1″, and 3″
Gerson Blend Prep tack cloth #020008C
SAS Safety 66518 Raven powder-free disposable nitrile gloves
Masking paper

PAINTING PEARL

When pearl gets mixed into a solid color, it turns it into a pearl color, but it may still retain the opacity (the opposite of transparent; you cannot see through it) of the solid color. In chapter 10, we mixed pearl into black and created a solid pearl color. In this chapter we mix pearl into clear basecoat to create a transparent pearl paint.

The mix ratio of pearl to basecoat is up to the painter. But you don't want so much pearl that it thickens the paint or tries to clog the paint passages in the gun. This is where test panels come in handy. It doesn't take much pearl to get a nice effect. The Miata is a fairly small car, so I'm going to spray three medium coats of white pearl. I'll pour out 2 quarts of DBC 500 and mix in 2 teaspoons of pearl. Then the mixture is reduced 1:1 with DT885 reducer as the booth temp is around 80°F.

A light gray primer was used on this car, but white is a tough color to use as a cover. I wanted to be sure there were no dark spots showing through, so I sprayed on two coats of DP50LV epoxy as a sealer. The epoxy was mixed 4:1:1 with DP401LV and DT885 reducer. I waited 15 minutes between coats. Then I waited an hour before spraying the white basecoat.

For this Miata, an undercoat of DP50LV will be sprayed over the sanded primer. Next I'll apply a white basecoat, DMD1683 reduced 1:1 with DT885. For the pearl, I'm mixing PPG PLRX Silver Crystal Pearl into DBC500 Color Blender. The DBC500 will be a carrier for the pearl powder.

DARK OR LIGHT BASE?

Light basecoat colors tend to require less pearl than dark basecoats. If you use 1 teaspoon of pearl powder for a dark base, double that amount for a light base.

- ¾–1 teaspoon of pearl powder per quart of clear basecoat for use over light basecoats
- 1–2 teaspoons of pearl powder per quart of clear basecoat for use over dark basecoats

I precleaned the Miata with DX320, tacked off any dust with a Gerson Blend Prep tack cloth, and sprayed the epoxy sealer. The DP50LV put down a nice white surface, so it did not take much white to cover it. I applied two coats of DMD1684 to the car with a 10-minute flash time between coats.

I tacked the car again to remove any dust that may have landed and applied the first coat of pearl to the surface of the car. I walk the car, starting at the top at the back end and walking toward the front, keeping a steady pace and even distance from the car. When I reach the front of the car, I move the gun down a bit and walk to the back. The gun is moved back and forth along the car. This is called "walking the car."

When I finished one side, I spray either the rear or front of the car, whichever end I am at. Then I move to the other side and repeat the process. I sprayed the second coat up and down, rather than back and forth. I sprayed the third coat of pearl moving the gun in a diagonal direction. Changing the direction of paint application helps to keep the coverage even. When coverage is inconsistent the pearl will look blotchy. The darker the pearl color, the harder it can be to get even coverage.

WET PEARL

Don't spray pearl too wet either! Never lay down a heavy coat of pearl. In fact, when trying out your test panels, spray some heavy coats of pearl and see what happens. The paint starts to run together and look blotchy. You want to lay down nice, medium, even coats of paint. Practice and perfect your technique before you try it out on your project.

HAIRY PEARL IS NO GOOD

Hairy pearl is not a known technical term. It's a name I made up for what happens when pearl paint is sprayed too dry, which is one the biggest problems when painting pearl. If the pearl is sprayed on too dry, it lands on the surface as overspray and a rough, gritty surface starts to form. Once the surface gets gritty looking, the endless depth of the pearl effect is lost. What causes hairy pearl?

- Holding the gun too far from the surface
- Air pressure too high
- Gun speed too fast
- Not enough overlap in the paint pattern

Take care to watch closely as you paint pearl. If you see a rough gritty surface starting to form, stop painting and see what you are doing incorrectly. How can you fix a rough pearl surface? Allow it to dry out. Then dry-sand the surface with 600 or 800 grit, respray the basecoat color, and respray the pearl. This is the correct way to fix it. Some painters have tricks, but I'd rather do it right.

To finish it off, I sprayed a light, mist coat on the car. It's not really a coat of paint, just a very slight dusting. This just adds a bit of pearl on the surface that will stand up and really catch the light.

Here's the pearl all sprayed on the car. The car should sit for an hour before the clearcoat is applied.

Here's the car all clearcoated and ready for delivery. The white undercoat and basecoat really give it a crisp, bright look. And the Crystal Pearl is very clean and white. There are no yellow tones at all. Spraying pearl is pretty easy, but it helps to be familiar with the process and always take your time.

Here's a pearl orange on a Ford Mustang. Pearl colors give a very bright glow to the body lines and curves on a car.

Pearl colors can also be mixed up to combine a colored pearl with a silver pearl, like the silvery, mint green pearl on this Ford F150. Play around with pearl powders to create your own custom colors.

PAINTING CANDY

Candy colors are a little more challenging to paint than pearl colors because flaws and spraying/coverage inconsistencies tend to show up more than with pearl. Spraying candy on a car is hard for a first-time painter, but it can be done. Here again, is where practice comes in.

Before you paint a car with a candy color paint, make sure you have a good idea of the spray technique, how fast you need to be moving the gun, and the amount of overlap. But what can make or break a candy paint job? The way the gun is spraying. That spray pattern has to be even and unflawed; otherwise, it will be very difficult if not near impossible to get an even coat of candy on the surface. But it helps to mix your candy paint light on the candy.

Picking the Right Basecoat for Your Candy

The choices are endless when it comes to the basecoat under your candy paint. Very fine metallics or pearl basecoats like PPG's Liquid Metal can give a sleek, elegant effect. Later in this chapter, you'll see a yellow car with a liquid metal basecoat. Courser, brighter metallics give a blingy, bright sparkle effect like the saddlebag in the step-by-step demonstration seen here. This is where it helps to look a paint chart and see the different effects various bases have. Or play around with a few and come up with your own custom basecoat to use under the candy.

How Much to Mix?

It's very easy to start out too dark with the candy tone. Start out lighter, as you can always add another coat. Dark steaks can be a big problem when painting large surfaces like cars or trucks. Start with a light candy mixture; you can always add more candy to the mix if it's way too light or add another coat. Some painters add candy toners to urethane clear. If you do this, check to make sure the products are compatible with each other. This is another example of a good time to spray test panels beforehand. If if any problems come up, it is always better to find out on a test panel and not on the car.

Please know that you can order candy premixed from an automotive paint supply store. I mix my own colors but for the DIYer, it may be easier to look at a color chart and simply order the candy basecoat already mixed up. PPG's Vibrance Line of Radiance II offers a wide selection of premixed candy colors.

The PPG Radiance II candy color I'm using is called Orange Glow DBC 61079. If you are mixing the candy yourself, start out by adding a half ounce of DMX 211 Radiance II toner to clear DBC500 color blender. The candy paint mix is reduced 1:1 with DT885 reducer. Dip a paint stick into the mixture and see if it's the tone you want. Then add another half-ounce until the candy is the desired intensity. Color should appear rich to achieve color density in three to five coats. Remember, always start out lighter. Don't go too dark with the candy; otherwise, it might have dark streaks from the gun pattern.

The metallic or pearl basecoat is just as if not more important than the candy color. The amount of sparkle or bling the base has is up to you. A fine, medium, or coarse metallic may be used. Aggressive pearl powders or flakes may be added to give the base even more bling. Any color of metallic or pearl may be used under candy. Gold metallics tend to give candy a warmer tone than silver. Use a purple metallic base under a candy red to get a rich, deep burgundy. Put a green metallic under a cherry candy to get a sparkly purple with a depth that looks endless. Play around and experiment with candy and pearl colors. Liven up a candy color by adding a little pearl powder to it. But know that adding pearl to candy will mute the effect of the candy, so go very lightly with the pearl if you try this. This is the painter's chance to do something unique and different.

THE NUMBER RULE OF CANDY PAINT

Don't mix your candy too dark! You can always add more candy to the surface, but it's brutally hard to take away. In fact, it's nearly impossible.

SPRAYING CANDY ON THE JAMS

Use care when spraying candy on door jams, hood jams, trunk jams, and similar parts. When painting the jam, aim the spray gun so the paint lands on the jam surface and not on the exterior surfaces. Otherwise, you will end up with dark lines along the edges.

This is going to be an orange and black two-tone paint job with a graphic border separating the two tone. The black has already been painted, clearcoated, and sanded. The top half of the graphic has been taped off and the lower section under the tape will be covered with masking paper.

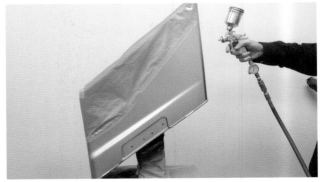

The parts were set up in the spray booth and tacked with a Blend Prep cloth to remove any dust. I sprayed the orange areas with PPG's DBC 33896 sterling silver basecoat (reduced 1:1 with DT885) using a SATA Minijet 3000B spray gun. This paint gun has great coverage, and two coats covered the black completely. The dry time between coats was 15 minutes. As I'll be doing more than two coats total of basecoat, I'm giving the layers of paint plenty of time to gas out in between applications of paint.

HOW TO AVOID DARK SPOTS IN CANDY COATS

One of the problems with spraying candy is that it will puddle around bits of dust or debris in the paint surface. Unless you have a pristinely clean spray booth, this problem is difficult to avoid. The best way to deal with it is to be prepared and watch for it. But know that sometimes it cannot be avoided.

- Make sure to tack and check the surface before the metallic base is sprayed.
- Check for dust bits landing on the paint as the base is being sprayed. If any fibers or dust lands on the surface, wait for the surface to dry and pick out the fiber with a pair of tweezers. I use Uncle Bill's Sliver Grippers.
- After the metallic base is completed and dry to the touch, check the surface for dust bits. Try to pick them out. If you can't get them out, very carefully nib sand the dust by folding a piece of sandpaper and sanding the dust with a corner, but be careful not to sand into the base.
- If you see any dust landing in the candy as it's being sprayed, try and pick it out, but again, use care. Sometimes it's best to just leave the dust alone and have a slight dark spot.

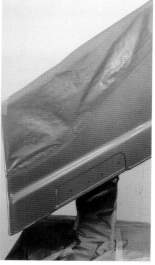

On the left, the first coat of candy is sprayed into the saddlebag using a SATA 4000 RP spray gun with a 1.3 nozzle set. I'm applying a medium coat with a 70% overlap, working my way back and forth across the part from side to side. Note how light it is. I prefer to do four or so coats of candy paint mixed lightly rather than two or three coats of candy mixed heavily. After waiting 15 minutes, the second coat of candy was sprayed onto the parts. I changed direction and sprayed diagonally, up and down, working my way across the part. Note the subtle color change.

After the second coat, it's looking pretty good, so it's time to match it against the color chip. Never trust your eyes to check color without comparing it to the sample or chip. The color had looked very close until I put the chip next it. I was about halfway there. It still needed more candy orange.

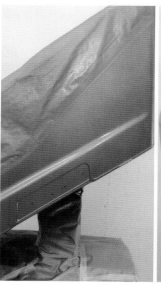

I applied the last two coats of candy. Again, I change gun direction with each coat of paint. On the left is the third coat, and on the right is the fourth and last coat. The color change is so subtle. By doing it this way, I play it safe, avoiding the possibility of dark streaks from using a candy that is mixed too dark.

I waited about an hour and then removed the tape from the parts. The parts were allowed to gas off for another hour. Then I cleared the parts with two coats with DC2000 mixed 4:1:1 with DCH2015 hardener and DT885 reducer. Make sure to use the reducer best suited for the temperature in your paint area. Here's what it looked like after the urethane clear.

DOUBLE-CHECK YOUR COLOR MATCH

In chapter 10, I talked about spraying your color process on a spray card at the same time you are spraying the car or parts. It's a little extra insurance to help the color match. The color may match in the booth, but will it match in the sun? It's helpful to check the color match in the sun to make sure the match is correct.

Don't just check to make sure the color matches where the sun hits. Check to make sure it matches on the flop (the dark angle). Here, I checked the saddlebag against the PPG color chip, and it matched on the flop.

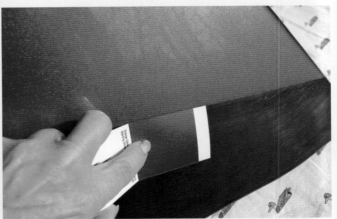

CANDY COLORS THAT BLEED

Some candy colors can tend to bleed up through coats of basecoat that are applied over them. For example, say you paint a car with candy cobalt blue, put a few coats of basecoat clear over it, and then spray some white lettering. Chances are pretty good that the white lettering may turn sky blue once you try to clear it again. The way to avoid this? Use a two-part urethane clearcoat over the candy colors. The urethane locks down the candy, and the colors won't bleed up through any artwork or topcoats.

Candy colors that tend to bleed include purple/reds, cobalt blue/red shade blues, burgundy, purple, and purple blues.

CANDY PAINT ON CARS

How different is painting candy on cars than on bikes? Well it's a little different in that it's harder to get even coverage on large surfaces. Again, practice before painting candy on your car or truck. Get used to the way candy sprays and get comfortable with the layering technique of changing spray gun directions to obtain even coverage. You can even use these techniques when spraying the primer and sealer. Make sure you walk the car and figure out the best plan of attack for spraying your car. Refer to chapter 10 for more information on creating a spray plan. Do not just go for it and spray it on your car!

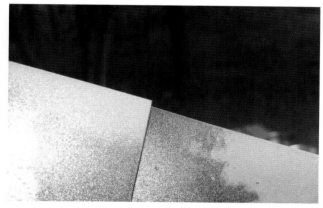

Left: Next, I sanded the parts with 800 grit, airbrushed a metal effect graphic between the two colors, and clearcoated the parts. This is the finished saddlebag. **Right:** One coat of candy can make a big difference. These two sprayout cards were both painted with a silver base with candy black layered over it. The sample on the left has two coats of candy. The sample on the right has three coats and is darker.

Here are all the finished parts together. See how all the candy is the same tone? The coverage is consistent. Making sure that each part receives the same amount as the others is the hardest part of spraying candy.

Here is an incredible candy paint job on a legendary car. The metallic basecoat under the lime candy is PPG's Liquid Metal. Liquid Metal is a specialized pigment designed to achieve a polished metalized final appearance. It can be used as a stand-alone metalized finish or as a ground color for other PPG Vibrance topcoats to create special effect finishes.

An amazing candy apple red paired with a black combines to create a show stopping two tone. The darkness of the black is a great contrast for the candy.

The use of both candy and pearl is a powerful combination on this Cadillac. You can see the pearl particles in the paint sparkling up through the candy layers. Gene Winfield is the painter behind this incredible paint job. Candy is the perfect paint for doing fades.

There are endless ways to use candy and pearl paint. Chapter 8 talks about flop. Candy paint tends to flop pretty dark. That means when the candy panel is viewed from a sharp angle it looks dark. It's one of the things that gives candy its richness. But can a painter make candy flop lighter? Absolutely! In this picture, the tank from the candy paint detailed in this chapter is on the bottom. The tank on the top was painted with the same orange only it flops light. This was done by first painting a white undercoat, followed by painting an orange pearl basecoat, followed by two coats of candy orange—only the candy orange had much less candy toner in it than the tank on bottom. Yet it still has the same orange tone due to the orange pearl basecoat.

Chapter 13
Flaking Out with Flake Paint

Back in the '60s and '70s, flake paint was everywhere—on vans, cars, speedboats, and motorcycles. It was bold and brassy, the perfect base paint for the wild, experimental artwork being done at the time. Then it faded away. But over the past few years, custom painters are rediscovering flake paint and its endless possibilities.

Most paint companies have their own line of flake paint. Most of the time, it comes dry, in a jar, and needs to be mixed with paint, usually clear paint. The flakes are made from a very thin polyester. They are offered in different sizes from super brilliant and big to a fine

MATERIALS & EQUIPMENT

SATA 100 BF HVLP spray gun
SATA agitator cup
SATAjet 3000 B minijet spray gun
Paint materials of your choice
Gerson Blend Prep tack cloths
Evercoat mixing cups
PPG sprayout cards
PPG Prep Plus wipes
PPG DX320 precleaner
800 sandpaper

Flake paint is very popular for those wild multilayer lowrider-style paint jobs. But for many of these cars, the flake is a major accent color, being one half of a two-tone paint scheme or used as an accent color.

Left: The first step is spraying the surface with a color that is similar to the end result color. Make sure you have a properly prepped surface—either sanded primer or sealer ready for basecoating. Tack rag the surface to remove any dust or debris. This bike tank will be a dark gray, so a black basecoat is the first color I sprayed. **Right:** Now for main trick. Get out the coarsest basecoat silver you have. If you are applying a gold flake, use the coarsest gold metallic available. If you're going with a silver or colored flake, try PPG Vibrance 33896 sterling silver. Or if you have a mixing system, use PPG Deltron DMD650 and mix it with DBX1689 basecoat converter. If you are going with a colored flake, find the toner that goes best with the colored flake and mix it into the silver metallic, creating a color that is the same shade only a little darker. My flake color is dark charcoal, so black is mixed with the silver. The metallic mix is pretty close to the charcoal flake in the bottle.

flake that's a little bigger than pearl particles. Modern flake comes in many colors, is thin, and lays down flat, requiring less clear to level out the surface. Flake paint ranges in size from ultra micro flake .002 inch to bass boat big flake .62 inch. The most popular size flake is .15 inch.

The two biggest problems with painting flake colors are the rough surface of the freshly applied flake paint and the mess that results from the application. I use a few tricks to make the flake process somewhat easier.

I'll address the cleanup first. Flake is heavy stuff, and unless you're using a downdraft booth (a booth with the outtake filters right in the floor beneath the car), it's a pain to clean up. The flakes are heavier than metallics or pearl colors, and they tend to land everywhere. The floor will be covered with them, and no matter how thoroughly you clean up, they'll try to get in every coat of paint you spray in the months after. So when planning out paint times, take into account the time it will take to clean up from the flake.

One trick to help keep the oversprayed flakes under control is to cover the floor with masking paper to catch any loose flakes. Simply roll up the paper when you're done. If you're attempting to spray flake in a garage, go out and get some disposable drop clothes. Drape them over everything, even tool boxes and benches. In fact, if you choose to spray any paint in your garage, cover everything with drop clothes and hang up plastic to

DON'T FLAKE OUT!

OK, now that you know how to clean up flake, let's see how to spray it.

Test, test, test your technique and the products being used. Do not simply start spraying flake on the car or parts. Practice on a spare part, a junk fender, anything you can spray paint on. It is very easy to create a mess when spraying flake, so get used to how it sprays.

Test your colors. If you want to layer candy over the flake, test that to make sure your process is successful. You don't want to layer on too much basecoat at one time. That is a big no no, and it's easy to get caught up in spraying the flake, not realizing just how much paint is going onto that surface. If the basecoat is applied too heavily, it takes forever to dry. One of the worst things you can do when painting is to spray clear urethane over a basecoat that has not gassed out enough. This oversight can result in wrinkling. Sometimes, it may look OK at first, but the next day the surface will look dull and rough and feel rubbery. Solvents from the basecoat, which are now trapped beneath the hardened urethane, were trying to get out. That ruined the glassy urethane, and now there's a mish mash of soft layers of paint. Always read the P sheets and test.

cover the walls. But never spray paint in a garage that is attached to your home, especially if the garage is located under the house. Know the laws on what you can and cannot do in your neighborhood.

To clean up from flake, I first grab the shop vac and vacuum the floor and walls and any cobwebs that might

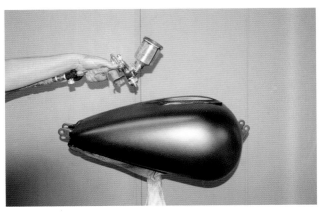

I loaded the charcoal metallic into a SATAjet 3000B mini spray gun and applied two medium layers to the tank. If you tried spraying the flake directly on the black surface, you can see bits of the black base between the flakes. By having a coarse metallic base under the flake, any spaces between the flakes are filled up with this sparkly base. This means less flake is used, and it helps give the flake a bottomless effect.

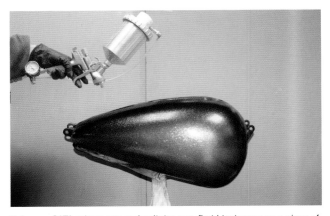

Using my SATA primer gun and agitator cup, first I test spray on a piece of masking paper taped to the wall. What does the pattern look like? Does the flake have an even distribution of material? Once I'm happy with the testing, three layers of flake are sprayed. Don't go too heavy on each coat! Spray a medium wet layer. Don't try to build up full flake coverage with one coat. If you are using a gravity feed spray gun, remember not to use a filter inside the cup. Many disposable paint cups, like SATA's RPS cups, have little filters in the bottom of the cup. The flake will not get through that filter. After you are done spraying flake, wearing a clean disposable glove, lightly brush your hand over the surface to loosen and remove any flakes that are not lying flat.

have gathered in the corners. Next, I remove all the filters from the ventilation system in the booth, both the intake and outtake. They won't be used again. Then I sweep with a soft bristle broom, carefully looking to see how much flake is still there. The next step is mopping the floor, again looking to see how much flake remains. Like I said, flake clean up takes time.

Next, mix the flake with clearcoat. A variety of different clearcoat paints can be used. Many painters use basecoat clear, and that's what I'm using here. But clear urethane can also be used. When using urethane as a midcoat (that is, over a basecoat and under a clearcoat), PPG recommends that their VM4401 gold and VM4402 silver flakes spray better in a medium solid clear. For example, flakes used with DC2000 two-part clear will make the finished product much smoother than if you decided to mix the flake in DBC or BC solvent basecoats or waterborne midcoats. For PPG's Ditzler Big Flake, the company recommends using 14 oz. clear to 0.2 oz. flake or, for those with a paint scale, 400 grams of clear to 8 grams of flake. For the DIYer, I'm using 2 level teaspoons (1 oz.) to 1 mixed quart of clearcoat.

But remember, too much flake in the mix will tend to clog up your spray gun and will lay down pretty rough. You want the flakes to lie down nice and flat to reflect the light effectively. Make sure to leave time between coats for the coats of paint to flash off. Whatever paint and flake you use, get the P sheet for the flake and paint and follow the directions closely.

Make sure to wear a disposable paint suit with a hood. And maybe even shoe covers or junk shoes, because you and your shoes will be covered in flake.

If you want to add candy layers over the flake, you can add candy concentrate or dye to the clear. Just be sure that any candy concentrate and clear are compatible. This

is where testing before you spray comes in handy. Know how thickly you can layer the products being used and how many layers can be successfully painted in one day. For my tank, I mixed a little Radiance II DMX black into the clear basecoat and sprayed one coat over the flake.

The flake layers might look a little dull because basecoat clear dries dull. The flake will need clearcoating

For those wanting to spray a colored flake and then candy over, check out this mini hood. I sprayed on red flake then layered over it with two layers of red candy urethane, then I cleared it with two more coats of urethane clear.

HANDY HINT

You'll need special tools for spraying flake. The following have worked well for me. I use a SATA 100 BF HVLP spray gun (my primer gun) fitted with a 1.7 nozzle set with a SATA agitator mixing cup. A hose runs from the gun regulator to a quick disconnect fitting on the lid of the cup. The lid has a paddle that reaches down into the cup. Air propels the paddle and keeps the flake mixed.

With gravity feed guns, the flake has a tendency to settle in the gun's paint chamber; remember, you're not using a filter in the cup. If you suspect this is happening, hold a bundled rag over the gun nozzle and pull the trigger. It will force air through the paint chamber and into the cup, clearing out any clogging flakes. This trick can be used to keep the flake mixed in the cup if an agitator cup is not used. Just give it a zap before applying each coat. Just apply a small dose of air; do not pull back all the way on the gun's trigger.

Here's what the tank looks like after the urethane clear has dried down for a day. The surface looks a little bumpy, but that's because I was careful not to flood the clear on the surface. This is the part that is tricky about working with flake. It's tempting to just layer on tons of paint material at once. But that's a bad idea. Paint needs time to dry.

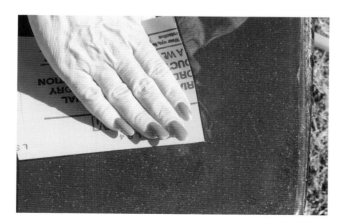

Once it's dry, scuff with a gray 3M Scotch-Brite pad, then wet sand with 800, being careful not to sand too much and break through any flakes or any flake layers. The Scotch-Brite will scuff up the low areas in the surface, and the 800 will take down the high points. Watch carefully as you work. If there's candy under the clear, say a layer or two of red candy was sprayed over the flake and you see red washing up as you sand, that means you've sanded through the topcoat clear into the candy and are about to go through into the flake. Here I'm sanding with 800 grit on the hood I sprayed with red candy. Leveling out the surface of the flake is a combination of clearing, sanding that clear, and repeating until the surface is smooth and glassy.

with a topcoat clear. The clear layers will build up the paint thickness and help level out the flakes. Use a clear that is compatible with the basecoat paint.

If you get any light spots in candy flake jobs, retouch carefully with candy and an airbrush. Either way, once you've got the flake and/or color coats under the first round of clear, it should only require one more round of three to four layers of clearcoats. Now, artwork or the finishing clearcoat can be applied. Refer to chapter 24 for doing artwork over flake paint. But give those coats time to dry out (a day or so) between rounds of paint.

After sanding the tank, I clearcoated it with three layers of Vibrance VC5200 clearcoat. That was sanded with 800, and I did a layer of red flake flames and striped them, followed by two more rounds of clearcoat. Here's the finished charcoal flake tank. This was not a paint job that was done in one week.

Prismatic flake must be pretty popular for roofs, as here's another roof that it was used on. PPG's Vibrance Prizmatique can be used to create this kind of effect. I'm guessing the painter here put down a gold metallic base, layered a gold flake with prism flake in it over that, taped off the darker stripes, and sprayed those with a transparent candy.

Using large-sized flakes for painting the roofs of hot rods and lowriders is pretty popular, and for a good reason—it looks wicked cool. The roof of this street rod is one of my favorite custom-painted roofs. A color-changing prismatic flake base was laid on, and then a huge flame was taped off. Next, the painter taped off a Mexican blanket design, then sprayed on black stripes and then candy color stripes that allow the flake to show through.

Red flake flames look great on this Dodge Magnum.

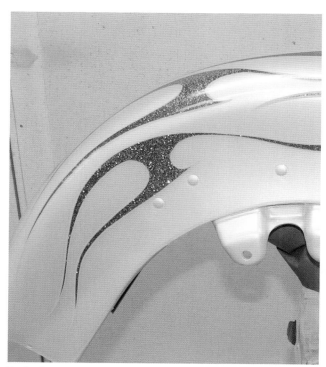

For the flames on this off-white pearl, I added some Prizmatique flake to some purple flake.

Flake works great for filling in graphic effects like the dark blue flake in this graphic.

Here's a lowrider with graphics by Craig Fraser. The hood and top surface of the car were layered with flake, and then Craig applied the graphics.

Flake doesn't always mean retro graphics on a bike. Here are classic-style graphics over an intense purple flake base.

I dig lowrider-style paint. And leave it to a lowrider to cover a vehicle with flake—check out this firewall. Wild stuff!

Chapter 14
Creating Custom Colors

Many hot rodders see a color they like and want that color for their ride. I have received multiple requests for burgundy-and-champagne two-tone over the years, and for good reason: it's a great combination. But go to most car shows, and you'll see at least at least one champagne pearl and some kind of red two-tone. Why not be unique and have a color all your own?

One of the reasons people tend to stick to factory colors or colors from a paint company's custom chart is that it's quicker and easier than creating a custom color. But given the right circumstances, a custom color can be relatively easy to create and spray. Custom colors give painters a chance to have fun and to be creative. They can also allow a painter's work to stand apart from others'.

Custom colors can be as simple or as complex as a painter wants them to be. Sometimes creating a fantastic shade is as easy as changing or adding an ingredient or

HANDY HINT

Custom colors can make your work stand out from the crest, but always document the mixture of your color. Have pen and paper next to you as you're mixing. Write down everything you add—even if you add the same color twice, write down each bit as you mix it in. For example, if you add 10 grams of white and realize it needs another 5 grams, note this on your mixing sheet. If you need to pour off some color because the mixture is going in the wrong direction, write down what was poured off. Always take the time to document every detail as a custom color is mixed.

two in a formula; sometimes it's simply spraying any base color and laying a pearl mixture over it. Other times, it's creating a color from scratch, starting with a base and mixing until you get the desired effect. Anytime you deviate from a formula, you end up with a

Color can be an art form in itself. The right combination of one-of-a-kind colors can bring a vehicle to life. And with patience and creativity, creating those unique colors can be one of the most fun things about painting. Custom designed colors can also complement and emphasize custom fabrication as on this wild street rod.

custom color. Here are a few simple ideas to help create, mix, and spray a custom color.

SIMPLE CUSTOM COLORS

Many times, a painter needs the color to be simple but also unique and eye-catching. A recent job in my shop required those very things—the color had to be unique, yet easy to mix, easy to touch up, and easy to blend. And it had to look a mile deep and stand out in a crowd of custom bikes. The job had a total of 39 parts that needed paint, so the color had to remain consistent throughout the job. In fact, there were so many parts that they had to be painted in batches. And many of the parts required artwork. That meant those parts needed to be sanded between rounds of clearcoating to level out the paint layers of the artwork. Chances are with so many parts, some edges would get sanded through and need touching up. I needed a color that was very easy to spray. But what makes a color easy to spray?

For this color, I started out with PPG's Vibrance Perfect Purple. I changed the formula slightly and made up three different samples. My customer picked her favorite, the middle sample. I mixed up 2 quarts of the color. Her factory paint was in good shape, so it was cleaned and prep sanded with 600 grit. Next, the parts were based using PPG's DP90LV epoxy primer, and then three coats of the custom purple were applied. Next the parts were clearcoated with PPG's DCU 2021 clear. Simple and quick.

Here are just some of the parts laid out in my airbrush studio. At this point, out of 39 parts, 22 pieces were completed, needing only to be buffed. But 17 parts needed artwork. Some edges were sanded through, and I did find a few places where the paint application was not as perfect as I had wanted. Because my color was accommodating to work with, it was easy to respray or touch up any parts and have them match all the others. Notice how the color changes from different angles. The parts on the left side of the picture have a bluish tone from the camera flash, while the parts on the right look more purple. Colors like this can drive a painter crazy. This color changes slightly. It would be extremely difficult to match the color without knowing the specific paint formula. Despite this, the color was easy to paint as it covered well and was very easy to touch up.

Some of the parts are assembled on the bike. The tail section is combined of four different parts. The color matches perfectly where they come together.

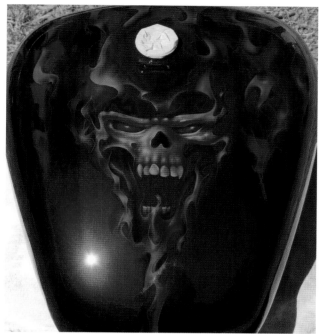

Many customers want black as a base yet at the same time they want some kind of color. Using the process in the last step, I created a simple custom color that from most angles looks black, yet when the sun hits it, it lights up purple. This effect can be done with any color, I just used purple here. Start off with a black basecoat. Then pour some clear basecoat in the mixing cup. Pick out a pearl color with the amount of desired sparkle. Add a very small amount to the clear basecoat and make one quick pass with this mix. Do not overdo this step. Then mix a small amount of candy toner to clear basecoat, creating a tinted clear rather than a full strength candy. Apply a coat of this mix over the pearl and look at the effect in the sun to check the result with the test sample you (hopefully) made. Always make sure to spray out a test sample to test the color mixtures and your process. You can also make this black pearl candy effect as bold or as subtle as desired by varying the amount of pearl that is applied.

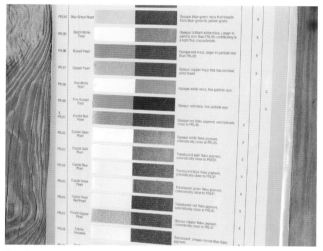

Here's another great way to create a simple custom color. For a sweet trick effect, try mixing pearl with a solid color. To create a blue pearl black, add blue pearl to black basecoat. This is the pearl section of the PPG Tinting Chart. The right side of each color chip shows the pearl mixed with black basecoat. One trick is to try mixing two pearl colors together to create a new color. Don't hesitate to experiment with what's lying around the shop. Try mixing pearl with a blue or yellow. Maybe you have a whole bottle of an oddball pearl powder that you seldom use in regular paintwork. Adding this to a base color or mixing it with some clear basecoat and adding a little candy toner, might create a really cool color that is uniquely yours. But make sure to document the formula!

- The color stays pretty much consistent through two to four layers, no matter the air pressure or the application.
- The color covers well. After two to three coats there's no blotching or unevenness.
- The color does not require a specific basecoat. It sprays great over a medium gray primer or sealer.
- The paint formula has only a few ingredients and mixes up uniformly each time.

Some painters hesitate when it comes to custom colors because they're more difficult to work with than premixed custom paint. You have to be more careful and attentive in the process, and mistakes are easy to make because of the brutal schedule of a paint shop. Keeping to the paint chart often gives painters one less thing to worry about. Custom colors are not for every project or even most of your projects, but when time allows and that unique project arrives at the shop, playing with custom colors can be the best option.

For the DIYer, you don't need a great deal of painting experience to create your own custom colors. You just need to take your time. Some say passion is the enemy of precision. Many times, we get so caught up in the excitement of a project that we rush through some primary steps in an effort to rush the final result. This is when

For this next example, a simple change to a stock paint formula made a big difference. Sometimes a custom color is discovered by accident. For this two-tone tank half, I picked two colors from the Vibrance Collection, 908354 Rattlesnake and 908359 24 Carat. Both of these colors use pearl powders from PPG's line of Liquid Crystal Pearl. Rattlesnake uses VM4102 Emberglow, a bright sparkly orange pearl with a slight greenish tone depending on the angle it's viewed from. It's a wild color. 24 Carat uses VM4101 Emerald, a green pearl. The problem was, I did not have any Emerald Pearl. So I substituted the Emberglow pearl for the Emerald pearl. And it actually worked to my advantage. Because both colors now used the Emberglow pearl, they better complemented each other. And both colors were easy to mix up and spray. They only had a few ingredients, and they covered fast.

Always, always spray a paint sample or samples. Don't trust what you see in the mixing cup or on the paint stick. Paint can change as it dries, and many times colors spray out lighter than they will be after they dry. Spraying a sample gives you an idea of how well your color will cover. Use multi-toned sprayout cards—they'll help show how many coats it takes to cover thoroughly. Too many times painters skip this step only to find out the hard way that their color needed an adjustment or a specific base needed to be applied first. Instead of taking a few precautionary steps, they take a shortcut that ends up costing a day or more of work and hundreds of dollars in materials. Sprayout cards are cheap, effective tools when working with custom colors.

horrible mistakes are made, like not carefully testing your color on sprayout cards, or writing down every change you make in the process of a color application, such as documenting the number of coats of paint. Another big mistake as a result of impatience is not waiting for a sunny day to judge your colors. Take that extra time—in the long run, you will be glad you did. Another day or two of waiting to paint your car or bike will not be the end of the world. Don't make a rookie mistake.

One tool referred to in this chapter is the paint scale. Not many DIYers have one, but they come in handy. Mixing cups with measurements on them are inexpensive and easy to use. They can be used to keep track of the ingredients in a custom paint formula. They're not as precise as a paint scale, but if you are only using liquid ingredients and not pearl powders, you can keep your measurements pretty much consistent if you need to mix more of your color. In any case, always try to mix plenty of color the first time, especially if you are using mixing cups to keep track of your formula.

COMPLEX CUSTOM COLORS

Designing signature colors is a great way for painters to make their mark. I've developed many, but my favorite and most well-known is an orange pearl that I designed

10 years ago. Over the years, I have tweaked the formula, trying to take it to the next level. It had been a few years since I had used it last, so when a customer was looking for a wild orange color, I knew it was time to try a remix of this very bright orange. But what makes it a complex custom color is the custom mix candy orange that I planned to lay over it.

Think about the color you want to create. Then look over the chart and find the mixing bases that have the effects you're looking for. If you have those bases in stock, pour a little of each in a small cup, mix them,

Unlike collision shops that use a paint scale every day, some custom painters don't have one. I was one of them! In fact, some of my custom painter friends don't even own a paint scale. We figured most of the paint we bought came premixed, so we lived by the custom color charts provided by paint companies. We played around custom mixing some of it, adding some of this to that. And we tried to document it by using measurements on mixing cups—4 ounces of this mixed with 10 ounces of that. It works pretty well, and that's why I did it that way for over 25 years.

Then I bought a mixing scale and wondered why it took me so long to buy one. It changed the way I mixed paint and made life easier. The mixing scale is the handiest tool for creating custom colors. I can mix up more of a custom color and know it will be exactly the same as the first batch I mixed. Some painters feel you don't need a mixing scale if you don't have a mixing system. This is not true! Over the years, you accumulate cans of paint, toners, pearl powders, and such and end up with many of the components of a mixing system. The scale allows you to accurately document creating special mixes.

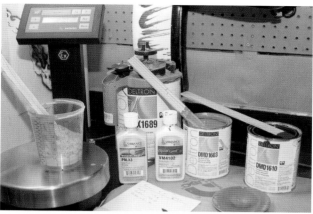

The first step in any custom color is checking the tinting or toner chart. On the toner chart, I look for orange colors that are the kind of tone I want—bright orange but not leaning toward red. Maybe more toward yellow. Using an old part that was painted a similar color, I find two toners that might work. The main toner that is very close, DMD1603, is actually not an orange but a red shade yellow. The painted piece is next to the red shade yellow. Look along the three sections of the color chip. The full tone section on the left is very close in tone, but the section of the chip on the right, where the toner is mixed with silver, is very washed out. Five color chips below that chip is DMD1610 transparent orange. The full tone section of the chip looks almost brown, but on the right side, mixed with the metallic, it looks more orange. It just needs some yellow to warm it up. This is how the chart is used, going back and forth between colors, finding the right match of characteristics for the desired colors.

These two toners, 1603 and 1610, will be the base of this custom pearl. Next, I need to find the actual pearl powders. Two very different Vibrance Pearls will do the trick. PLRX03 gold pearl has a brilliant crisp sparkle, a stronger kick than regular pearl. VM4102 Emberglow is a little larger in particle size, and the Liquid Crystal pearls reflect light differently due to their unique shapes. This pearl also changes color a little and gives a vivid, dazzling sparkle to my color. This is the fun part of creating your own colors—mixing in fun things like Crystal Pearls. I also add some DBX1689 to thin out the mix. Bit by bit I add the ingredients to the mixing cup, writing down the amount of each item. Then the scale is zeroed out and I add the next item until everything is mixed and carefully documented.

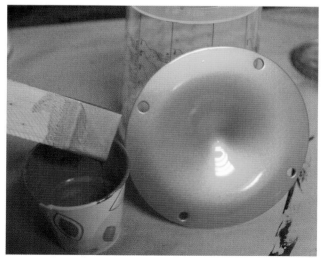

The next step is checking the color on the stick. It is close to my old color, but by using the different pearls gives paint more sparkle, more bling. Comparing also shows that the two toners selected were correct and the pearl combination is doing what I had hoped—it's got a great look. But if the color had not been right, this would be the time to go back and add or refigure the formula.

Several sprayout cards are sprayed with my custom mixed base pearl and numbered. Now to figure out the mix of the orange candy that will go over it. I don't want too many layers of candy over the base, just enough to richen it up without taking away from the unique sparkle it has. DBC 500 color blender will be the base for the candy. A small amount of DMX211 orange candy dye/toner is added to the DBC500. Then it's mixed with reducer and two coats are sprayed onto the #1 sprayout card on the left. It's a little too dark, so a mix with less 211 is made up. Two coats are sprayed onto the #2 orange basecoated sprayout card in the middle. This time, the color is perfect, bright and rich. The sample on the far right is just the orange pearl without any orange candy. Note how much lighter it is than sample number #2. And the candy color itself is actually much lighter than usual candy colors. It's more like a tinted clear. Look at the big difference just a little bit of candy makes. But that's what great about custom mixing candy colors, they can be as light or as deep as you want.

There's one general rule when it comes to mixing up any color: it's infinitely better to mix too much paint than to get three-quarters of the way through a job only to run out. Plus, if you need to mix more color and you want to be sure the color is identical, it's great to have a little extra to compare it to, stick to stick. The bottom line is to mix plenty of color. This is not the place to be cheap.

and see if it starts looking like what you're aiming for. Sometimes you can create a cool color by using paint that you have around. For example, mixing two similar pearl colors together can create a new color, like mixing a purple-blue pearl with a hot pink pearl can result in a bright medium purple pearl. Applying a candy purple tinted clear over it will richen the effect and give it depth. Applying a light cobalt blue candy over a green shade of blue metallic can yield a bright blue. The color won't be as purple as candy cobalt blue over silver, but it will have the deep richness of cobalt.

Next, I make sure I have enough paint for the project, and I'll mix more color if need be. The great thing is that I have the original mix right there and can compare the new mix to the previously mixed paint. I'll place the mixing cups side by side and compare stick to stick. Yes, I have the formula, but maybe I made a mistake without realizing it. Maybe I added something but forgot to write it down. Comparing the mixes helps catch any mistakes in the formula. Remember, it easy to make mistakes while painting, and catching those mistakes early in the job makes it much easier to remedy them.

Here's the color sprayed on the project. It's a perfect match to the sample. Always spray your test samples exactly as you would spray the vehicle or parts. But keep in mind, the surface of a car or truck is very different from the small surface of a test card. Bend the card and see how the color appears on a curved surface. Be 110% sure of your color before you spray it on a vehicle. Don't rush through the testing and sample stage. And make sure to look at your color in different kinds of light.

CREATING CUSTOM COLORS

A PAINT TRUTH

What do you do when you don't follow the rules? Sometimes we don't always mix up enough color, or we're in a hurry and for some reason don't accurately document the mixture of a color only to run out of paint and need to mix more. First off, stay calm. If you're using uncatalyzed basecoat, unofficially, you have pretty much an unlimited window to recoat. Uncatalyzed basecoat will usually bite into or stick to uncatalyzed basecoat. This is one of the advantages of not using hardener in your basecoat. It all depends on the product you are using. So you may have some time to try and figure out how to reproduce the formula. But what if you can't? Or what if your basecoat has a tight recoat window? Then it's time to improve the formula. Create a new version. Similar but slightly different. The end result will be pretty much the same.

Sometimes, we as painters are too critical for our own good. We focus so hard on a task that we lose track of the end result, which is to create a high-quality paint job that will impress. So when something goes wrong, embrace it. You never know, you may even come up with a color that is better. Some of the best custom colors are discovered completely by accident.

A COLOR TRUTH

The kind of light a paint is viewed in makes all the difference. This photo shows why it's always a good idea to wait for a sunny day to judge a color. These chips are all the same color, but the top half of the photo shows the chips in direct sunlight while the bottom half shows the same chips in the shade. The chip on the right appears bright and light in the sun but muddy and dark in the shade, and you see none of the pearl sparkle in the shade. Always judge your colors in several kinds of light.

Here's another example of a complex custom color. The customer wanted a WWII theme on his bike. I didn't want to do the usual solid olive green, so I designed a candy olive green. I wanted the basecoat to have a lot of sparkle, so I used the coarsest metallic I had: DMD650. I mixed it with DMD614, a blue toner, and came up with a steel blue metallic. Candy yellow was layered over it, resulting in a candy olive green with lots of kick and depth.

Chapter 15
Troubleshooting Paint Problems

About 35 years ago, I bought a book on custom painting. Over the years, the part of the book that I used most was the chapter on troubleshooting problems. But paint technology has changed vastly, as have the paint problems and their solutions.

One fact I keep repeating throughout this book is that all paint is different. A successful solution to a problem that works for one brand of paint might not work for another. Get the P sheet for the paint being used and follow the guidelines for that product. If you misplace it, you can usually download one from the paint company's website. Know the phone number for the tech line of the company whose products you use, and don't hesitate to call them or your paint supplier when you have a problem. When you speak to them, be honest about what is going on, especially if you took a shortcut or did not follow the guidelines. You would not be the first person not to follow the rules. It's their job to help you, so use this resource.

Here are some common problems and some remedies that have worked for me. But remember, each situation is different and what works for one problem might not work for another.

COLOR MATCHING AND REPAIRS: HALOS

Chapter 8 presents color matching in depth, but one thing that can be an issue when doing a repair are halos. A halo is the result of sanding through coats of paint when repairing chips, cracks, and dents. The edges of the paint layers are revealed. The halo effect happens when new paint reacts with the edges of the old paint. It is usually caused by the solvents in sealer, primer, and basecoat, which are used to match the color for the repair. They can react with the sanded through edges of the urethane used for the original paint's topcoat.

Avoiding this unwanted reaction is one reason why waterborne paint has become so popular in the collision industry. The waterborne primers and basecoats, simply sit on top of the edges of the sanded layers without irritating them. And as waterborne dries so quickly,

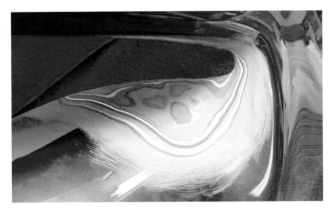

This photo shows an example of halos. There had been a large bubble of lifted paint on this plastic part. The lifted paint was removed and the broken edges sanded down. If the broken edges are not sealed down, they will ghost through the new paint, resulting in a halo, which is caused by slight impressions that show in the paint.

there's little chance of the new paint shrinking down and those edges ghosting through the new paint over time.

But what if you're not using a waterborne product? For my shop, the best solution I have found is to seal down those edges with a skim coat of plastic filler. Chapter 5 shows the simple steps I use for this problem.

CRAZING OR CRACKING

Newly applied paint will crack or craze for a number of reasons. It could be a chemical reaction for an incorrect mixing ratio: if too much activator/hardener is used, or if the correct ratio is not properly mixed, defects may appear in the finished dried paint film.

- If the parts were just removed from a colder section of the shop, and your booth or spray area is warmer, give the parts some time to heat up. Painting cold parts in a warm area with paint that is the same temperature as the area can result in crazing or cracking.
- Painting over an improperly prepared surface can also cause crazing and cracking. If the substrate

Notice the slight lines running across this surface? They are actual cracks in the paint.

you are working on has cracks or other issues, those issues will come up through the newly applied paint. Never take the shortcut of thinking you can simply fill cracks with paint or catalyzed primer. The damaged material must be completely removed and the area repaired.

The repair for crazing and cracking can be vexing. Some painters have made saves in this area by recoating the part with overreduced paint. I do not recommend this course of action and have not made any saves in the crazing dept. The best solution is to remove any cracked material by sanding down the cracks, sealing, and starting over. I don't like putting hours of artwork into basecoats that cause me doubts. In my early painting days, I made a few trips to the sandblaster with crazed parts.

WRINKLING

Wrinkling is usually caused by trapped solvents or repenetration when newly applied solvents reach down into a painted surface and react badly with the paint layers below. Wrinkling is another problem with multiple causes.

- Using the wrong temperature range of reducer can cause wrinkling. Some painters mistakenly use a cold (fast) reducer to "dry" their work quicker. This is a bad idea because the top dries faster. The bottom of the layer (or coat) just lies there while the drier, top layer acts as a lid. As a result, the solvents can't evaporate and they just lie there, soaking into the layer below. If you recoat before this layer has dried, at the very least it wrinkles; at the worst it lifts clear to the primer and maybe even to the metal.
- Piling on coats of paint can also cause this problem. Perhaps you recoated too soon or it's way too hot to be painting. The bottom line here is that for whatever reason the top of the paint skinned over and trapped the solvents.
- Other causes for wrinkling are bad catalyst and uncured or soft urethane.
- Wrinkling can also happen when painting basecoat over a thin layer of urethane clear which was over

basecoat. It begins when solvent from the top layer of basecoat gets through urethane clear in a thin or broken spot and resaturates the basecoat under the clear. There'll be a layer of catalyzed clear between two wet layers of basecoat. All the affected paint must be removed. Having mish mosh layers of catalyzed and uncatalyzed paint, clear, primer, and sealer is unstable. This is why urethane should never be applied too thin. The thin coats of urethane clear get sanded and are almost gone in places.

• Some company's products can be more prone to wrinkling. This is due to the "temp" of their solvents. Some paints are pretty "hot" and thoroughly penetrate the layers below. Time between coats is crucial with products like this. The window between coats is very strict. Wait a few minutes too long, and the paint wrinkles. Lay on a coat too heavy, and the paint wrinkles. This is especially problematic with urethane paints. I try to use paints that are very painter friendly. When I use a new product, I put it through a few tests, trying to make it wrinkle on a sample part. This is why testing your paint products is so important. A few hours of testing can really save you time, money, and your sanity. There's no telling what may happen down the road even if it looks good. This is what happens when trying to take shortcuts. If you have any doubts, remove all the paint, right down to the substrate.

What do you do if the paint wrinkles? I have never been able to save paint that has wrinkled. Again, I hate doing something, having it look OK, then a few days, whammo. . . . It's showing the wrinkled effect again, but now it's under all kinds of clear and the customer is due to arrive shortly.

In cases where it's just a bit of wrinkling on one part, I let it dry and remove the damaged paint by sanding. Then, I let the part dry out, in case any of the undercoats are soft. I look very closely at the paint layers. Are there tiny wrinkles in them or is the paint soft? If I have any doubts, I'll take the affected area down to the metal, removing those doubts. Then, I use flowable polyester filler to cover up the edges of the layers I sanded through because those separations between the layers might show as halos through the basecoats I'm about to reapply. Next, I sand the filler, lay on some two-part primer, sand, and then apply epoxy primer sealer immediately before spraying the new basecoat. Make sure you give the epoxy enough time to dry. The PPG DP90LV I use says to wait at least 15 minutes but

Runs are a reality in custom painting. Even experienced painters run their paint occasionally.

no more than 12 hours. I wait 30 minutes. Finally, I look very closely around the edges of the repair for tiny wrinkles after I resume paint application.

What if the entire part is wrinkled? Strip all the paint from the part. Start over.

RUNS AND SAGS

Runs and sags can be caused by paint that has been applied too heavily or overreduced for the conditions. Maybe the wrong temperature reducer was used and the paint is drying too slowly.

To fix the problem, carefully sand the high spots. I wrap 600 grit sandpaper over Motor Guard Company's aluminum sanding blocks (Run Blockers) and slowly wet shave down the sag, taking care not to sand anything other than the run itself; it's too easy to get a light spot around a run that was sanded away, especially in candy. I take down the run with the hard block then softly sand the whole area with a lighter grit paper, using a Meguiar's sanding backing pad.

Beware if the candy paint run is along a fender edge. Chances are you might sand through the candy creating a light spot. When that happens, I leave the run alone and do my filler clearcoats. The clearcoats build up the area around the run. Then, it is sanded later and there's less chance of getting into the candy coats. That's when I softly airbrush some candy in the light areas. The great thing is, if too much candy is applied, it can be sanded off and airbrushed again without affecting the original candy coats. This can also work for pearl colors.

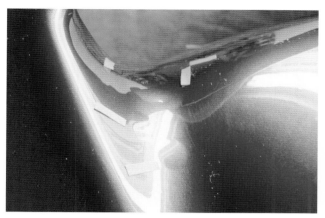

Look closely at this pearl blue paint. Notice the bubbles? They're lifted areas of paint. To find the cause, the bubble must be cut away. The lifted paint has to be removed anyway. The next picture shows what caused these bubbles.

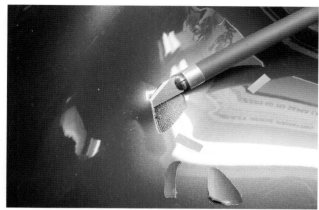

The bubble has been cut into and it's easy to see what's under it. Check out the weird pattern in the black paint underneath. It's wrinkled. That means some kind of solvent was trapped. The trapped solvents wrinkled the paint below, then those solvents pushed up on the paint above. Whoever painted this part either piled on coats of paint without leaving enough time in between coats, improperly reduced the paint, or improperly mixed the paint. For whatever reason, the bottom line is something caused the black paint to wrinkle and then they quickly painted the blue paint over it, which lifted.

Same part, different area; different cause, same problem—lifted paint. The large lifted paint bubbles on this area have been cut away. This what was underneath the big bubbles. Look at the black areas. See the problem? The black is shiny. It shouldn't be. The blue paint did not stick to this area. There are several reasons why this will happen. Waiting too long in between coats of paint and missing the recoat window. Most paint manufacturers recommend recoating basecoat within 12 hours. Longer than that and the newly applied paint might not stick without first scuffing the surface. Not properly preparing the surface for paint. Paint will not adhere to shiny paint; it needs a tooth to stick to. The black paint that shows should not be so shiny.

Here's another example of lifted paint. This time the paint and primer are lifting right off the plastic material of this dash. This is what happens when plastic is not prepared properly. Some plastic materials require special chemicals to soften the plastic and help the paint adhere to it. Now, some kinds of plastic don't need that kind of prep. Refer to chapter 7 for more information. This plastic dash obviously needed plastic prep and adhesion promoter.

Try a different technique for big drips off the edges of parts. If—and only if—the paint is still soft, I use a new razor blade to shave off the run, then carefully sand the edge smooth. If the paint is hard, then the run must be sanded.

LIFTING PAINT

Any number of reasons can cause lifting paint (delamination) or bubbles. Whenever a painting cus-tomer or painter sees lifted paint, it's always bad. There is no easy fix.

What is the remedy for any kind of lifted paint? Remove all the lifted materials. Find out why the paint lifted. Remove any questionable material. Sometimes this remedy will require removing most or all of the paint on the affected panels. Then repaint. See chapter 5 for more information on repairing small areas of lifted or cracked paint.

Here's an example of serious delamination. There were no large lifted bubbles as there were no trapped solvents below the white paint. What happened was the gray sealer was allowed to sit for too long before the white basecoat was painted over it. The painter missed the recoat window.

WHAT IS THE RECOAT WINDOW?

The recoat window is the length of time paint can be recoated without first scuffing or sanding the surface. A product's P sheet will list this information. The amount of time can vary with the product.

HANDY HINT

Always keep current on new products. You never know when some little item will be out that may come in quite handy. For example, sometimes very small chips can happen as a vehicle is going together. Then, I have to take my little paintbrush and try to touch it up. I have found two tools that work much better than a paintbrush. The first is the Micro Tip from Carworx. It's great for those excruciating little chips. The Touch-N-Go Precision Applicator from EZ Mix is also pretty neat. Use the syringe to pull up the paint, attach the tip, and the paint flows through the tip and into the repair area. I use these two timesavers more often than I want to admit.

OTHER KINDS OF BUBBLES
Small Bumpy Bubbles

Sometimes, you'll see a small bump in the paint that almost looks like dust. If you poke at it and it flexes inward, it is a bubble. Somehow the paint did not stick in that spot. Moisture or water in your air source can also cause bubbles, and water may be trapped inside. If you see a whole bunch of bubbles, get out the 400 grit paper and take down the surface, removing all the affected paint. Look carefully at the primer layer. Did the problem start there? Are there any suspicious areas or marks in the primer? If it is only one or two bubbles you may be able to save it.

Using a stencil knife, dig out the bubble. Try to determine what caused it. Then wrap some 220 grit paper around a pen and carefully sand out the pit you dug, smoothing the edges the best you can. Sand the area around the pit with 400 grit paper. Dab some polyester filler in the pit, making sure it runs over the edge. Let it dry well. Sand and feather it without going through to the edge or disturbing the surrounding

surface. You don't want deep scratches in the paint you are trying to save. Tape and paper off the area, and spot prime it with a two-part primer. Wet sand. Now, spot in the base color.

This kind of repair only works for solid colors and some metallics, and there's no guarantee it will fix the problem. If there are any candy layers, I recommend redoing the entire basecoat process from scratch—unless you're a whiz at repairing candy.

Do the lifting bubbles appear all over the part? Remove all the paint. Start over.

Sometimes, lifted paint bubbles that only appear over areas where bodywork was done were caused by problems with the bodywork. Usually, the problem is with the hardener that was used with plastic filler. Maybe it's old or just bad. If this is the place you're at, remove the affected materials and start over. Start by removing all the filler. Don't try to spot repair. Problems related to sanding through all the paint layers will haunt you. So just give in and remove all that paint and bodywork. Buy new filling material and try again. Don't use what you did before or just buy new hardener, especially if the material you used was over a year old.

Itty, Bitty Bubbles or Solvent Pop

Tiny bubbles locked in the clearcoat itself are usually caused by solvent drying problems. I normally run into this problem with candy and clearcoats in the summer when it's hot and the humidity is high. The paint has skinned over in those areas before the solvents gassed out. The remedy is to stop painting, let it dry, and sand the affected areas. Sand away the coats containing the bubbles, then repaint. This time make sure you're using the proper temperature reducer for the conditions, not waiting too long in between coats, not applying the coats too heavily, and not doing too many coats in one day. On hot, humid days, I try to be done with my candy and/or clearcoat process in an hour or less.

STRANGE MARKS UNDER CLEARCOATS

Mystical fingerprints can sometimes appear in the paint under the clear weeks or months after a job is completed. The cause is usually someone touching or handling a part with his or her bare hands. There could have been some kind of contamination on the hands, or sometimes all it takes is the natural oil on our hands to leave an invisible fingerprint. Invisible, that is, until the sun hits it, heats it up, and causes a chemical reaction that turns the fingerprint white. This is why I never touch parts ready for paint with my bare hands. I also wash my hands frequently throughout the work day, especially in the summer when it's hot and sweaty.

The remedy for these strange marks is not easy; it just involves hard work. Some situations might require repainting the affected areas. Some colors can be spot repaired. But take note, sometimes rework can cause a shadow with certain light colors that have tons of clearcoat on them.

If a spot repair is not possible, I wait for a sunny day, and wet sand the part in the sun with 600 grit paper, carefully rinsing and watching as I go. What I'm doing is sanding down through my clearcoats to the surface or layer that the fingerprint is on. Hopefully it's sitting on top of a clearcoat, not under or in the color coats. The clearcoat is where marks usually happen. If that's where it is, I sand it off then feather the surrounding layers of clear. Then, I spot spray the area with filler clear (I use urethane clear) until it is level. Finally, I reclear the whole part.

If the mark is under candy coat, all I can say is good luck with spot repairing it. You may have to start over. Or if there is artwork in that area, maybe the artwork could be extended to cover the fingerprint.

CONTAMINATION

So many different things can cause contamination, but they all have one thing in common. They should not have been on the surface to be painted. Products that contain silicone or oil, like waxes, rust penetrating oil, tire shine, and hand lotion, will contaminate a painted surface. You won't know the surface is contaminated until paint is sprayed over it. Then it's easy to see. The contamination can get on the surface in a number of ways.

- A painted surface was not precleaned properly. Wipe it and clean over and over until it squeaks when you rub it.
- The cloth used to clean the surface had some kind of contamination on it.
- Someone was spraying rust preventive, oil, wax, or tire shine, and the material traveled across the shop and landed on the surface to be painted. A neighbor might have been grilling next door and the oils from the grilling traveled into your garage.

The fix for contamination is to sand away the affected paint and wipe the surface with precleaner.

This motorcycle fairing was ready for paint but the cloth used to clean it was contaminated. It's easy to see how the contamination was wiped across the surface. All the black paint was sanded off the surface, and the gray primer was wiped several times with precleaner.

Hopefully that will fix it and the surface will be free of the contamination. This is why precleaning a surface before painting is so critical.

FISHEYES

Fisheyes are also caused by contamination. They appear as round, concave impressions in the surface of the paint. Sometimes you get a bunch of fisheyes, but usually there are only a few. They mostly appear on the top surface of a part because some tiny microbe was floating around in the air and landed on the part. The microbe of contamination will push the paint away, and the result is a little pit or hole in the paint.

The cure for fisheyes can vary depending on the severity of the fisheyes. Sometimes during clearcoating, they can be leveled with a layer of clear. Other times the fisheye is so severe that no matter how much paint is applied, the fisheye will not level. The only thing to do then is to allow the paint to dry, sand it level, and reclear. Small, shallow fisheyes in finish clearcoat might be able to be sanded flat and buffed. If in doubt, sand and reapply the clearcoat.

SAND SCRATCHES OR SAND SCRATCH SWELLING

This problem mostly happens with pearl and metallic basecoats. The paint settles into scratches and the scratches appear as lines in the paint. When they are very bad, they may even be visible as scratch impressions on the surface.

Causes

- Sandpaper with a grit that was too coarse was used for the sanding before the basecoat.
- A piece of grit, dirt, or small debris got trapped under the sandpaper as the primer or substrate was being final sanded.
- The wrong ingredients were mixed together for the basecoat, leading to a chemical cause. This chemical mix can adversely affect the surface, causing the coating on that surface to swell or wrinkle.

Remedies

- If you are spraying sealer, then apply another coat of sealer. It may help smooth the scratches, but it will not completely fill them. If the scratches are deep enough, the primer should be resanded and followed by spraying sealer.

Sometimes when painting molded plastic or fiberglass parts, you will see some odd reactions when the part is painted, even though it was properly prepared. This is usually attributed to some mold release material still left on the part. When parts are molded, the molds are sprayed with a material that helps to release the part after it's molded, so the part won't stick to the mold. Once in a great while, some of this material will remain on the part after it's been cleaned. In the few times it's happened to me, the affected areas are sanded down, reprimed, and painted.

- If the problem was found while you were spraying basecoat, stop painting and allow the basecoat to dry. Then, dry sand the areas with a very good quality paper like 3M Purple 600 grit. Next, you can either spray another coat of sealer or try applying the basecoat again. Make sure to review the P sheets for the sealer and basecoat to see if sealer can be applied over the basecoat.
- If the basecoat has already been sprayed and this problem is found after the painting is complete, there is no fix short of sanding and repainting the affected areas.
- If the paint is soft and you can see scratches, it may be a chemical reaction of some kind. The best thing to do is remove the affected materials and start over. Don't put good paint over bad. It never works.

DRY SPRAY

Paint is going on very dry no matter the gun setting.

Always check the vent hole on the paint cup to see if there's a blockage. If you can't see light through the hole, then its blocked. Clear it out.

Chapter 16
Airbrushes and Other Forms of Torture

Tools for creating custom paint artwork are like any other tools in the shop: they are accumulated over time. You don't need everything in this chapter to create artwork. But start off with getting the essentials. Then build up your collection over time.

THE ESSENTIALS

I'll start off with a handy tool most folks have already, and that is your computer and printer. Using graphics programs on your computer like MS Paint, PhotoShop, and for the advanced users, Corel and Adobe Illustrator, you can create design drawings, print artwork patterns, print out paper stencils you can cut by hand, and use the Internet to research ideas for your designs.

The computer is the most valuable tool in my studio. And here's why, 20 years ago, I knew the location, quality of copies, and hours of every copy machine within a 30-minute drive from my home. I'd break the speed of sound trying to get to one with great enlargement and reduction capabilities before they closed. There were times when it felt like my life depended on it. Copy machines saved me hours of resizing drawings by hand. They took all guesswork out of it. Then someone invented personal computers, along with scanners and printers, and suddenly I was working much more efficiently. If you don't have a computer, most drug stores and many other places have copiers that will reduce and enlarge drawings or photos.

Check out the top half of this photo. The colored design you see on the side of this truck is actually a paper pattern I made using a computer and a printer. The actual pattern was printed using the MS Paint program on my computer. The pattern is made up of over a dozen pieces of paper that were taped together. On the back side of the paper, I traced the design with a pencil. Then I flipped it over and taped it in place on the truck and drew along the lines of the design. The pencil on the back side of the paper transfers the design to the surface of the truck. That makes it quick and easy to tape off the design and have it exactly like the drawing. This method takes much of the guesswork out of getting a design on a vehicle. The bottom half shows the artwork painted on the truck.

Where would the custom painter be without airbrushes? The best airbrush for custom painters are dual-action airbrushes that are versatile. Dual action means the trigger serves two functions. To control the air, you push down. The air flow is fine-tuned by how far down the trigger is pushed. Pulling back on the trigger controls the paint. These SATAgraph 4 airbrushes are made in the USA and can spray from a fine line to a wide pattern. I actually prefer the workhorse airbrush over the super fine detail airbrushes as they put out more air, which means you can lay down a lot of paint quickly. For less air, simply don't push all the way down on the trigger. A good quality airbrush should give you a real fine line as well as spray larger patterns.

HANDY HINT

Be sure to get some airbrush holders to hang up those airbrushes. For many of the years I airbrushed, I used this small hanging style holder. Although, it works well, it can cause problems. The drawback is that it is very easy to knock the airbrush off the hook, and it happens to me all the time. For most custom painters, a better choice is the holder on the right from coastairbrush.com. It clamps to any bench or cart and holds two airbrushes. Make sure they are securely held. When one hits the hard concrete, it can be costly.

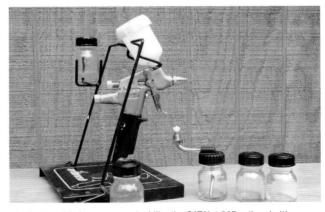

It's also great to have a spray tool like the SATAjet 20B artbrush. It's halfway between a mini gun and an airbrush. Its large round pattern is perfect for doing fades when painting flames and graphics. It has two cup variations: a gravity feed cup or siphon feed bottles for quick changes when using multiple colors. Five nozzle sizes from 0.5 to 2.0 allow for great versatility in spray patterns, from a fine line to wide fades. Some painters, like Ray Hill, use these instead of airbrushes. Some painters find them easier to use because they are held like a spray gun.

If you're using airbrushes, you have to have a way of hooking them up to the air. An air brush manifold is essential. You can buy them already made like this system from SATA. Or you can make one yourself. This one I adapted to run two more airbrushes. Note the gauge on this manifold. This is a high pressure regular air gauge, not one of those little micrometer gauges that goes on the end of a spray gun. Do not try and run a little gun gauge for your airbrushes. It won't control the air flow properly, and when you pull that trigger, you'll get a momentary high pressure blast of air until the line pressure adjusts to the gauge. Get a real air regulator and gauge and make a manifold yourself or buy a good quality premade manifold.

Colored pencils, markers, mechanical pencils, and erasers are low cost and very useful. Get more than one mechanical pencil. This way when you lose one, you have another immediately. They are very cost effective. Even though I do a great deal of drawing on the computer, I still do much of my drawing by hand. Make sure you get a good sharpener for traditional pencils.

These small tools are the backbone of my tool kit. Starting in the middle from the bottom: Mack Sword striping brushes, squirrel hair lettering brush, Mike Lavallee Pictorial Series brushes, and scissors. On the top are the different measuring tools I use. I rely heavily on a little 6″ machinist scale for lining up lettering stencils and checking measurements for graphics. I use rulers to measure but also as cutting guides. It's great to have a retractable metal tape measure, but also get a soft seamstress tape measure as that will go closely around the curves on sheetmetal. Lower right: Uncle Bill's Sliver Grippers are great for grabbing onto the edge of a stencil or tape and getting a good grip to pull it up. Plus they are handy in the paint booth if you need to quickly remove hair, bugs, or stuff that gets into your fresh paint. Next, fine line markers, mechanical pencils and erasers, and X-Acto stencil knives. The #11 is my favorite. Keep plenty of spare blades and change the blade often as they get dull fast. The tools are sitting on two cutting mats: a small green one and a large light blue one. A cutting mat is essential for getting clean cuts on handmade stencils.

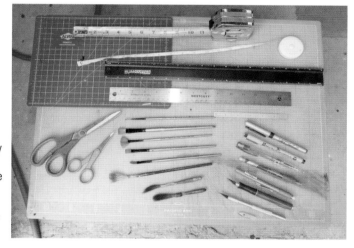

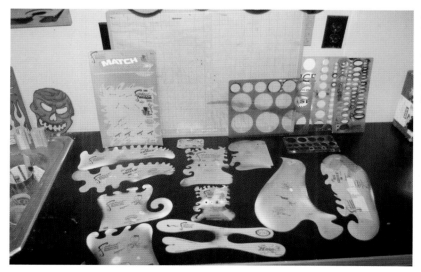

Artool Templates and drafting templates are great timesavers. Their ready-made curves are multipurpose. Use them as a hand-held shield to quickly mask off as you are spraying. Whatever certain size curve, circle, or shape you need, these templates can do it. And they are solvent proof. Template sets seen here: The Essential Seven, Matchmaker, the H Series, and The Master Series.

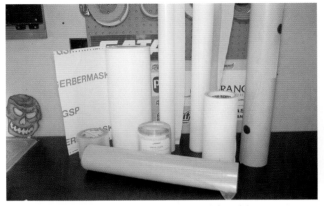

Masking and stencil materials are pictured from left to right.

1. GerberMask Ultra II is the main stencil material I use. I like it because it's easy to draw on, it cuts cleanly, and it works great over fresh basecoat without leaving any adhesive behind. I use it for all my plotter cut stencils and for freehand stencils.

2. TransferRite Ultra is a clear transfer tape that I use to mask off already painted details. I'll put a piece of transfer tape over the area, then carefully cut along the edge of what I'm masking and pull the tape off the area I want to paint. This way I have a clean, sharp edge right against the edge of where I don't want paint.

3. SprayLat liquid mask is brushed on and dries as a solid stencil that can be drawn on and cut.

4. Artool's Frisket Film is great because it's transparent and it cuts clean.

5. I use tracing paper to draw out and design artwork and graphics. I'll wrap it around a part and then try out designs directly on the part. I also use it to reverse designs. See chapter 21 for more info.

6. Sticky Mickey is opaque transfer tape that's great for masking flames and graphics. I use a lot of this!

7. Artool's Ultra Mask is a thick, stretchable material, which is great for round and irregular shapes. It has adhesive backing that will not release and will stay on your painting, even when retouch paint is applied.

8. Artool's Stretchmask is a very stretchable and flexible repositionable masking film. It's great for motorcycle tanks, helmets, and sharp corners on vehicles. It's a clear, thin film that cuts very easily and can be effortlessly manipulated and repositioned with your artwork always in view.

I use all of these. The reason why no labels are seen? This stuff gets used.

There's no such thing as too much light when you're doing custom artwork. I'll have two flood lights on each side of a car and still wish I had more. This is my workbench where I airbrush motorcycle parts. I have a three bulb Dazor Model 134E3 daylight lamp over this bench. Under it are a couple of the floodlights I use when working on cars. Buy some inexpensive portable lights.

Plastic solvent proof bottles are cheap to buy, very handy, and they travel easily. I keep much of the paint I use for airbrushing in these bottles. Notice how some of the bottles have tape on them. I put different color tape on lacquer thinner and enamel reducer bottles so it's easy to tell them apart.

HANDY HINT

One super handy tool to keep around is magnets. Magnets hold design patterns and stencils in place while you're aligning them and hold reference pictures and drawings on the car. They are a low cost, very useful tool you may not have thought of.

HANDY HINT

Here the image of a grim reaper is projected onto a hood. The room is nearly dark, and the hood is white while the reaper is a black outline. Yet, it is not as visible as you would think. Projectors are great, but they do have their limitations.

TOOLS THAT ARE NICE TO HAVE

Artool Custom Templates can help anyone to get wild results. They are so easy to use. Just tape off your graphic or flame, hold up the template, and spray. Instant special effects. Here are just a few of the ones I use. Check out artoolworks.com for a full list and pictures of their templates.

Easels are great when doing artwork on hoods and trunk lids. It puts the surface at the perfect angle for working and holds the part securely.

For large surfaces, a projector can be very helpful. The top panel flips up to reveal a glass surface. Simply place the drawing or photo you are working from face down on the glass plate. Then place the projector the needed distance from the surface being worked on. The farther away the projector is, the larger the image will appear. The lens tube slides back and forth to focus the image. Once the image is displayed on the desired surface, just draw it on the prepped surface with a pencil or Stabilo pencil. Just like any other tool, the more a projector is used, the more effective the artist will become with it. I use an Artograph Super Prism projector. They run about $200.

FUN STUFF

Mike Lavallee is an amazing custom painter who pioneered the Tru Fire paint style and is constantly coming out with products that helps the average painter turn out above average paint jobs. His latest invention is his Killer GrungeFX Special Effects Masking Spray. It's a water-based product that sprays out a liquid mask that can be used to create random organic patterns for wild natural backgrounds for steam punk or worn patina effects. It's also great for filling in graphic areas or shadowed backgrounds.

Simply shake the can of Grunge and press either the Fat Splat or Fine Splat tip (both tips come inside each GrungeFX can), spray the surface, allow it to morph into shapes, and airbrush a contrasting color. Then wipe away the Grunge. You can achieve endless of one-of-a-kind textures on your surface for airbrushing solvent-based paints. This product cannot be used with waterborne paint.

Having a small compressor just for doing artwork can be very helpful in situations where compressed air is not available. Badger's TC910 Aspire Pro is very small and portable, has a 1 gallon air tank, puts out 57 psi, has a regulator and two airbrush holders.

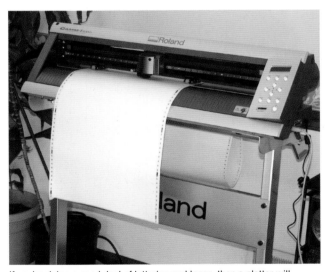

A rolling cart is very handy for custom car projects but it also works for custom paintwork, I clamp airbrush holders on my Summit Racing cart. I can keep bottles of paint and other tools right there on the cart. The pressure regulator sits on the shelf below and I can roll it anywhere. I can even fit a small Badger compressor on the bottom shelf if I need to bring my own air.

If you're doing a good deal of lettering and logos, then a plotter will make life much easier. I did custom paintwork for over 20 years before I got one, but once I had it, it completely changed the way I worked. It expanded the kind of work I could do and drastically shortened working times of much of the artwork I did. This is a Roland GX-24. It's not cheap, but if you're serious about doing custom artwork on cars and bikes, it's a worthwhile investment.

Chapter 17
Painting Traditional Flames

I love painting flames, and I'll tell you why: flames are pretty easy to paint. Painting them is a time-consuming task, but they are fun. The number one thing to remember when painting flames is don't rush through the job. Have fun painting flames. Enjoy and savor every moment. When you paint flames you become part of a tradition that is over 50 years old.

For these old-style hot rod flames, I'm going to use a new technology paint, PPG's Envirobase High Performance (EHP) waterborne paint. In fact, EHP was used for the basecoat black on the Durango hood 24 hours before doing the flames. EHP can be recoated up to 48 hours after it is applied. After 48 hours, it must be scuffed before recoating. So there was no need to scuff before painting the flames. Please refer to chapter 11 for more information on waterborne paint.

The first thing to do is to have an idea of the style of flames you want and have reference pictures handy. In 2012, I flamed a Factory Five 33 Hot Rod on MuscleCar TV. I'm going to duplicate that style of flame on this hood. I want the flames to match somewhat on each side of the hood, so I will lay them out on one side, then transfer the design to the other side and tape the flames.

Here's a trick that can be used to get a mirror effect when you want both sides of the design to match. I use this trick all the time to get both sides of a design symmetrical or have designs on both sides of a vehicle match—any time I need to reproduce a mirror effect. For this project, I want the three outboard flames to match on each side. The center flames will be random.

continued on page 167

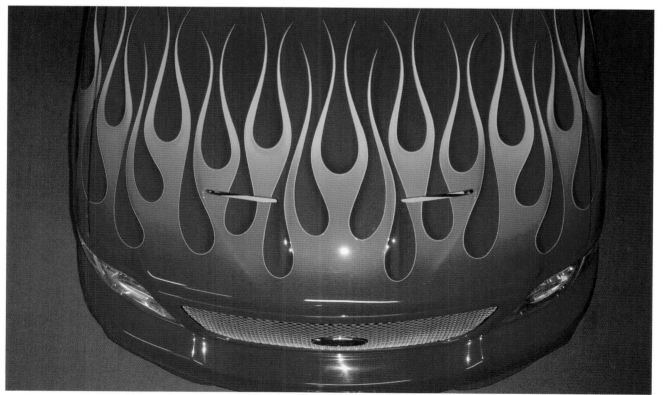

New truck or old car, it doesn't matter. If done correctly, traditional flames look great on anything—like this F150 flamed by Ron Gibbs. This is a reverse hot rod flame. On regular-style hot rod flames, the bright colors are at the front part of the flame, like in the example in this chapter.

MATERIALS & EQUIPMENT

Equipment
SATA 4000 HVLP spray gun
SATA Dry Jet
SATAjet 20B artbrush
SATAgraph 4 airbrush
Stencil knife

Materials
SATA RPS cup system
FBS 48405 ProBand fine line ⅛″ orange tape
FBS 48063 K-UTG ¼″ gold crepe tape
FBS PT-43 48720 ¼″ crepe masking tape
FBS PT-43 48720 performance tape
FBS ProMask
¾″, 1½″, and 2″ IP aqua masking tape
Evercoat blue polycoated masking paper
PPG Evirobase High Performance T400 white
PPG Evirobase High Performance T433 brilliant orange
PPG Evirobase High Performance T425 permanent yellow
PPG Evirobase High Performance T426 warm yellow
PPG Evirobase High Performance T435 salmon red
PPG Evirobase High Performance T441 carmine
Vibrance VWM5556 waterborne midcoat
Mechanical pencil
Tracing paper
Evercoat polycoated masking paper

I started by laying out the flames on one side of the hood using FBS 48405 ⅛″ ProBand fine line orange tape. But a problem arose. I started on the right side of the hood, and as I worked across to the left, the flames started getting squeezed next to each other. I like the layout and shape of the flames; I just need to move the two flame licks on the left over.

I ran a line of FBS K-UTG ¼″ gold crepe tape down the center of the hood. I placed a piece of tracing paper over the flames and traced the inside edge of the tape around the flames with a mechanical pencil. Next the paper is flipped over and taped onto a window. I traced along the pencil line with a pencil. This paper will act like carbon paper.

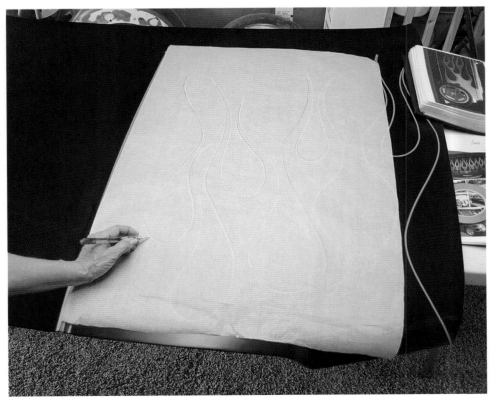

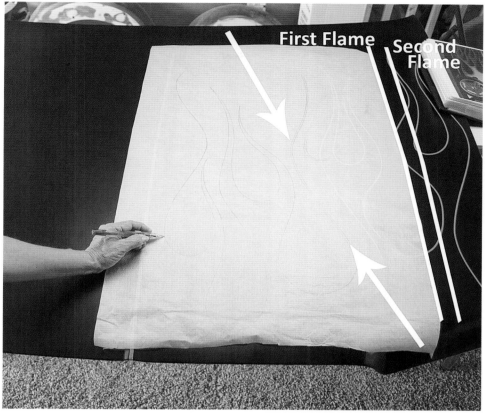

I flipped the paper back over and placed it on the hood. Note the white arrows and lines on the photo. As I want the two fire licks on the left side of the paper to be more on the left, the paper is lined up on the hood so that the flames on the paper are at the same level as before, but they are moved over to the left by 4˝. The line the arrows point to is the line that used to line up with the third flame. I traced the first flame pencil line on the left onto the hood. Then, I moved the paper to the right about 2˝ and traced the second flame. The white lines on the right show where the paper lines up for the first flame and where it is moved over for the second flame.

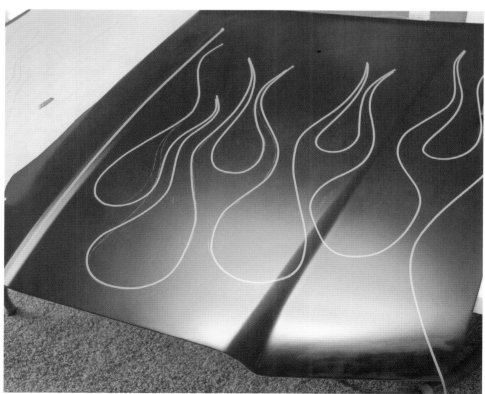

Following the transferred pencil lines on the hood, I taped off the two left flames. Now the flames are more evenly spaced. Note how I changed the shape of the first flame slightly. It's actually only half the flame. The left half of the first flame still needed to be taped off. Next, I'll tape off the flames on the left side of the hood.

RESHAPING THE FLAME

Say you like your flame, but one part of it needs help. You don't have to completely remove the tape to edit the flame. On the left side, the bottom of this fire lick is too thick. Instead of redoing the whole flame, I simply added some tape on each side, narrowing the bottom of the lick as seen on the right.

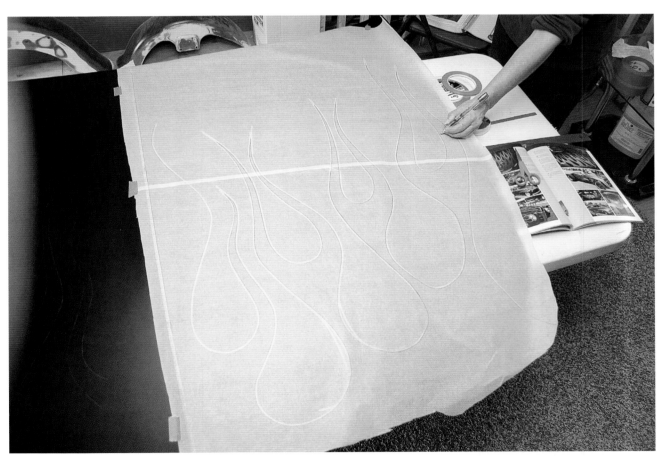

I laid tracing paper over the right side of the hood and traced the flames. The tape along the center line and the front edge were used as location reference points so I could line up the paper on the other side of the hood.

THE BEST WAY TO PAINT FLAMES

There are two ways to paint bright colored flames over a dark basecoat.

- Option #1: Painting flames over the basecoat. This is the most common way to paint flames. But it tends to leave a thick paint edge. First a white or light colored base must be applied to cover the black. Next the main flame color goes on, and many times, the flames have a candy or colored fade inside the flame. There might be 6 to 10 coats of paint by the time these flames are done.
- Option #2: Painting flames over a light or white sealer, then masking off the flames and painting the basecoat. This sounds like more work, but in the long run it's actually less. A white sealer is applied to the car. The flames are then taped off and the basecolor is sprayed. Then a candy or colored fade is airbrushed on the flames. There still is a paint edge, but it's not as thick. The tape is removed, and now the flames are masked off and the dark basecoat is sprayed. This builds up layers of paint around the flames, evening up the two levels of paint. For example, say the flames have six coats of paint and the basecoat has three or four. That means the flames are only two coats thicker than the basecoat and there's less of a paint edge that needs to be leveled and filled.

It takes less clear coat to level out Option #2 than Option #1. Option #1 would require several rounds of clear urethane in order to level it out. Option #2 would only need one round of clear to level out the paint edge of the flames. This hood started out as a dark color, but if the hood had been in primer, I would have sprayed it with a white sealer and then painted the hot rod flames.

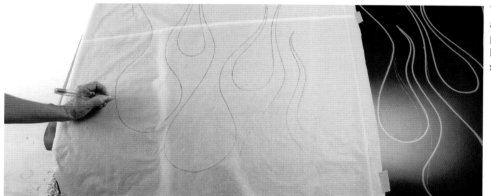

The tracing paper was flipped over and lined up using the reference points. Then I traced along the pencil lines, transferring the design to the surface of the hood.

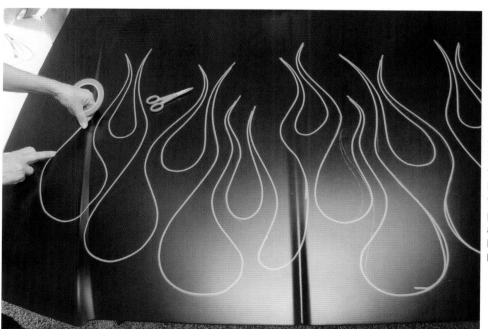

The flames on the left side were taped off by following the pencil lines. I decided to have the center section of the flames random. The three outboard flame licks on the left side are a perfect match from the left side, but center three licks have a random pattern. The trick to taping smooth lines to is pull the tape tight while taping around the curves. One hand holds the tape, steering the tape along the line and pulling the tape; the other hand presses it down on the line. If the line gets bumpy or uneven, simply pull up the tape and try again. It takes a good deal of practice to get smooth lines, so don't get discouraged if your lines need some rework.

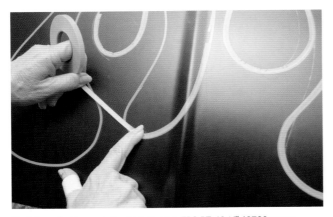

Next, I needed to mask the flames. I ran FBS PT-43 ¼″ 48720 crepe masking tape along the curves. FBS 48063 K-UTG ¼″ gold crepe tape was run everywhere else along the flames.

Here are the PPG Envirobase High Performance Products that were used for the flames From the left are the T494 Thinner and EHP Basecoats: T400 White, T409 Deep Black, T435 Salmon Red, T425 Permanent Yellow, T426 Warm Yellow, T433 Brilliant Orange, and T441 Carmine. In the middle is Vibrance VWM5556 waterborne midcoat, which is clear.

I used a combination of ¾″, 1½″, and 2″ IP aqua masking tape and Evercoat blue polycoated masking paper to mask off the flames. Now the flames are ready for paint. Take the time to go back over the tape and masking to make sure there are no little gaps or open spaces. Make sure all the tape edges are stuck down the surface. Every time I do this, I always need to add tape and I find places that need to be pressed down.

Hot rod flames need a bright yellow basecoat. But yellow is a very transparent color. It does not cover well. So, I used white as a basecoat under the yellow. After performing a viscosity test, EHP T400 is thinned down about 12%. I used a SATA 4000 HVLP spray gun with a WSB nozzle set and an RPS mixing/spray cup. I sprayed three coats with a 75% overlap. The paint is blown dry between coats using the SATA Dry Jet. The coats are sprayed medium. I looked over the hood and sanded away any dust that was sticking up above the paint as these will cause dark spots in the color fade.

I sprayed T425 Permanent Yellow next. It was also reduced about 15%. Two coats were sprayed using a 75% overlap. We made sure to dry out each coat before proceeding with the next.

Continued from page 161

The warm yellow, orange, and reds will be mixed with the clear 5556 midcoat and become somewhat transparent. The colors in EHP waterborne are very concentrated. This bright effect against the black base will be very bold and striking. The formulas for the fade colors are as follows:

- First Fade Color: Brilliant Orange T433 mixed 1:1 w/VWM5556
- Second Fade Color: Warm Yellow T426 mixed 1:1 w/VWM5556
- Third Fade Color: 2 pints Warm Yellow T426 and 1 pint Salmon Red T435 mixed 1:1 w/VWM5556
- Fourth Fade Color: 1 pint Warm Yellow T426 and 1 pint Salmon Red T435 mixed 1:1 w/VWM5556
- Fifth Fade Color: Carmine T441 mixed 1:1 w/VWM5556

Now comes the fun part, spraying the fade. Spraying a fade takes a little practice, and if this is your first time, then please try your fade technique on a practice panel. I started out with the orange, using a SATAjet 20B Artbrush. I started at the tip of an end flame and ran the Artbrush along the edge, fading the orange toward the center areas of the flame. You're looking for a nice even dispersal of paint, not too grainy, not wet. Just soft and even. Keep it light, don't go too dark; you can always add another layer. I went around the entire outline of the flames. When the water had dried out of the paint, I added another soft coat.

The next color to go on is the warm yellow. This fade will extend past the orange toward the center of the flame and is concentrated toward the front of the hood. It softens the transition between the yellow base and orange.

All the color mixes were thinned down 15% with T494. Make sure to strain each color after mixing and before you spray it! The RPS cup system has a special strainer for waterborne that snaps into the lid. For the airbrush colors, just strain them into another mixing cup then pour that into the airbrush, artbrush, or minijet spray gun. If you do not have an artbrush, then a mini spray gun can be used. Just adjust the pattern, material flow, and air pressure for a small pattern.

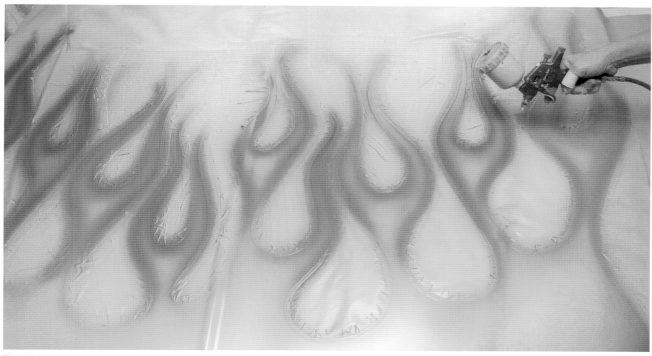

The third color combines two parts of warm yellow and one part of salmon red with the clear midcoat. It's a little darker than the orange. This color is sprayed along the edge but does not extend as far into the flame as the orange. This color does not come all the way to the front of the hood.

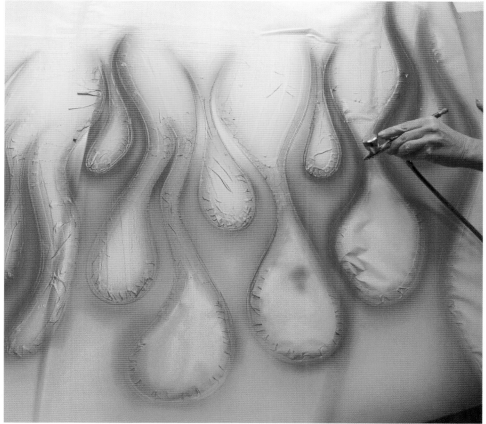

The fourth color is very much like the third only a little darker and redder. I sprayed it along the edge using a SATAgraph 4 airbrush, not extending into the flame as far the third color. And this color stops at the base of each flame; it does not go around the curves that connect the flames. The darker colors are concentrated along the edges.

The last color is the carmine red. I airbrushed it right along the edge of the tape in a very thin line and it does not extend past the base of each flame.

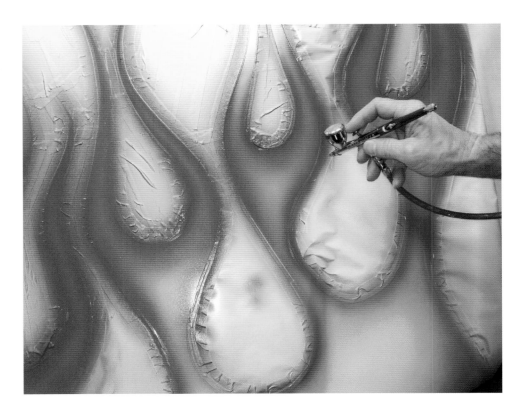

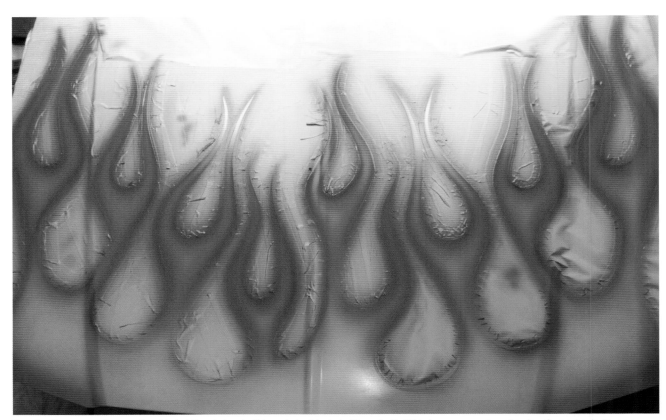

Here the flames are all sprayed and faded. Your fades don't have to be this dark. It's perfectly OK to have more yellow showing. Or maybe don't use any red and simply have a nice orange fade around the flames. Your hot rod flames can look however you want them. There are no rules.

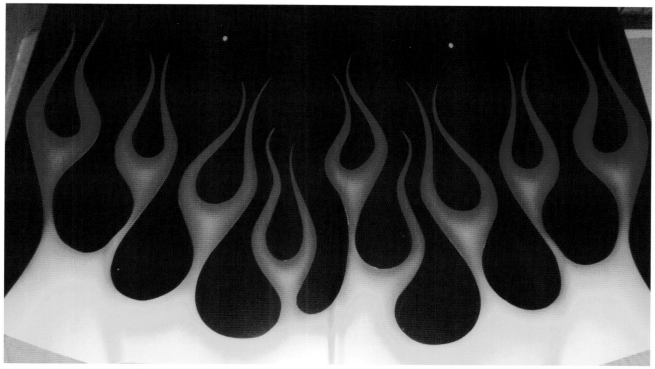

The tape has been removed and the flames are ready for pinstriping and clearcoat. Be sure to go over the surface and erase or sand away any remaining pencil marks. Pinstriping adds a crisp, clean edge to the flame. It gives the flame even more dimension. Pinstripe colors for hot rod flame jobs can be whatever you feel will go best with the flames. Blue is very popular for hot rod flames. But lime green would also look great.

For the flames on the Factory Five 33 Hot Rod, we went with a dark red pinstripe. The flames on this car were actually done first over white sealer, then they were masked off and the black basecoat was sprayed. The paint on this car was done with PPG's EHP waterborne. After the pinstripe was done, the flames were clearcoated, allowed to dry, sanded with 800 grit, and finish clearcoated. To see more examples of flame paint, refer to chapter 9.

REMOVING THE TAPE

When removing tape from any kind of artwork, always pull the tape back over itself, "cutting" the paint film as the tape is pulled. How long you need to wait before removing the tape depends on how much paint was applied and how thick the paint layer is. This waterborne was pretty thick, so I waited about 3 hours before pulling the tape. The best way to figure out when it pull it is to test it. Pull up just a little bit and see if the paint is rubbery and tears. If it does, then wait a while and try again. The tape should pull up nice and clean, cutting a clean edge of paint. If you wait too long the paint might be brittle and break off as the tape is being pulled. This brittle breaking paint is usually only a problem with solvent-borne paint, not waterborne. Keep a stencil knife handy; if the paint does not cut easily when the tape is pulled up, carefully run the stencil knife along the edge of the tape, cutting the paint edge.

FLAME VARIATIONS

This photo shows several very cool flame variations. On the left the truck, the flames start out as reverse or inverted flames that turn into a regular flames. The truck on the right features multilayered flames. Note how the top layer is darker than the bottom. The bottom flame layer is pretty interesting. It starts off white and then turns orange with very little yellow.

Chapter 18
Creating and Understanding Ghost Flames

The term *ghost flames* gets tossed around quite a bit in the custom paint world. What are ghost flames? Ghost flames are any flames that are somewhat transparent. The flames can be easily visible yet still fairly transparent, or they can be nearly invisible and only visible from certain angles. This covers a lot of ground.

The trick to doing very light ghost flames is simply spraying as light a line as possible around the edges of the taped off flame or spraying a very light layer of paint over the whole taped-off flame. "Ghost" means hard to see but visible. Traditionally, the perfect ghost flame is one that can only be seen from certain angles and in certain light. Usually they are just a little lighter in tone than the base paint. For example, you'd airbrush charcoal pearl for the ghost flame on a black basecoat.

On a candy blue basecoat, you'd airbrush a light blue pearl. The reason for using pearl instead of a solid color is that pearl dusts on with nice even coverage,

MATERIALS & EQUIPMENT

¹⁄₁₆″, ⅛″ fine line tape
Masking tape from ⅛″ to 2″ American masking tape
600 or 800 grit sandpaper
Pencil eraser
Transfer tape
Tracing paper
Pencil
PPG sprayout cards
PPG Prep Plus wipes
PPG DX330 precleaner
PPG DX320 precleaner
Gerson Blend Prep tack cloths
Paint materials of your choice
SATAgraph 4 airbrush
SATAjet 20 B artbrush
SATA 3000 B minijet spray gun
SATA 4000 HVLP spray gun
Evercoat paint mixing cups
X-Acto knife

This sweet '68 Camaro RS features a traditional ghost flame paint job. The flames don't jump right out at you. They are subtle, almost completely transparent. From some angles, the flames are not readily apparent. They were done using pearl paint, which helps them look very ghost. Pearl is the perfect paint for doing ghost flames.

where solid colors can break up and appear inconsistent. Plus pearl has that shimmery effect that makes it very effective for ghost flames. Ghost flames work great over pearl or metallic basecoats. Or for candy color, try putting the flame directly over the metallic base under the candy. Or you can even mix a few ghost flames under a regular flame paint job. A neat trick is to do a reverse of the color order above: use a dark color for the ghost flame on a lighter color base. A good example would be a black ghost flame on a dark blue candy basecoat.

Ghost effects also work great when they are painted in multiple layers. Using handheld shields and lightly spraying one layer of flames after another is a quick way to create a cool effect that will work for many kinds of artwork. Try it as a fade in over a candy or pearl basecoat or inside a graphic such as a taped off tribal graphic, flame, or panel.

continued on page 178

GHOST FLAMES ON A LIGHT SURFACE

This Miata is not the kind of car that is usually flamed. Old street rods and '60s and '70s muscle cars are mainly the canvas for flames. But hey, why not? The first step taken in this process was to take a digital photo of the car. That's used to create a blank drawing so some flame designs can be made. Usually, I load the photo onto my computer and use a graphics program to white out the body of the car. As this car was already white, all I needed to do was print out a few black and white copies. The low tech way to do this would be take a photo of whatever vehicle you want to flame and make an enlarged copy at any copy place. Then, cut out the body of the car using an X-Acto knife, place the altered copy on the scanner bed of the printer and make all the blanks you want.

First, I drew some tribal flames on the copy in pencil. In this case, I only did one drawing. The first version was perfect, and I knew it when I drew it up. For most flame projects, the painter will want to see how different colors will look. So make several versions using various colors combinations.

For playing with colors for ghost flames, I simply draw on a copy with colored pencils, tracing over the flame outline. But for all those keyboard commandos out there, this step can easily be done on the computer. I'm too impatient. The customer wants the flames to be very ghost. So we decide against going with any colors. The flames will simply be a bright white. The color of the car is white pearl, so how will white flames show up against white pearl? I'll use bright white basecoat and it should contrast just right, as white pearl appears darker from an angle and white basecoat is bright from any angle.

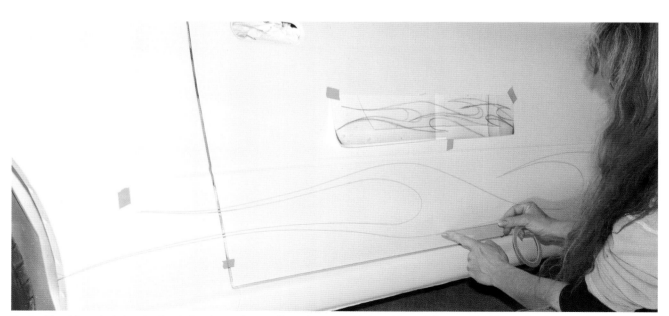

The traditional flame technique involves laying down a flame outline using a very thin tape. I tape off flames with 1/16" green fine line tape. Some folks use 1/8" masking tape or blue fine line tape. Some use 1/16" green fine line tape; while others like to use FSB orange tape. I find for certain things, I like the 3M 218 1/16". Then, for some flames, like very curvy ones, the FSB 1/16" or 1/8", works great. I think folks just use what works best for them. The flame area of the drawing is enlarged and taped over where I'm laying out the flame so I can easily reference to it as I am taping. Arranging the flame design to best fit the contours of the panel is the hard part. Don't just rush through it. It is quite unpleasant to untape a car after hours of work and layers of paint to see that the design looks awkward or just doesn't complement the line of the sheetmetal. I enjoy painting flames and like to have fun with designs.

HANDY HINT

Less is more when it comes to ghost flames. Ghost flames are all about creating an impact while using very little paint. Think soft images that fade into the base paint. Try playing around with ghost flames before you paint them on any project vehicle. Take a junk fender, hood, or old sign, paint it black or white, and experiment with paint mixtures. Get a good idea of what it takes to hold a steady movement with an airbrush down a long taped-off line. Play around with the distance between the airbrush and surface. Always test your paint mixtures and techniques. Find the right combination of factors to create your perfect ghost flame. Don't get discouraged if it takes a while. Remember, relax and be patient.

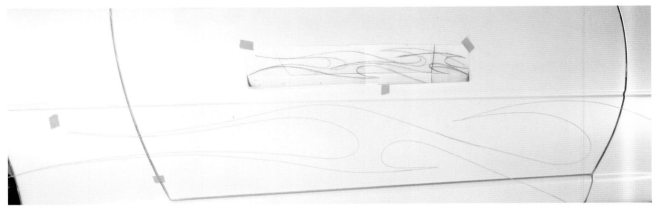

I like my flames to have a random symmetry. The design should be nicely balanced, not too generic, not too uniform, but not too busy. I use two methods to lay out flames. With the first, I lay out the flame with ¹⁄₁₆″ green fine line tape. I prefer it over blue fine line because it's stiffer and lays down a "smoother" flame line. It leaves a crisp, sharp line, which is perfect for ghost flames or metal effect flames that will not be pinstriped. Masking tape is the second method. Most folks who use masking tape will pinstripe their flames. Once the flames are laid out, take a very short break. You don't want the taped corners to lift. Go get a cold drink. Then go back and look at your design. Always stand back and study it. It's too easy to miss something obvious when only looking at it close up.

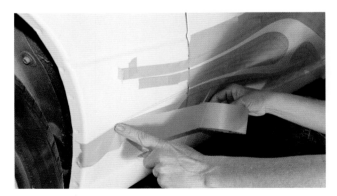

Masking off the flames can be done by several methods. Each has its advantages and disadvantages. Either transfer tape or regular masking tape can be used. Using transfer tape is faster but it involves cutting into the fine line tape. Press too hard with the knife and you'll go right through to the paint surface and maybe leave a cut mark. Real care must be taken not to cut too hard. Here I'm using masking tape. There's not much flame area, so it will not take long to mask these flames. The car's color is light. It will easily show flaws such as cut marks in the surface of the paint. I start off with the ¾″ tape overlapping the fine line tape and run it around the flames. I'll use ½″ masking tape or narrower for tight areas like between the flame licks. Here I'm using 2″ masking tape to quickly get the job done.

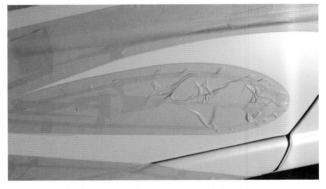

Try to use methods that save time. Sometimes this involves using materials that cost more money, like using 2″ masking tape to quickly tape off odd-shaped areas. What good is it to save on materials if it takes longer to do the job? And always check your tape edges after you lay them out to make sure the tape isn't puckering up or lifting on the edges. I use my fingernail to burnish down any lifting or bubbling tape edges. The other thing to watch for is tiny little spaces that haven't been covered by tape. I take two breaks away from my work while laying out flames. The second break to take is after the flame is taped off. When you go back to look at it, you'll find lots of small areas that paint will sneak through. This technique for taping off flames can be used for painting flames other than ghost flames, like traditional (or hot rod) and airbrushed flames.

Now it's time to tape off the other side of the car. Take some measurements from the flame to points on the car, like from the top of the flame to the top of the door panel and from the bottom of the flame to the bottom of the door. Transfer these measurements to the other side of the car using pieces of tape to mark those areas. Then take your drawing, flip it over, tape it to a window, and trace along the flame. Now you have an exact reverse design of your flame for the other side of the car to use as reference. This will act like a carbon copy and make it easy to reproduce a mirror image of the flame.

HANDY HINT

Sometimes, when I'm doing ghost flames or graphics and spraying the paint lightly at a low pressure, I won't tape off the entire panel. I just use a "spraybreak." I simply bend the outer area of tape back, directing the paint away from the surface of the vehicle.

HANDY HINT

Ghost flame paint can be adjusted in several ways. You can adjust the mixture of the paint, or you can adjust how fast you move the airbrush. If the flame paint is too much, then either thin down the paint by adding a reducer or using less pearl in the mix. You can also try moving the airbrush faster. If the paint is too thin and doesn't show up enough, add a little more pearl or paint to the mix or move the airbrush slower. Sometimes, it takes a combination of adjusting the paint mix and the airbrush speed. Make sure you test before you spray the vehicle, especially if you are doing ghost flames for the first time. The trick is to find the right balance of paint reduction and airbrush movement.

Starting at one end of one side of the taped off flame, I aimed the airbrush at the edge of the tape and moved along the tape edge until one complete edge of the flame is done. The movement must be smooth and steady. No jerky movements. You want a soft, consistent fade.

Now, get out the airbrushes and make sure they are clean. One little bit of old, dried paint blowing out of the airbrush will have you back at the previous step. I mix up some PPG DMD 1684 basecoat white and reduce it about 200%. It's best to have the basecolor of your vehicle, in this case white pearl, sprayed on a sprayout card with a piece of tape on it. To see if my flame paint is too light, too heavy, or just right, I'll spray a quick pass on the card and peel back the tape.

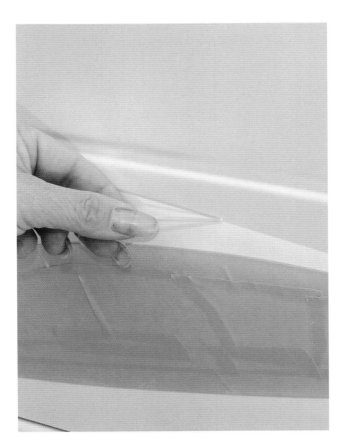

HANDY HINT

When painting ghost flames, especially on light colors like white, the surface has to be flawless. No boogers, no bugs, no specs of colored dust, nothing. When painting flames or any graphic, most of the time, the design area will be receiving several layers of paint, and while it's never a good idea to paint over noticeable flaws, small stuff can sometimes disappear under the new layers. But very little paint goes on when applying any kind of ghost image, so take care to start with a flawless surface.

If you missed something and it's showing up in the ghost flames, it can be repaired. If the basecoat is a solid color, then the repair is easy: simply spray on more base color to cover the flaw. If you're working with a pearl or candy color, then you'll have to judge the type of fix on a case-by-case basis. Pearl colors can sometimes be repaired by airbrushing some basecoat and some pearl. The same thing goes for candy colors.

After the flames are airbrushed, I carefully removed the masking materials, leaving the fine line tape in place. Always pull the tape back almost across itself. This usually cleanly "cuts" the paint edge. I'll wait 15 minutes before removing the tape as the paint is so thin that it dries very fast. But if you're doing any other kind of flame you should pull up the tape a little and see if it breaks cleanly away. If it doesn't, then wait some more.

Here's the first layer of flames. They look pretty good.

I masked off the second layer and repeated the process is repeated. Make sure to carefully look over the flame area and see if any flame paint or overspray got past the tape. If so, carefully wet sand it off. But remember, you can only use this technique of you have clearcoated over the basecoat. When you are done with the flames, be sure to remove any left-behind adhesive from the tape. Wiping down the surface with a gentle precleaner like PPG 320 will remove adhesive and any fingerprints that were left on the surface.

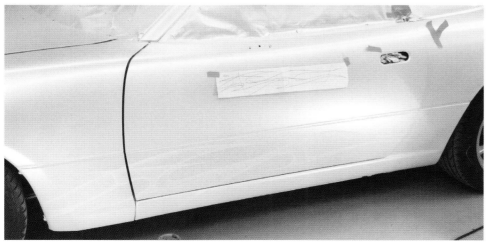

Here are the finished flames. They came out great. Not too noticeable, but when the light hits the car right, wow. It's harder than it seems, but once a painter gets used to doing ghost effects, they can be the perfect artwork answer for vehicles that need some kind of artwork but not too much. See chapter 26 for clearcoat information.

GHOST FLAMES ON A DARK SURFACE

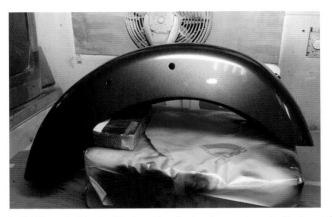 

Left: This project is a fuel tank and two fenders for a motorcycle. The basecolor here is a very dark gunmetal gray that almost appears black from certain angles and in different kinds of light. I'm going to do a very subtle black ghost flame. It will be so ghost that it can only be seen from certain angles. First, I wet sand the clearcoat over the base with 800 grit sandpaper. **Right:** Next, I needed to figure out the mixture for the black by varying the amount of reducer in the mixture. Then I had to find the perfect speed to move the airbrush along the taped edge. I reduced PPG DBC9700 black 1:1 with DT895 reducer and sprayed the sample on the left. It was too dark and thick. I added more reducer to the mixture, reducing it by 125%. I sprayed the sample on the top right. The spray is fine but I'm moving the airbrush too slow; it's still too dark and the fade extends too far. I sprayed another line beneath it. Again, too slow, as it's too dark. For the sample in the middle, I sped up the movement of the airbrush. The fade is light and short. Perfect.

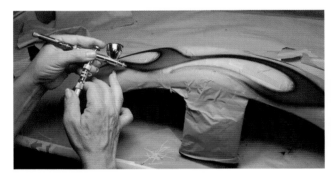 

Left: The quickest part of the job is airbrushing the flame. I started at one end and moved down to the other. Then repeated on each edge of the flame. And it's done. Notice how minimal the black fade is. It sure doesn't look there's much there. **Right:** I removed the tape. The ghost flames stand out on the sanded surface of the paint. It's hard to tell from this photo how close I came to getting the flames to look almost invisible. To check and see if the flames are what you want, wipe some precleaner across the surface. This will give the surface a shine and you can judge your flames. That's what I did.

Here are the flames after they were clearcoated. Wow, what a difference. It's the exact effect I was trying for. The flames are only visible on the place where light hits the surface. At an angle, the flames cannot be seen.

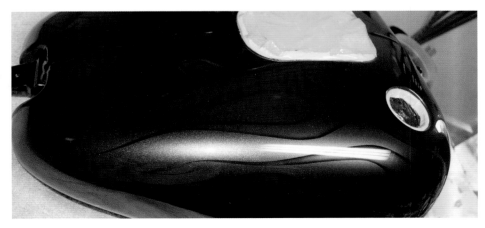

NOT SO GHOST FLAMES

Here are some flames that are between a ghost flame and a solid flame. The technique is very similar to airbrushing ghost flames, but these flames are much more visible. This example shows them painted with a solid color around the edges then layered with a candy color. It's a cool technique, and by using different colors and kinds of paint, you can get unlimited ghost flame effects.

This old Chevy truck features two layers of ghost flames. These flames are not as ghost as the flames I painted in this chapter. Also, these are not faded flames. These were painted with a spray gun, which sprayed an even layer of paint across the entire flame area. That's the beauty of ghost flames, you can make them as bright or as noticeable as you like. These flames were sprayed with a pearl that slightly changes color, which works well across the big, round hood and fenders.

Now here's a trick ghost flame. The flame was done under the red candy using silver marbleizer. If I were doing something like this, first I would spray the silver basecoat, tape off the flame, spray black, then apply the marbleizer, and spray the red candy. And it's a pretty neat flame design, kind of backward.

Is it a ghost flame with a pinstripe or a traditional flame? That depends on whom you ask. But all three colors in this paint scheme are very similar. Dark purple pearl basecoat, medium purple pearl flame, and light purple pinstripe. Very subtle but eye catching at the same time.

Chapter 19
Painting Real Fire Flames

Real fire flames are one of my favorite things to paint. The reasons why are simple. They can be airbrushed relatively fast, a minimal paint edge means fewer layers of clearcoat to level them out, and the freedom of the design allows for a great deal of creativity. Best of all, if you need to make a change midway through the process, it's pretty easy to do so.

Do not try your first real fire attempt on an actual project. First play with some test panels. Get to know what color mixtures will work for you. Develop the technique, and find your style of real fire. Everyone's real fire is different.

Real fire that looks real is the right combination of freehand airbrushing and template use. Mike Lavallee likes to say, "Dark to light," with your colors and "Loose to tight," with the airbrushing technique. Mike is the pioneer of the real fire technique, and the methods he developed have inspired most painters who airbrush real fire.

MATERIALS & EQUIPMENT

Materials
PPG 61457 Poppy Orange DBC basecoat
PPG 83032 Sunburst Yellow DCB basecoat
PPG DBC500 color blender (clear basecoat)
PPG DBX1689 basecoat converter
PPG Vibrance DMX 210 red candy toner
PPG Vibrance DMX 211 orange candy toner
PPG Vibrance DMX 212 red candy toner
Plastic mixing cups
Gerson Blend Prep tack cloths
PPG Prep Plus wipes
PPG DX320 precleaner

Tools
Mike Lavallee Tru Fire Artool templates
Mike Lavallee Tru Fire 2nd Degree Artool templates
Artool Matchmaker templates
Artool Essential 7 Templates
SATAgraph 4 airbrush
SATAjet 20 B artbrush
SATA Minijet 3000B spray gun
Evercoat paint mixing cups
Solvent-proof plastic bottles

Real fire flames can be fun to paint, once you learn the technique.

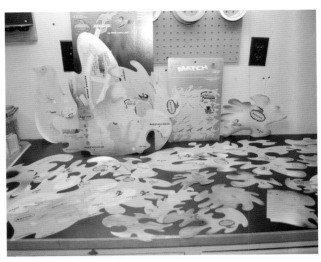

The main colors used for real fire are orange, yellow, candy red, candy orange, and candy golden yellow. Using PPG's Deltron paint system, I've mixed up the two solid basecoats, 61457 Poppy Orange and 83032 Sunburst Yellow, and put them into solvent-proof squeeze bottles so they are readily available. The three candy basecoats—red, orange, and yellow—are made using DBC500 clear basecoat. Into this, I'll add a candy toner. For the yellow, it's DMX 210; red, DMX 212; and orange, DMX 211. I mix these into plastic mixing cups. As for how much toner to mix into the clear basecoat mix? The easiest way to judge is to use a paint paddle. Dip the paddle into the paint, then see how dark or light the candy is against the wood grain. Find the good medium between too light and too dark. This is where playing around with test panels will help you understand how to exactly mix your paints. Although it's tempting to jump right into your project, don't rush through this practice part. Don't work on the project until you are happy with your fire.

To help give the fire its free-flowing shapes, the technique requires templates. Some painters make their own, but I use the same templates designed by the Tru Fire man himself. Mike Lavallee of Killer Paint has spent thousands of hours over the years developing his technique for real fire, and he uses a combination of Artool Templates, The Essential 7, Matchmaker, and Mike's own line of Tru Fire templates: The Original Tru Fire and Tru Fire 2nd Degree Burn. I use all four sets of templates in my real fire. But I have been painting real fire for almost 10 years now and have been collecting these templates over time. If you could only afford one set, I'd recommend the Tru Fire 2nd Degree Burn. The templates seen here get used a lot and not just for real fire, but anywhere a sharp, clean edge is needed. If you're doing any amount of custom artwork, invest in some good quality templates.

PAINTING REAL FIRE OVER DARK BASECOATS

The victim here is a 1998 Corvette. I did several Photoshop drawings for the customer, and this is the one she picked. To create a real fire Photoshop drawing, upload a photo of anything with real fire flames on it. You can even use photos of actual fire. Select and copy the real fire areas of the photo and then paste them onto the photo of your project. Use the Free Transform option in the Edit menu to make your fire bigger or smaller or to change the shape of it. The Smudge Tool is also handy in reworking the fire. Sound confusing? You can also create a blank drawing and then use colored pencils to draw your fire. Refer to Finding the Most Effective Design in chapter 9 for more details on creating blank drawings.

Here is the Vette. The wheels, the door and trunk jams, everything under the hood, the underside of the hood and trunk lid, and any openings in the body of the car like the side coves have been masked off and the car has been wet sanded with 800 paper.

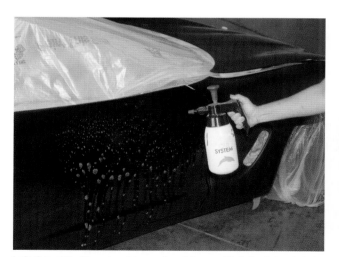

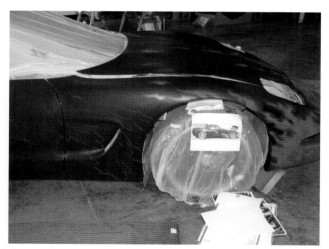

Left: One of the biggest problems when doing any kind of paintwork, but especially artwork on a plastic or fiberglass car, is the static electricity. Everything wants to stick to the surface, and overspray from airbrushing can be a real problem. One solution is to use an anti-static solution on the car. Some can be sprayed on and left. Others are sprayed on and wiped off. Here I use a water-based cleaner as the anti-static solution. It is sprayed on very wet and then immediately wiped off. Make sure it's completely wiped off. But use care; too much wiping will build up more static electricity. **Right:** The drawing of the car is taped right where I can see it as I work. You can see where I already have started airbrushing the fire. To start the flames is pretty simple. Lightly sketch them out with the airbrush using the orange basecoat. This is where the loose part of the technique comes in. Keep it simple, not too many hard lines. One of the biggest mistakes people make is starting off with too many hard lines.

TWO MAIN QUESTIONS FOR AIRBRUSHING REAL FIRE

One often asked question is how much do you need to thin down paint to airbrush real fire? It's one of those questions that will be different for every painter, but here's a good rule to follow. If the paint comes out of the airbrush too grainy, reduce it a bit. If the paint is runny or not leaving a clean, solid color line, then add more paint. It will take a few tries to find a happy medium.

The same advice goes for air pressure. Mike Lavallee airbrushes real fire using over 65 lbs. That's too much for me. I usually run about 45 lbs. Play around with a test panel and try different air pressures to see what works best for you.

The next step is to take the templates, find curves in the templates, line up the matching curves, and spray a little color. Look carefully here, and note how the curve of the template lines up with the side of the flame. But see how only the left half of the curve has paint on it? I only airbrushed orange against part of the curve. This will help give that flame lick a randomness. Carefully observe the other fire licks in this photo. Note how parts of the lick are sharp (a stencil was held up against it while the color was sprayed), while other parts are fuzzy (the fire lick was freehand airbrushed). Then in some places I'll use a combination of both, spray it freehand and fuzzy then lightly airbrush the color against the template in the exact same spot.

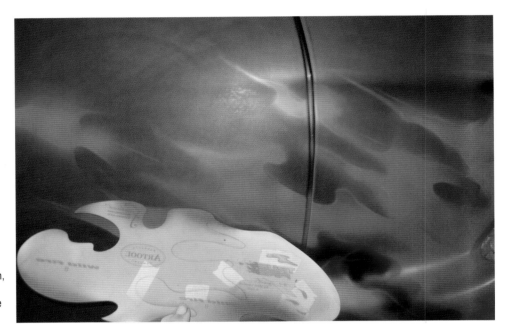

The one thing you don't want to do is for the fire to start to have a pattern to it. Don't try to be too precise with the fire. Just let it happen. For example, in this picture I'm airbrushing a fire lick on the left of the template. But notice where the bottom right side of the template is? It seems to fit the curve of that fire lick also, so I'll spray a little orange on there too while the template is on that location. Keep it spontaneous. Draw a flame outline and only fill in part of it.

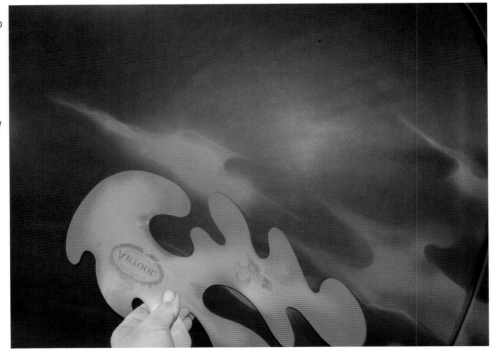

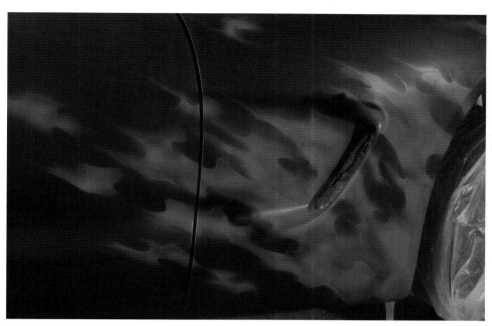

This is the result of the first layer of fire using only the orange basecoat. It already seems to have a good natural flow to the fire. And that is very important; you want the fire to have a very natural flow. This basic technique will be repeated with each of the colors of the fire. Only with each successive color, the layers cover less and less area.

A WORD OF WARNING

The spraying technique for real fire produces a great deal of overspray and it must be carefully removed after each round of color.

1. First use a tack rag and wipe away any overspray.
2. Then, using a gentle precleaner like PPG's DX320, carefully preclean the surface, and then thoroughly wipe off the precleaner left behind. If you're having a hard time removing overspray, try a stronger cleaner like PPG's DX330.
3. A water-based cleaner will also help remove any static electricity that has been building up.
4. Repeat these steps throughout the job after finishing each layer of color; otherwise, the overspray will ruin your work. Keep the tack rag, the cleaner, and the box of wipes handy. As you move around the car, they need to follow you, just like the airbrushes and paint.

If you are tense when you're painting real fire, your fire is going to look tense and structured. It won't look natural. If you're getting frustrated, clean out your airbrushes and walk away. Take a break. Maybe have an adult beverage. If the customer is breathing down your neck about the job, let him know that hassling you is going to show in the job. Doing custom artwork is not like doing bodywork and paint. There is only one way to do bodywork and paint; artwork involves creativity. So try to shut out the stress with custom paint projects, especially if the source of stress looks at you in the mirror every morning.

The next step is spraying a coat of candy red basecoat over the fire. Use care. If sprayed too heavily, it will muddy up the artwork and obscure the detail. If sprayed too lightly, the candy may appear grainy. This is where doing the test panels will really come in handy; they will help you to find that perfect mix of paint and spray technique. Remember, you can always add another coat, but it's much harder to take a coat away. To apply the paint, I use a SATAminijet 3000 B, which is a mini spray gun, not a full-size gun. One or maybe two medium light coats should do the trick. Two coats of red candy were sprayed on over the fire. Compare this picture to the previous photo. Note how it's not that much redder than the orange that was sprayed. It just needs to be a little red.

Now build up another layer of orange fire using the same techniques, a combination of freehand and template work. See how I created a new layer off of the first fire layer? I'll take unfinished ends of the first layer and continue them with the second layer as well as starting a few new fire licks. Now you can see the color difference that the candy red created. It's not a big dramatic difference as subtle differences are what make real fire paint look real. And yes, this is the opposite side of the car. It was a long day. Again, it's very easy to overdo it. Work on it a little, then step away and see how it looks. Remember to tack rag and wipe the surface with precleaner to remove any overspray after you are done with this layer.

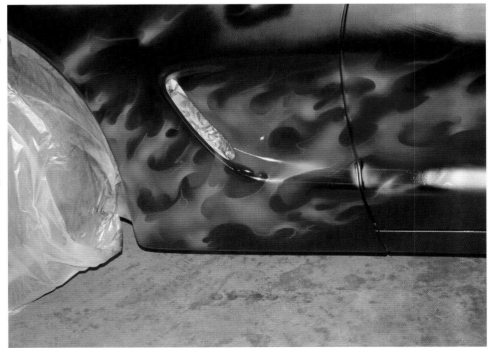

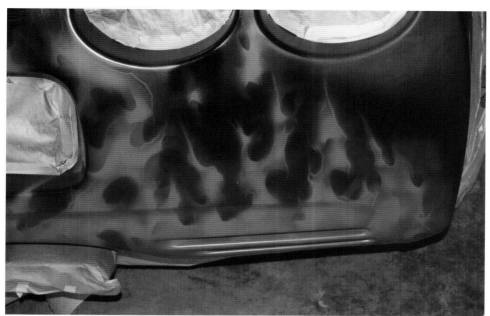

Now here's a photo of what not to do. Here, I covered up most of my red with the orange. I'll have to go back and spot in some red candy to even up my colors.

OOPS!

See the straight yet fuzzy orange line my finger is pointing to? This is a place on the side of the car that, for whatever reason, overspray decided to stick to. As the basecoat of the car is a solid color, and not a candy color, this problem is easy to fix. I simply need to airbrush a little of the black basecoat to cover it. I'll use an Artool template to cover the orange fire right next to it, so the black overspray doesn't land in the orange. If I were working over a candy basecoat under the flames, I would need to cover that flaw by adding a fire lick in that area.

Using the mini gun with the candy orange basecoat mix, spray a light to medium coat of candy orange over the second layer. Not a whole lot of orange candy toner was used in the mix. A little goes a long way. Notice how the color changes are not very big. But that's the trick, subtly building up layers of color. Remember to tack rag and wipe the surface with precleaner to remove any overspray after you have sprayed the candy and it has dried for a few minutes.

189

Now it's time to start airbrushing the yellow fire layer. Be careful spraying the yellow as yellow is a funky pigment; it can come out very grainy. This is another place where you'll be glad you played around with the test panels and found the right mixture of paint and reducer. Using one of the 2nd Degree Tru Fire templates, I built the yellow fire licks off of parts of the orange ones. In some places, the fire runs along the same line as the orange but then goes off on its own. Look closely at the lower right part of the picture and you can see how the yellow builds off the layer below it. And remember to keep it random. In some places, a short lick of yellow fire works great; in other places, longer licks fit the space. Keep it random yet balanced. Note how a few of the orange fire licks have just a small accent of yellow. In some places, I sprayed along the edge of the template; in other places, I aimed the airbrush away from the edge so the edge is softer.

The door on this '67 Firebird shows another good example of the yellow layer building off the orange. For instance, look at the area the blue arrow is pointing to. The bottom line of the fire lick will run along the orange, but the top line of the lick is a new line, not directly or running along the orange fire. There will be more yellow fire at the front of the vehicle. It starts to flicker out as the fire progresses toward the rear of the car. Once all the yellow is done, tack rag the surface and give it a good cleaning with the precleaner and wipes. Inspect the entire black surface to make sure there's not yellow overspray.

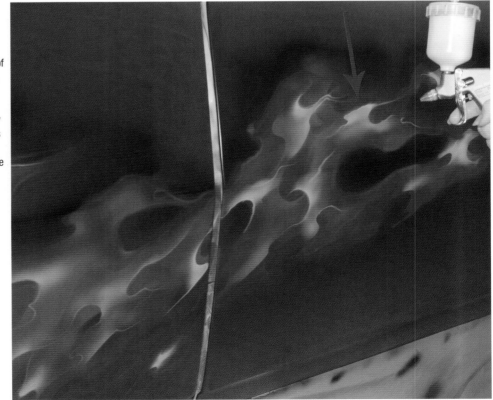

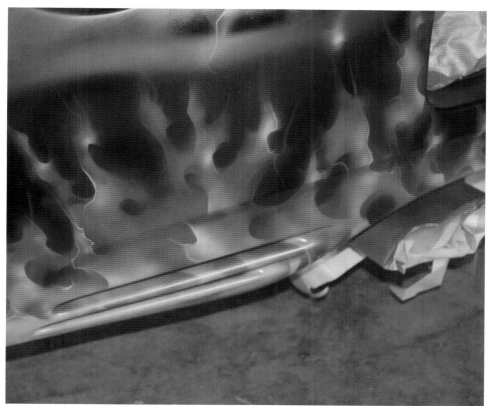

Using the candy yellow clear basecoat mix and the SATAjet mini spray gun, I sprayed a medium coat over all the fire. Here at the rear of the car, you can see how the yellow candy makes the colors really pop. Don't spray too heavily or it may muddy up all the wonderful subtle color effects. Too heavy a coat of basecoat clear softens the paint underneath and the colors tend to "melt" into each other a little.

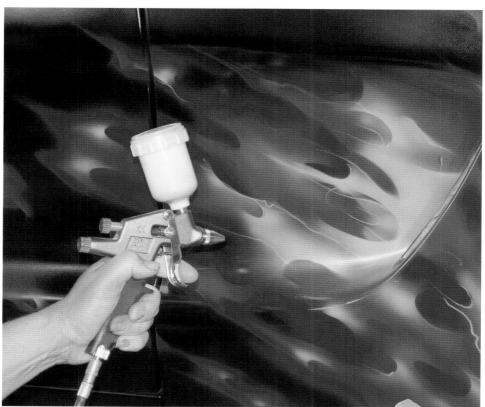

Another trick to help the random feel is to airbrush a little orange candy over parts of the yellow, giving it a richer, deeper look. I'm using a SATAjet 20 B artbrush. Don't overdo this step.

Now I want to accent the yellow fire with a slightly lighter yellow. I mixed a little white into the yellow color and sparingly accented some of the yellow fire by adding some of it to a few of the areas of yellow fire and building a few small new licks of fire.

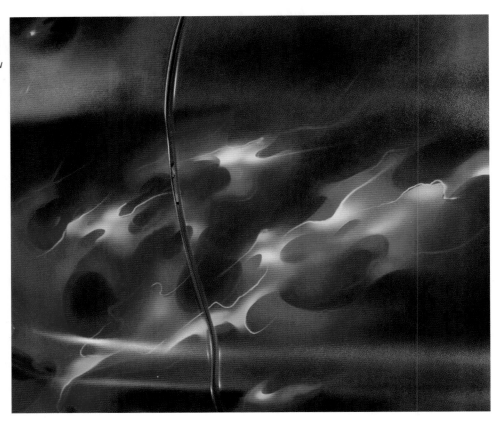

Here is another good example of how the new yellow layer is built off the layer beneath it as well as forming out into a new layer. Look closely at the inside edge of the fender. I'll have to go back and make sure to airbrush the fire to wrap around that edge. Pay attention to little details like that. They are easy enough to overlook.

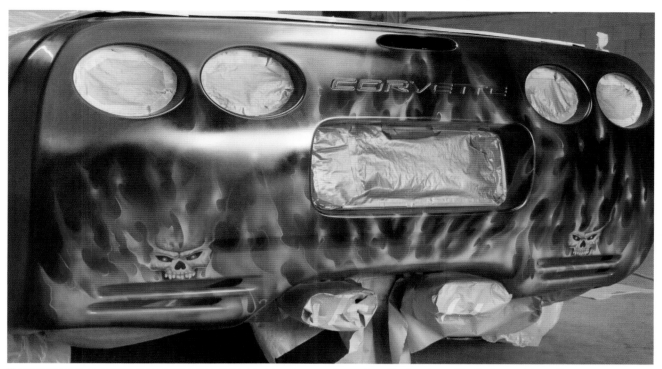

The next step is to go over the car and make sure all the artwork wraps around any edges, like the edges of the fenders and doors. Here, you can see where the artwork stops at the bottom edge of the rear of the car. The artwork need to be wrapped around and under. Also in this photo you can see how I masked off the exhaust and behind the openings on the rear bumper cover.

For some vehicle models, especially older cars and trucks, the step of wrapping the artwork around edges should be taken a step further. For example, on this '39 Ford, it's very difficult to cleanly and sharply airbrush into the area where the front fenders meet the hood sides. The angle where they meet is very sharp. On this kind of project, for the best result, remove the parts and then airbrush the fire past the line where the parts meet up. Here, the fenders have been removed. The fire will now be painted to go past the hard line seen on the bottom of the hood sides.

I'm airbrushing fire past the line. Look closely and you can see how the fire is very fuzzy next to the line. Extending the fire will clean that up. I'll do the same thing on the fenders, and the fire will be sharp and clean into that joint.

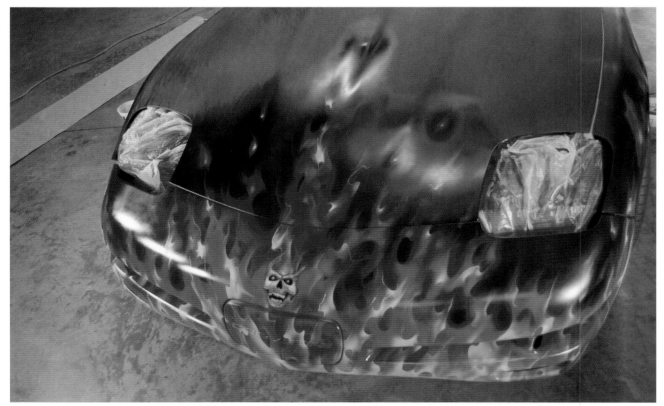

Now that the fire has been painted, the car must be thoroughly gone over and every bit of overspray must be removed. On most cars, I'll carefully sand the large areas where there is no fire, staying away from the edges of the fire. On solid colors, you can blend in any areas that visibly show where you sanded away the overspray. On candy or pearl colors that you cannot spot in, you have to use a combination of common sense and care. This is where you will wish that you had precleaned and removed the overspray after each layer of color. You can see in this picture, the dull unshiny areas on the hood are where I sanded away the overspray. Then I lightly sprayed some thinned-down black basecoat along the edge of where I stopped sanding.

COMMON SENSE

This step can be tricky. You want to remove any overspray that has settled and stuck to the surface without disturbing the soft transition between the basecoat and the fire. Common sense plays a big role here. For example, try this technique in an area that is not easily seen and make sure it looks good before you move on to a more visible spot. You may even want to test it on the test panels you painted. It's easy enough to make this correction on black or other solid colors as you can airbrush some basecoat along the sanded area. But with color that cannot be touched up, it's much harder. So for these kinds of jobs, create test panels from spare parts, and then try out your technique on them.

Here's a side view of the finished Corvette. I added a few skulls to the paint and the fire has a nice flow down the side of the car. Note how the size of the fire gets smaller as it goes back. One key to a good real fire paint job is to use the size of the fire to complement the shape of the vehicle.

The customer wanted more red and orange than yellow on the car. You can really see this on the hood. It gives a deeper, richer look to the fire. In other pictures of real fire paint in this chapter, you'll see how many real fire paint jobs have much more yellow. It's all a matter of customer preference.

PAINTING REAL FIRE OVER LIGHTER BASE COLORS

It's pretty much the same process to paint real fire over lighter basecoats. But how do you paint real fire over a basecoat that is lighter than the color of the fire? Here we are starting with a plastic T bucket body based in a light yellow. I have already painted a skull face on it. The fire will be coming off the face.

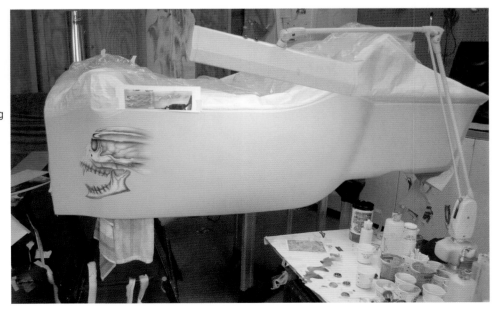

THE EASY WAY

Whenever possible, work with the parts off the chassis. For many projects, like T buckets and kit cars, the body is not that hard to remove. Talk to your customer or whoever is building the car. Use common sense, and look closely at the way the body is attached to the frame. Are the mounting bolts easy to access? Are there wires or cables that can be disconnected easily? This yellow T bucket was a running car, but my customer disconnected a few things so it was easy for me to unbolt the body and remove it from the frame. Not all T buckets are like this. I painted a T bucket a year later that there was no way to remove the body without a major hassle.

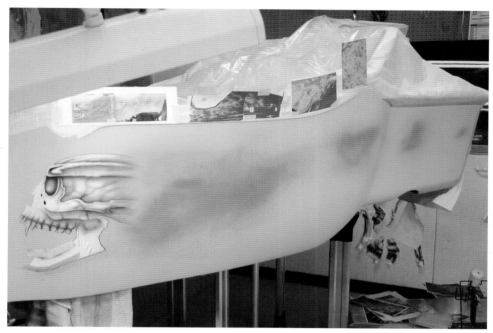

I'll only be using a few of the real fire colors. The solid yellow, light yellow mixture, and white basecoats, candy orange, and candy yellow. First I need to build up a slightly dark base for the fire to contrast against. I used a SATA Minijet 3000B to lightly spray a layer of candy yellow where I wanted the fire areas to be. Then candy orange is sprayed, but that will not extend as far as the yellow. Note how the candy yellow extends past the orange. I've laid out four areas: the big area behind the skull and three smaller areas where pieces of the fire will be breaking off. Don't forget to tack rag and then wipe with precleaner to remove any overspray that has traveled beyond the fire.

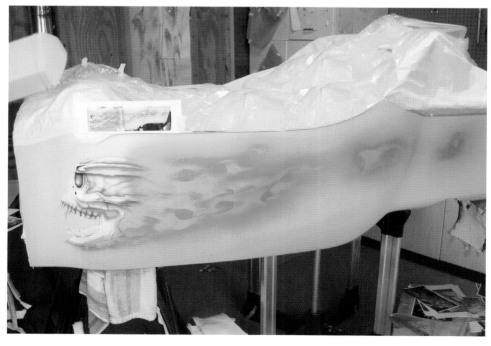

I airbrushed the first layer of yellow basecoat fire using the same technique as seen previously. Then I sprayed a layer of candy yellow over it using a SATA minijet. When working in spaces this tight, use a lower air pressure to keep the overspray from extending too far.

Using a SATAgraph 4 airbrush, I airbrushed candy orange on some of the outside edges of the yellow fire licks, and under the layer it is sprayed a little heavier. This gives the fire form and depth.

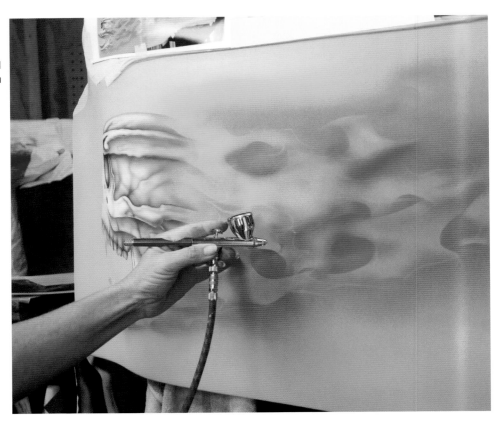

Here's the first layer. All the yellow has been shadowed with the orange candy. No solid orange was used here.

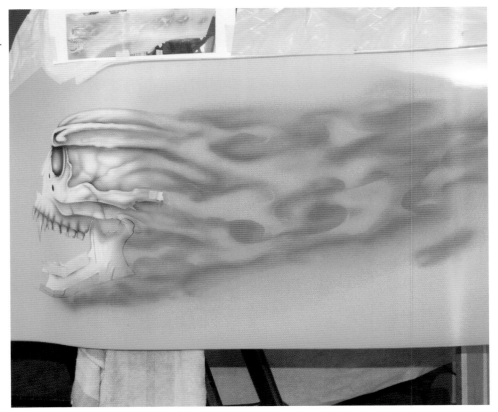

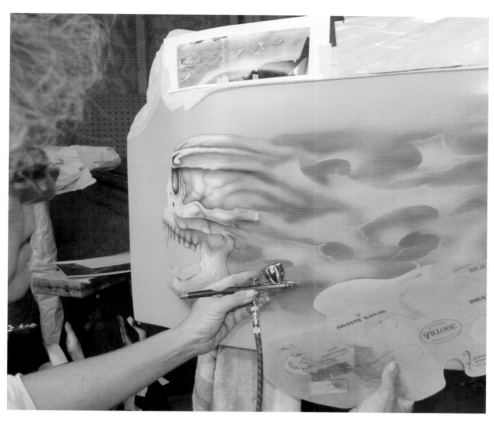

It's time to start accenting the yellow layer and building a new yellow layer with the solid yellow basecoat. I started by outlining the new fire licks. Start small and build slowly; don't cover too much of what you have. The layer is carefully built up by using the combination of spraying against the templates and freehand airbrushing. Once that is complete, a coat of candy yellow is sprayed over it.

Next, I accent the second layer with the lighter yellow. You can even add a few white accents over that.

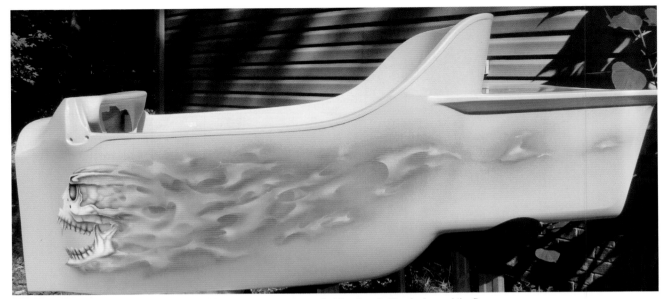

This is the end result. Again make sure to carefully remove any overspray that has traveled too far beyond the fire.

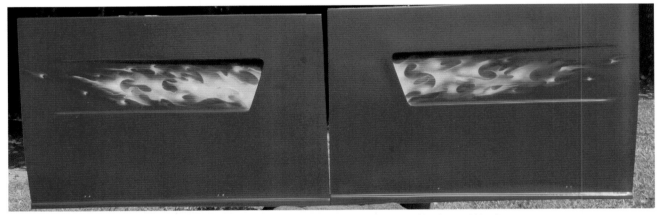

Real fire can also be used to complement detail areas on a vehicle, like the insets on these hood sides for an old truck.

Another cool way to use real fire is to work it into a classic paint scheme, like the rally stripes on this old Chevelle hood.

Here's the hood from the '39 Ford I painted. It shows how you want to keep your flame layers on the transparent side so the lower layers "glow" through the ones over them, giving the fire real depth. Less is more.

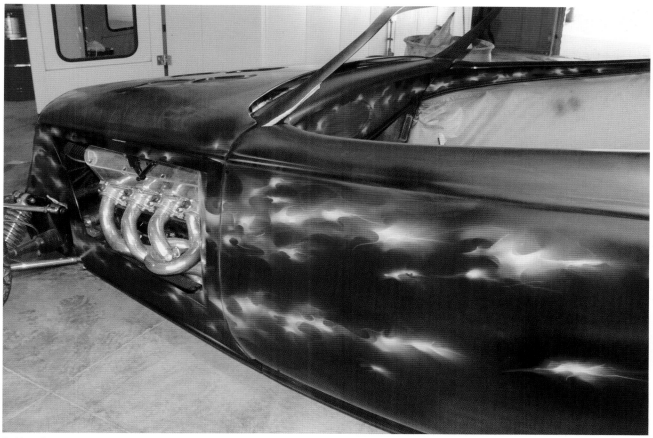

And here is yet another style of real fire flames. I painted this for a customer in Texas.

On Joe Gregory's 1965 Impala SS, I used a combination of traditional flames backed with real fire to split the two tone.

Here's some real fire on red basecoat on Paul B. Reeves T Bucket. When working over red, the fire is done the exact same way as it is when working over black. The red candy will help build a rich shadow under the fire and give it depth.

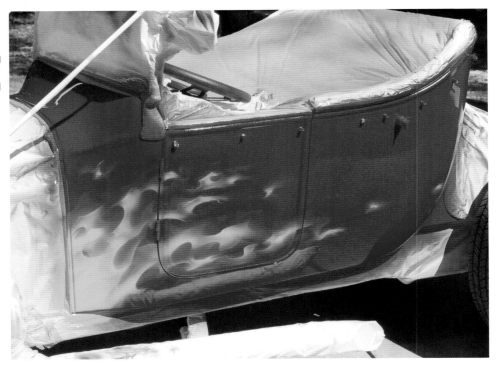

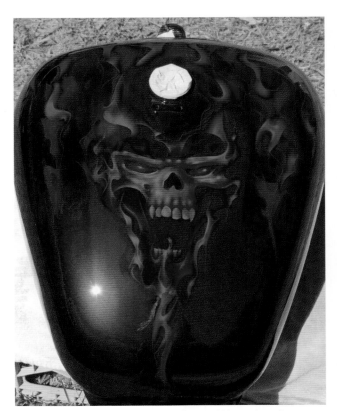

You can use any color for real fire. Here I've used blue and purple over a candy purple basecoat. All blue fire would look great too.

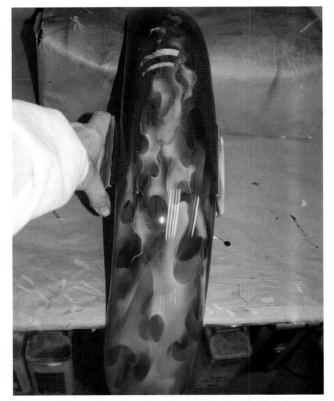

Here is another mixture of blue fire with orange/yellow fire. Note the loose, faded edges of the yellow and orange fire and how indistinct those edges are. Keep your fire technique very loose and unstructured so it has a more natural effect.

Chapter 20
Fun with Flag Graphics

Frank wants to have his bike look as though a flag is wrapped around it. I found a number of flag images online and studied the way, light and shadows play around the ripples and folds in the fabric of flags. A bone stock Harley Heritage is what I'm starting with.

One of the most fun and popular graphics uses a flag effect. It's easier than it looks and many customers ask for a flag design of some kind on their vehicles. Using a few simple techniques and a big dose of patience, most any painter with an airbrush can create this effect. This effect is very versatile as any kind of flag can be used. You can also use these low tech techniques to create a two-dimensional (a flat flag with no folds) or three-dimensional (a flag that looks like rippled fabric) artwork. Leave out the folds to create a graphic flag design.

Much of this technique involves shading to create the effect of fabric. This part of the technique can be used to create a fabric effect simply by airbrushing darks

I created blanks of the bike. Using the photo of the bike, I whited out the tank and fenders and printed out several copies. With colored pencils, I drew out the design. I did three drawings for Frank. This is the one he picked.

HANDY HINT

When you're trying to figure out how to create a certain effect, go online and use a search engine to bring up images of that effect. Look at them and think about how other painters have done that kind of work. Did they stencil it? Does it look like they freehanded it with an airbrush, or did they use a tiny paintbrush? Don't rush into any kind of artwork without first putting some time into research and planning. And always remember to test your technique before you try it on a vehicle.

NO RULES

You don't have to use a liquid mask to mask off the flag; any kind of fine line tape can be used. Simply trace your drawing directly onto the surface and run the tape along the lines. Tape off one color. When you are done painting that color, mask it off and paint the next color.

This picture is of a different tank but it shows this step. For the two parts of the bike that will be done with red and white stripes, I'm going to apply three coats of a liquid masking product. I always brush it on. Apply the liquid mask over paint that has been dried overnight and then wet sanded. After opening the can, thoroughly stir the mixture as much of the thicker product will have settled on the bottom of the can. Then with a flat, inexpensive paint brush, brush on a thin to medium coat, allowing for each coat to dry a little but not all the way, before brushing on the next. Be sure to clean the brush with water immediately after the last coat, or even between coats, if the mixture appears to be drying on the brush.

and lights under and then over a solid color. I'm using PPG's Deltron line of paint for this graphic. Water-based paint can also be used, but make sure to dry out each layer of color as it is applied. Although this example uses motorcycle parts, these techniques can be used to put flag graphics on cars and trucks, too. Flags can be used in countless ways to customize a project.

The best way is to start with either a black or white base. The technique is the same—build up a series of light and dark tones to duplicate the effect of rippled fabric. Here, I start with a white base that was sprayed and then sanded. Using a copy machine, I've enlarged the tank area of the drawing to be about the same size of the tank.

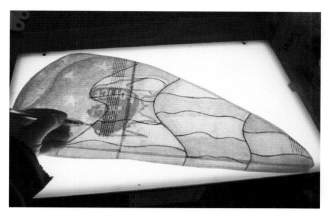

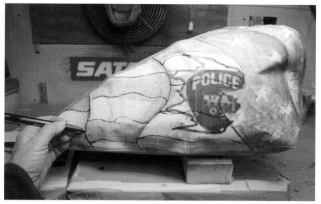

Left: Next, I flipped the drawing over and traced along the lines of the drawing using a light table or a window with a soft lead pencil. This drawing and transfer process is repeated for the rear fender as that will also have stripes on it. Note how the drawing is not transferred to the front of the tank. The areas with the stars will be handled in a different way. **Right:** Now I try to find the most effective placement of the drawing on the tank. Take your time when doing this. Back up and look at it from across the room. Is it too far forward or crooked on the tank? When I was sure it was exactly where it needed to be, I taped it to the surface. Then I carefully traced along the lines.

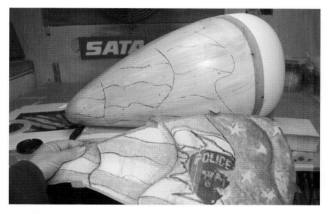

Left: The pencil lead on the back of the drawing creates a copy on the tank. I used this method to transfer the flag pattern on the rear fender. **Right:** This next step is not necessary, but I always do it, just to make sure all my lines are nice and smooth. I'll run a piece of fine line masking tape along each line then redo the line with a pen. This straightens out and smooths any imperfections. But remember, you don't want the lines of the flag to be straight. You're looking for a nice, balanced symmetry with a random look. You don't want it to look patterned and cookie cutter.

ALWAYS IMPROVE

The perfect time to do any design rework is when you're laying out the design on the vehicle. Remember your drawing is flat, but much of the time, the surface is not. The original flat drawing may need to be redesigned slightly to work better on the surface. And you might think of an improvement to the design itself. Here I redrew one of the folds to have more of a curve to it. It will give a more natural drape to the fabric of the flag. Don't be afraid to improve on your original.

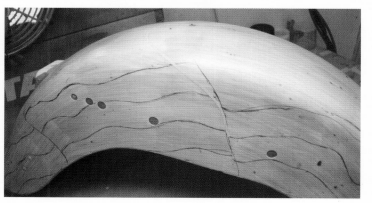

Now this tank has a dash that runs down the center, marked off with the blue tape. I'm going to run the flag pattern under it, but I still like to plan for what it will look like once the dash is on the tank. Note that I have marked which stripes will be red and white. Also at the top right of the tank, you can see where one of the stripes was edited. The stripes were looking too lined up/too uniform, and as the rippled flag is more random, one of the stripes was moved over to give the flag a more natural appearance. Remember, you can use a variety of masking materials to mask off the sections of the stripes. Masking tape and transfer tape can also be used. If in doubt, test your materials and technique beforehand on a panel or spare part. When doing this on a car or truck, the flat surfaces will make it easier to use masking materials like transfer and masking tape.

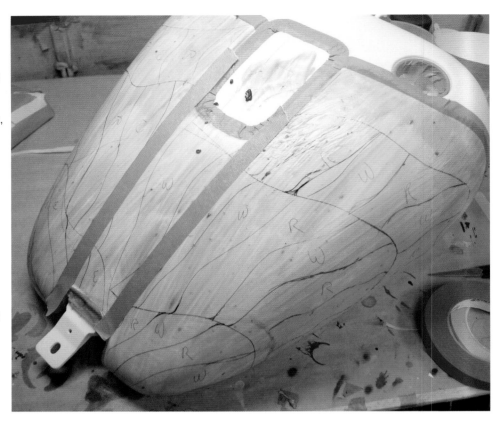

Using an X-Acto knife, I cut out the red parts of the flag, taking care to only cut through the masking film and not into the surface of the paint. How much pressure should be used when cutting through masking film? It will vary depending on how thickly it is applied. Use a slight amount of pressure when cutting. If it's not cut through, apply a little more pressure when cutting. Better to start off with less cutting pressure than too much. Using tweezers, pick out and remove the pieces of masking film for the red stripes. Watch closely to make sure that the areas are fully cut and that the rest of the film is staying in place and not lifting up with the red. Expect the mask to not be fully cut in all places. Keep the stencil knife handy and carefully cut any little strings that are still attached.

I CAN FIX THAT

What can you do if a mask or stencil does pull up? It's an easy enough fix. Simply trim off the lifted mask. Once the static connection is broken, the mask will not longer stick. Carefully place fine line tape in the area where the mask pulled up. Then, with the stencil knife, carefully trim the tape into the desired shape, literally patching the mask with tape.

DEBRIS IS THE ENEMY

Why are bits of dust such an enemy when you're simply doing just a little bit of shadowing? Tiny pieces of dust create shadows when the airbrush overspray hits them. This same effect happens to create dark spots when candy colors are sprayed. Dust is the enemy!

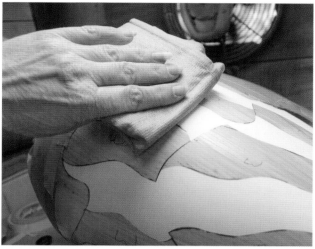

Make sure to gently run a PPG One Choice tack rag across the surface. Any pieces of dust or debris will be exaggerated once you start shadowing with the black.

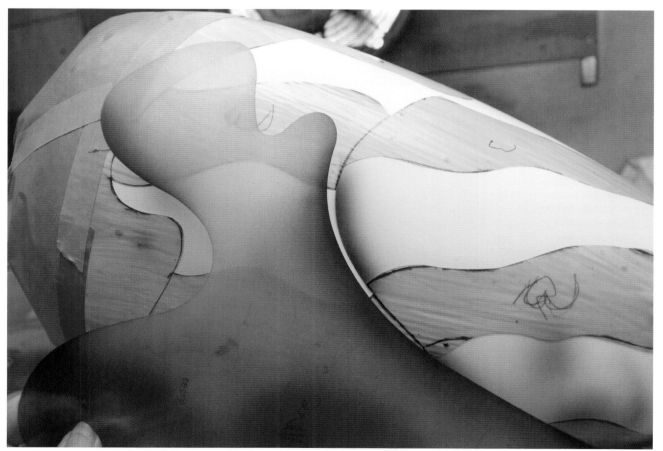

I laid out a few Artool templates and looked through them to find curves that match up with the curves of the hard-edged folds on the flag. Here a curve on The Bird stencil matches up very nicely with a fold. I thinned PPG DBC 9700 one part paint to two parts DT898 reducer. Remember, all these airbrush reduction mixtures will vary, depending on your airbrush, the air pressure, and how soft or hard you want your shadow to be. Play around with your mixtures, testing them out before you spray them on the surface. Here, I want the shadow to be very soft but very hard right along the edge of the fold (template) as if the fold was casting a shadow.

Next, I started to airbrush the ripples in the fabric. Remember, you can always add more. I started by lightly sketching in the shadows of the ripples. Study the reference photos you found. Don't just rush through it. Take your time, airbrush a little, then step back. For each shadow there will be a highlight. Note the soft shadow that runs alongside the hard shadow edge. See the white highlight right next to it? If you look at every shadow, there's a highlight near it. This forms a series of highs and lows in the fabric. This step is a little tricky as you want to slightly overdo the shadowing. Don't worry about losing the highlights. Note how the shadows correspond with the bends in the stripes.

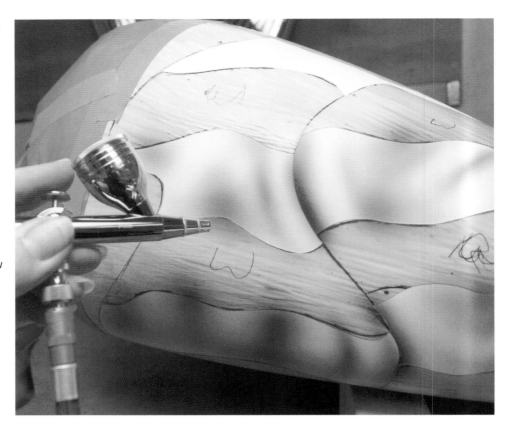

With white paint in the airbrush, I started accenting the highlights. Again, use a thinned down mixture of paint. You want to see an even, soft, nongrainy flow of paint from the airbrush. Aim the airbrush for the center of each highlight and softly spray. Here I accented the highlight that runs near the edge of a fold. Then I aimed the airbrush in the center of a high spot or raised area of a ripple and softly airbrushed white. This continued all over the surface. Now there will be a slight white overspray. I'll have to go back and reshadow the black using a little less air pressure. It won't take much black to reshadow those areas. Just a little will work.

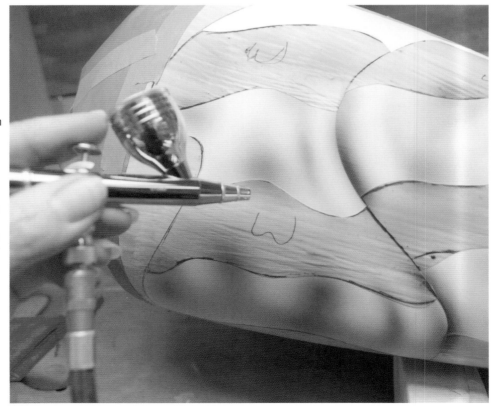

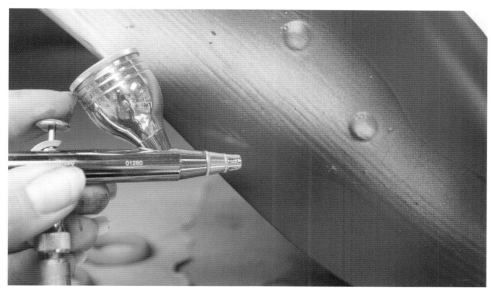

Now I'm ready to spray some red. Red is by nature a semitransparent color. Thin the red one part red with one and a half parts reducer. All mixtures will vary. You want the red to apply evenly, not grainy or spotty, going on smooth and flat. Spray on a nice, even light to medium coat. The lights and dark that were applied will show through the red. Just apply enough red for the surface to have a nice even coloring. A larger spray tool like a SATAjet 20B artbrush can also be used. Remember, if you apply too much red, it will cover up all those nice shadows and highlights.

The edge of the red is a little thick, so I'm going to trim it down using a razor blade. This is not an easy task for beginners. It takes a steady hand, and it's very easy to create a scratch in the red stripe. I hold the blade at a flat angle, so that it only makes contact with the red paint edge. If you try this, start with an area that is not easily visible, like under the tank. Why do I do this? It cuts down on my paint edge so it will even out better when clearcoated. Use care, as this is very difficult to do.

HANDY HINT

How long should you wait before removing tape or mask? There is no specific amount of time. Each situation will be different. These factors determine the amount of wait time:

- How many layers of paint were applied
- Thickness of paint mixture
- Kind of paint used. Urethane and water-based paint will dry slower than acrylic basecoat enamal. Water-based paints must also be dried out between coats.
- Temperature of the shop. Paint dries faster in warm shops.

The best thing to do when you're undecided about whether it's time to remove the tape or a mask is to pull up a little bit of the tape or mask. If it's rubbery or doesn't pull cleanly, stop and wait longer. Don't be impatient with this step, or you'll end up with a ragged edge that will look awful.

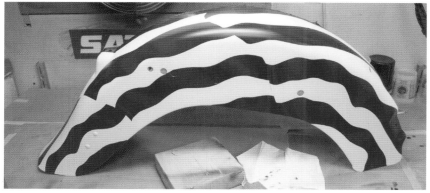

Here's what we have so far. Not what you were expecting, huh? You might think the way to have this done was to apply the red, then apply the shadows and highlights. But this way looks much more realistic. Later on, a little more shadowing will be applied. The folds and ripples in the flag can already be seen.

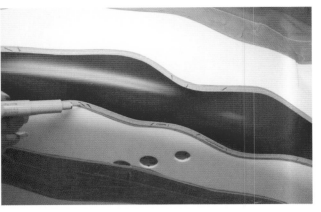

Once the red stripes were thoroughly dry, they are masked off to prepare spraying the white. I ran 3M ⅛″ fine line tape along the edges of the red stripes. Note how just a very thin edge of red peeks out from the edge of the tape. It's better to have the tape fully on the red. If you don't, then there will be bright white edge. Now the corners of each red stripe will have to be neatly masked. So the fine line tape is carefully trimmed with the X-Acto knife.

One thing that will help the flag to look realistic is for the shadowed areas on the white to line up with the shadowed areas on the red. I carefully marked the shadowed areas on the red with a permanent marker. These marks are made on the fine line tape. Once the red stripes were masked off, the marks were then drawn across the masking, making them easier to see. Now the shadows on the white will line up.

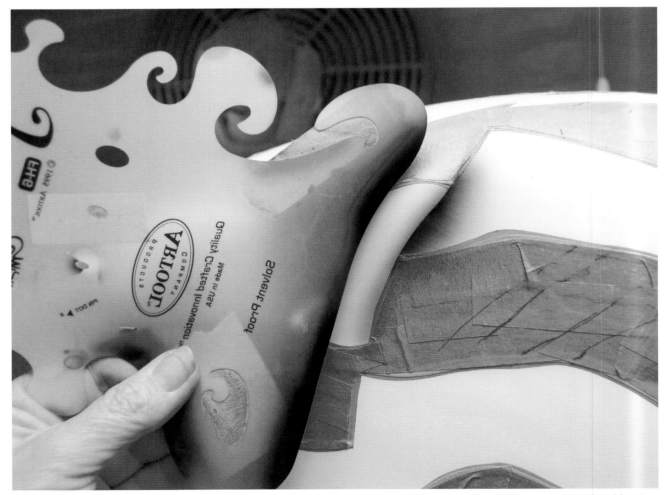

You can see in this photo where those lines were drawn. Now that the red is all masked off on the parts, the white can be shadowed. Here I used Artool Template FH-6 to create the hard-edged shadow that will run next to a fold in the flag fabric.

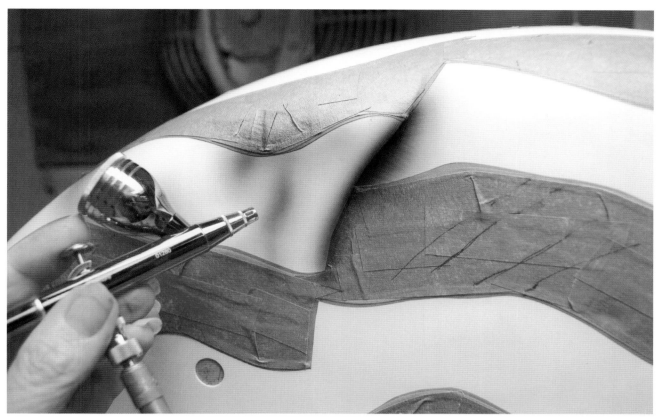

The dark shadows are lightly airbrushed in. Always remember to start with less. You can always add more; it's harder to take away. Note the location of the shadow and the curve of the red stripe above where the shadow is. I'm creating a sunken area by airbrushing several lines leading out of the center of that area. Plus note how this area is right after a highlighted area. On the right, you can see how the shadow lines up with a drawn line. Don't airbrush a hard line. Start with a very slight shadow lined up with the line. Then airbrush out from it, softly spreading the shadow across the area.

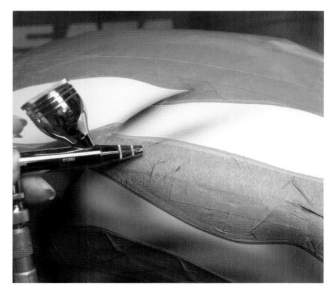

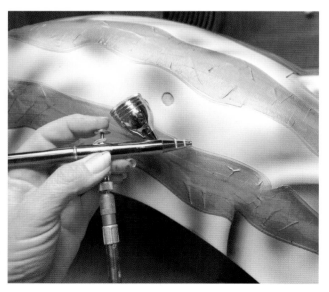

On the left, you can see how the shadow lines up with a drawn line. Don't airbrush a hard line. Start with a very slight shadow lined up with the line. Then airbrush out from it, softly spreading the shadow across the area. You can see the dark areas that have been built up. On the right, now it's time for the highlights. I start with some PPG DMD1684 basecoat white, which is thinned almost 200% with DT898 reducer. Again, test your pint mixture after you reduce it. Too thin, add more paint; too grainy, add more reducer. Now I lightly airbrushed white in the middle of the highlighted areas.

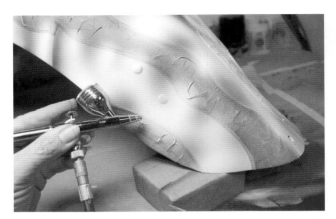

Left: Here I'm creating a highlighted area that is the opposite of the sunken area created three steps back. **Right:** Now you can see how it all comes together. It's all areas of darks and lights, shadows and highlights.

Left: Remember the hard lines of the folds? The highlighted side of each fold is masked off, leaving the shadowed side exposed. Now, the hard line of the fold does not go all way across the part. It gradually disappears at the top side. Note how the shadow ends in the middle of the uppermost white stripe. I softly darken the shadow starting there and moving the airbrush along the tape. The two shadows that form the sideways "V" are also darkened. This will be repeated with all the hard lines of the folds on the parts. **Right:** Here's another fold masked off. This one runs across the back of the fender. The bent tape forms a spray break that directs the overspray away from the surface.

I removed the masking and darkened the lighter shadows a little. Here I'm airbrushing a little black running down the length of this shadow. This way the shadow had more of a continuous flow.

NO WORRIES

Don't worry if something like this happens. Simply retape it and respray it. Here I taped off the red stripe, airbrushed a little white to cover the hard line of white, toned it down with just a touch of airbrushed black, and sprayed some red. All gone!

The front fender will have the blue with white stars part of the flag. First, I sprayed the fender with the PPG basecoat white and two layers of PPG DBC 17696 hot blue. Next, I figured out how the folds of the flag will fall across the fender and taped them off. Why did I put a bend in the 1½˝ masking tape? This bend is a spray break and will direct the overspray away from the fender, which is a great method to use to quickly mask off areas when you're doing light shading that does not produce much overspray.

Now, with the red, most of the shadowing was applied *under* the color. But the blue is not transparent like the red, so here the shadowing was applied *over* the color. In order to keep the shading soft and natural, I needed a dark blue for the shadow. DMD1684 was mixed with DMD660 and DMX 220 and thinned down almost 200%. This created a dark blue that will complement the hot blue basecolor.

I sprayed this mix (left) lightly along the tape and then airbrushed the hollows and low areas. I followed this with a light airbrushing of thinned down black. On the right, the tape is removed from the long fold I taped off. I sprayed a shadow along the top side of the fold. You can see how the dark blue and the black are creating the illusion of depth in the surface.

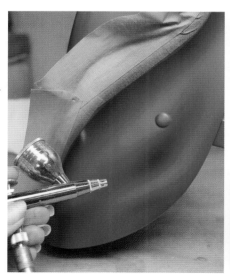

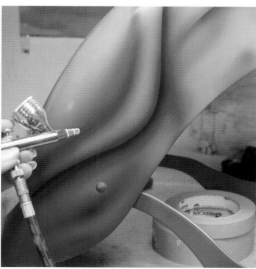

Some of the shadows need to be darkened up. Be creative. Here I cut a piece of cardboard to go along the curve of the fold. On another place, I used an Artool template, Mike Lavallee's Tru Fire Wild Fire A. They aren't just for doing real fire.

Above: For areas that needed a little more spray than the airbrush, I used a SATAjet 20 B. It's like a big airbrush and works great for blending colors into larger areas. **Right:** Because the dark blue shadowing might tend to bleed through any white sprayed over it, I sealed the colors down by clearing the parts with PPG DBC 2021. The parts will then be wet sanded with 800. The fender looks good in the sun the day after it's cleared.

BEWARE COLOR SPECIFICS

Always know the specifics of the colors and toners you are using. There are some candy/transparent toners that will bleed up through lighter colors layered over them. Purple shade reds, cobalt/permanent/red shade blues, and purple candy toners may tend to bleed. This means if you spray some white over purple candy or a color tinted with purple candy, the white might turn light purple.

Left: Now it's time to put the stars on the flag. You can cut the stars out by hand or use a plotter. I created drawings of stars on the computer and used my plotter to cut them out. I used GerberMask Ultra II for the stencils. I cut out a bunch of stars and started placing them on the surface of the fender. Note how the star is stretched out? As the fabric billows and stretches, the stars on the fabric become distorted. Looking at my reference photos of flags, I saw the shapes of the stars and stretched the stars in different directions. This star is stretched horizontally, so it's placed on the edge of a fold. To help keep track of what star will fit what stencil, I numbered the stars and the stencils. **Right:** By placing the stars on the fender, I can plan the layout of the stars and get the most effective placement. They look lined up, yet there's a randomness to them. They would not be lined up perfectly on a rippled flag.

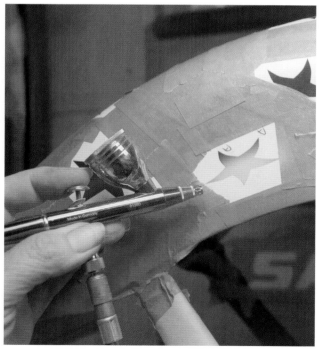

Left: I placed the outer stencil around each star, and removed the star with a pair of tweezers. The rest of the fender is masked off with aqua mask tape. **Right:** When spraying the white and black shading for the stars, notice how the stars are shaped. Always shade the star in the direction of the stretch. For the stars that are stretched horizontally, the white is sprayed across the middle of the star. Then the black is lightly shaded in on the top and bottom points of the star. Notice the half stars? Those are the stars that are on the edges of the folds. Don't go too thick on the paint for the stars, as this will build up a thick edge that will break off in places and make the edge of the star look rough. Go soft and light with the white shading. Once you're done, carefully remove the masking tape then peel away the stencil material from the stars. Gently brush the surface with a tack cloth to remove any loose paint edges. Inspect the surface of the blue for any overspray that has snuck past the masking and sand it away to remove it. Now the fender is ready for the first round of clear.

NO WORRIES REDUX

Beware! After the masking is removed, carefully look at the stars, especially the ones along the edges of the folds. Make sure the star comes all the way to the very edge of the fold and doesn't extend over it. If it does, then simply sand away the part that goes over. If it doesn't reach the edge, retape the star and extend it to the edge. Inspect all the stars and look for flaws and mistakes. When doing detailed work like this, expect to do some rework and fine tuning.

Remember the tank? The front third of the tank was masked off when I painted the stripes. I masked off the stripes and painted the blue and the stars.

Here's an unusual but effective use of a flag graphic. This CNC cabinet has a flag theme that carries throughout the cabinet and the machine parts located inside the cabinet.

Above: This gas tank also has a flag, but unlike Frank's tank, there are no overlapping folds. Don't hesitate to change the way a design plays across a surface. Always explore the design options. **Right:** Here's another view of this tank. The dash does not come all way down the bottom end of the tank so the design must flow visibly across the entire tank.

I clearcoated the parts with four or five coats of DBC 2021 urethane. Make sure that the first coat is light, as the weight of a heavy first coat will "grab" the artwork and pull it downward, literally "running" the artwork. Do the other coats light to medium. After they are dry, wet sand them with 800. Do not try to sand the surface perfectly flat; otherwise, you will sand into the graphics. Sand it gently then use a gray Scotch-Brite pad to dull up any shiny spots along the edges of the artwork. I can do any touchups needed at this point. And most of the time I find that I will have to touch things up. After the touchups, the clearcoating and wet sanding is repeated and the artwork is inspected one last time. Any last touchups are done and the parts are finish clearcoated with PPG DBC2021 with DCX61 hardener and the appropriate temperature DT reducer. Here are the parts reassembled on Frank's bike. I did additional artwork over the flag, commemorating Frank's service with the NYPD.

RESIST SANDING

When sanding in between rounds of clear, taking care not to sand into your artwork. Remember, the edges of the artwork are raised up.

- After the first application of clear, use a gray scuff pad to dull the edges around the artwork, then carefully sand the surface with 800 paper, but do not try to sand it completely flat.
- After the second application of clear, you should be able to sand it flat, but take care and watch the surface as you sand. Make sure you don't see color coming off.

Here's another view of the bike. See how the design flows across the bike? Good paint design always complements the lines of the vehicle. With the bike assembled, you can see how the graphic was designed to fit around the hardware of the parts. Always take things like bolt-on emblems, run lights, and taillights into consideration when designing the paint scheme.

Chapter 21
Graphics, Logos, and Anything Besides Flames

Some graphics, like those on this truck, can be laid out freehand on a vehicle.

Designing and painting graphics is one of the hardest tasks in custom painting. In this chapter, I'm going to give four step-by-step examples of painting graphics on a car or bike. These techniques can be used with any design. The thing to remember is to *think* your way through the process.

Using five simple steps, you can reproduce almost any graphic on a painted surface.

1. To create a pattern, use a computer and printer to resize the design to fit the surface area.

2. Transfer the outline of the design to the surface

3. Use a series of stencils, templates, and/or tape to mask off a single layer of the graphic.

4. Paint that area of the graphic.

5. Then, repeat the process for each layer or area of the graphic.

But, when trying to accurately reproduce a series of identical designs or a specific design, it helps to create a pattern to use when painting the design.

REPRODUCING A TRANS AM FIREBIRD GRAPHIC

This is an example of figuring out the graphics as you go along. When I started, I had an idea of how I would do this job. However, the high-tech process I thought would work did not work. In the end I had to do it all low tech and by hand. This process can be used as a low-tech way to reproduce any design, logo, or original car graphic.

It was a hot sunny day and by some miracle I was able to peel the original 1979 Trans Am Bird decal off the hood of a '79 Trams Am. It came off in one piece. The first step was to trace it and create a duplicate drawing. I had to get it flat and the only thing with enough surface area was this huge mirror. I laid the decal on the mirror. A photo of the graphic could have also been used.

HANDY HINT

The bird decal did not stay in one piece for long. It's old and very fragile. When it began to tear in places, I quickly taped the rips.

I'm going to use tracing paper to draw the bird, but the color differences between two of the bird colors are so slight, that they won't show through the tracing paper. I used a fine line marker to draw a separation between those two colors.

Left: Even though I'm using the longest roll of tracing paper I can find I still had to tape two pieces together. **Right:** Now, it's time to carefully trace all the lines. Take your time when tracing. It's tempting to rush through it but it's very easy to stray from the lines when you trace quickly.

Once the tracing is done, I taped it to the picture window on the back of my studio. It's way too big for any lightbox. And only half of it fits.

I taped a long piece of stencil material across the drawing. I'm using GerberMask as the stencil because it's thick and stands up to abuse. Because the stencil is so large, a lot of stress will be on it as it moved around and used. So it needs to be tough and sturdy.

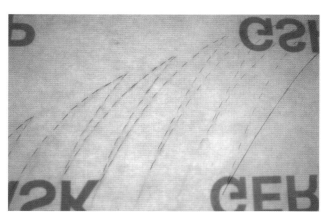

The long edges of the decal bird's feathers need to have smooth, even lines. Freehand tracing will not give me the results I want. So I came up with a little trick. First I drew dotted lines along the feather edges.

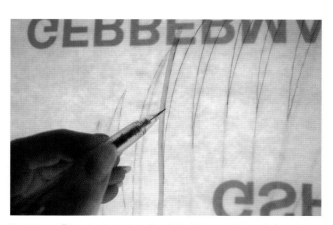

Next, I ran ⅛″ fine line tape along the dotted lines and I traced along that with a pencil. This gives me a nice, even perfect line. And it really didn't take that much longer than freehand tracing. But it's a much better result.

This dotted line, fine line tape, then trace method works great for other areas too, like this big round curve where the bird's wings meet up with the bird's body.

What if you needed to do something like this at night? By the end of this project, I ran out of daylight. A floodlight clamped to the top of a ladder placed outside the window—a common sense solution—solved that problem fast. Now if only I'd had the common sense to not take this paint job.

Bit by bit I worked my way tracing across the bird, adding more Gerbermask as I go, taping it together.

The bird is all traced. But thinking ahead, I know there's a chance I might be cutting the stencil apart. So using a long yardstick I drew a grid across the bird, separating the feather groups. This way if it gets cut apart, it's easy enough to line up the pieces. This also helps to see that the measurements along both sides of the bird are the same, which is very important. One small mistake at this point can turn into a big headache later on.

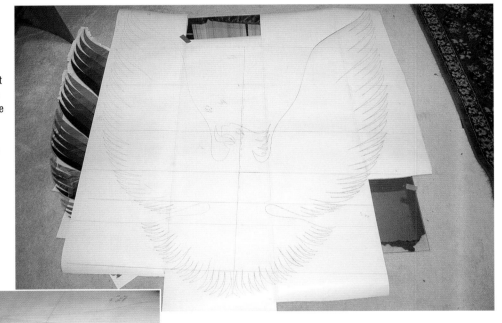

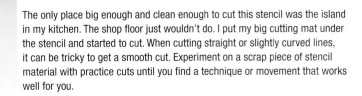

The only place big enough and clean enough to cut this stencil was the island in my kitchen. The shop floor just wouldn't do. I put my big cutting mat under the stencil and started to cut. When cutting straight or slightly curved lines, it can be tricky to get a smooth cut. Experiment on a scrap piece of stencil material with practice cuts until you find a technique or movement that works well for you.

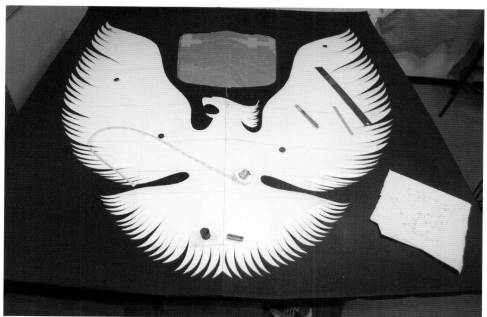

The hood has been wet sanded with 800 and is ready. Using measurements taken from the original decal before it was removed, I placed the inner stencil or cutout of the bird on the hood and secured it with magnets. On the lower right is the paper I wrote the measurements on. The main measurements are from the top of the wings to the top edge of the hood, from the bottom of the tail to the front edge of the hood, and from each side of the bird to the side edges of the hood. I also made sure the bird was centered on the hood.

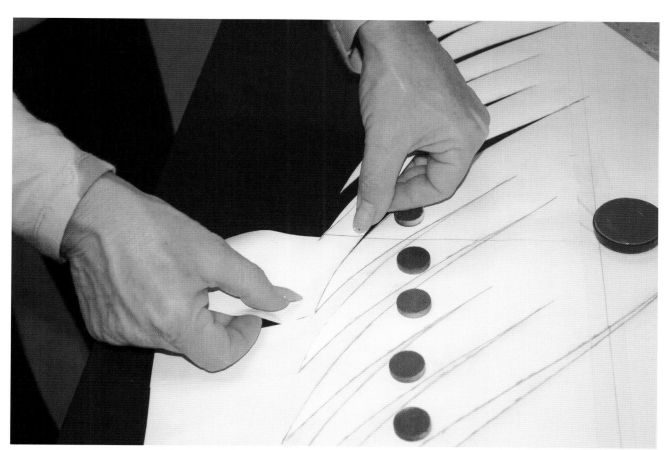

Sure enough, I'm going to have to cut the outer stencil apart. It's too hard to line everything up perfectly. Also the stencil is flat and the hood is not. It looks flat but the surface has a slight curve to it. I had to cut apart and put each feather tip in the stencil in place individually. You can see how the grid lines help make sure everything is lined up. This picture helps show how the pieces are placed, one by one. The feather ends of the inner stencil wanted to curl up, so I used magnets to hold them in place.

One side is done; now to do the other side. Look at all the magnets holding this down. Slowly I made my way around the bird.

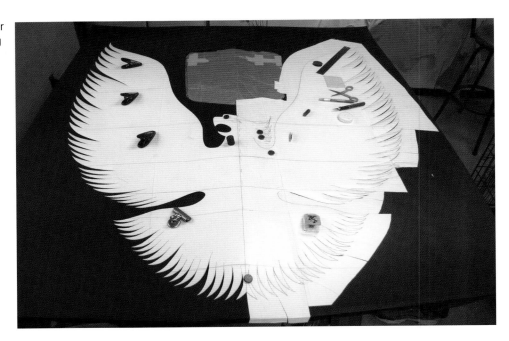

DON'T HAVE AN OOPS!

Always remember, no matter how carefully you place a stencil, little spaces will need to be taped. I ran tape over the places where the stencil pieces were cut apart.

The bird stencil is on the hood and the rest of the hood is masked with masking paper. This took a few hours.

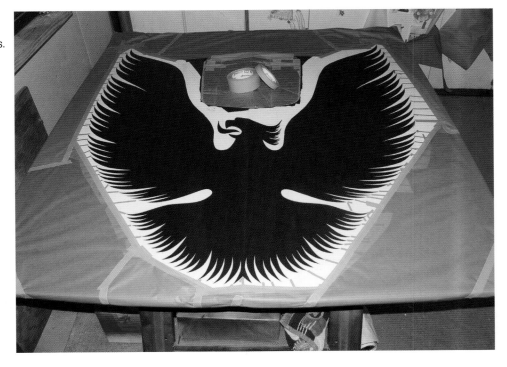

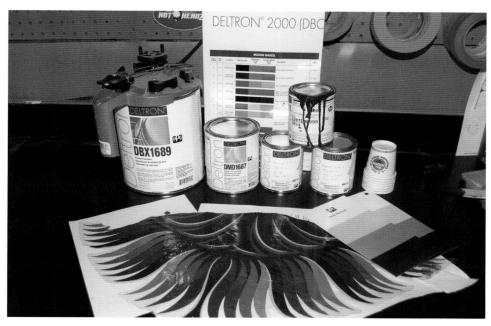

Chapter 8 showed (page 73) how the colors of the bird were matched. These are the PPG tints and ingredients that I used. You can see here how the tail came off the bird decal, which made it a little easier to have a small piece of the decal right there for quick reference. First, I matched the darkest color.

I sprayed three medium coats of the dark brown metallic over the entire area using a SATA minijet 3000B.

HANDY HINT

When working on parts with sharp corners, it's real easy to bump into them. To protect the part and yourself, wrap a folded, thick paper wipe around the corner and tape it in place, creating a pad on the sharp edge.

I flipped the tracing paper drawing over and I traced along all the lines in pencil. This will create a kind of carbon paper to transfer lines of the design to the hood. Note the inset on this picture. The bottom feather of each grouping of feathers—the one that is the background of the bird—is the darkest color. That is the first set of feathers. The area next to that bottom feather is the next area, which will be masked off. We'll call those areas Feather #2.

I lined up the tracing paper drawing on the hood.

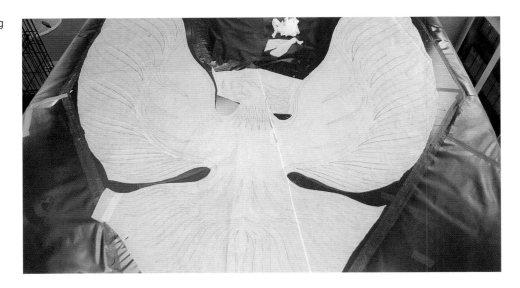

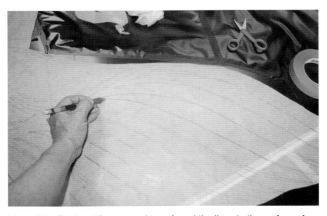

I traced the Feather #2 areas and transferred the lines to the surface of the hood.

I ran ⅛″ fine line tape carefully along the pencil lines on the hood left behind from the tracing.

Here's the second set of feathers, all taped off.

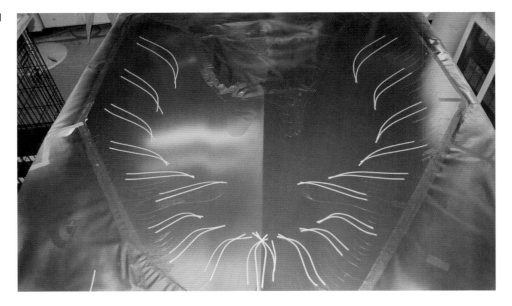

HANDY HINT

To help keep the main stencil from peeling when removing tape, pull the tape back toward any narrow points or ends of the mask. Note how I'm pulling the tape to the right, toward the little point on the end of the main mask.

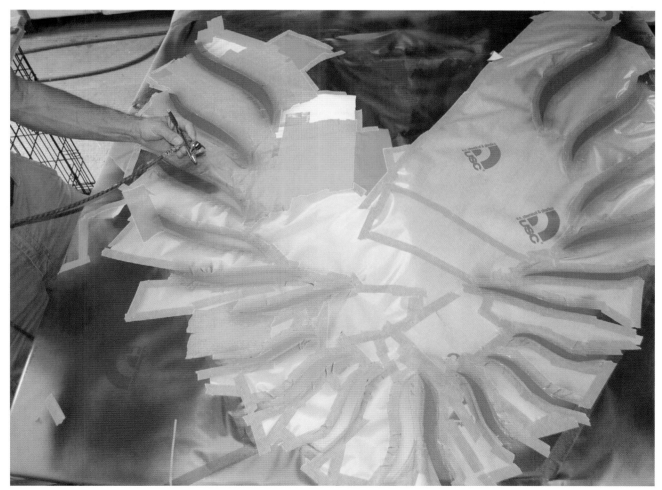

I masked the feathers using American Tape and blue masking paper and sprayed two coats of the next color using a SATAgraph 4 airbrush. The airbrush provides the narrow spray pattern needed. You don't want to get a big paint edge on these feathers. Spray medium even coats, not heavy ones.

I carefully removed the masking. I worked so I didn't pull up the bird stencil underneath. This is why using good quality masking materials is important. I traced the next row of feathers, call them Feathers #3, onto the surface and taped off and sprayed them using the same techniques as before.

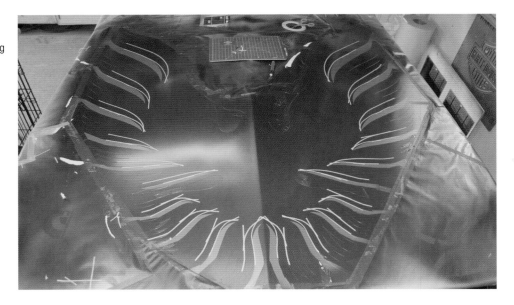

I laid out the next set of feathers, Feathers #4. But here's a little trick to help line up the stencil. One of the things with a graphic or logo this complex is that every layer painted has to be completely aligned to the other layers. If the drawing is not placed properly, it may line up in one place but not in another place. And the more layers that go on, the harder it gets to keep everything aligned accurately. So the inside tips of each Feather #2 were cut out. That cutout is lined up with the tips of each #2 Feather. Now, the next layer of feathers can be traced and transferred.

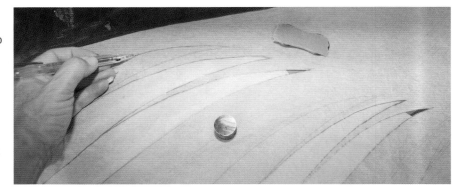

I sprayed the fifth and last layer of feathers. The SATAjet 20B works great for spraying the feathers, maybe better than the airbrush.

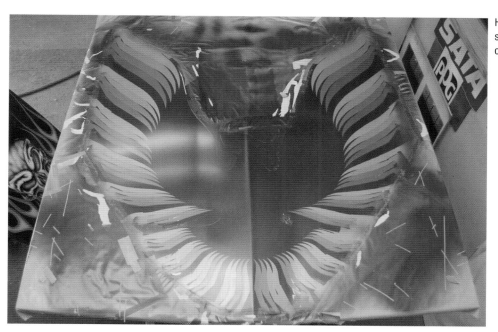

Here are the feather layers all sprayed. Next, I moved on to the body of the bird.

Using the cutout of the main stencil, I trimmed the outer wing and tail feather sections away from the body of the bird. Looking at the left side, you can see how the feathers are closely trimmed away leaving plenty of room around past the lines of the inner parts of the wings. Next, I cut the lines outlining the inner wings with a #11 X-Acto knife and cut apart at the top of each feather; refer to the right side. These pieces are then placed around the bird; refer to the left side of the photo.

Once the backing is peeled away from the cut stencil pieces, the pieces are placed around the bird's body. I masked the outer feathers and the tail. This is what my TA bird looked like at this point. This will be the new work area for the second step.

Using the tracing I made earlier, I created a new stencil for the first color layer for the head of the bird. This layer will end up as an outline but it's easier to do it as a solid layer then paint another layer over it, leaving the outline. The bird head is lined up and magnets hold it in place.

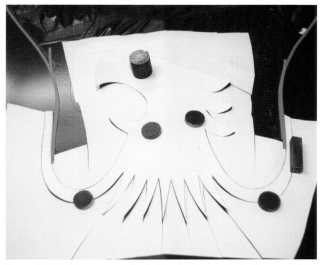

The main techniques seen earlier in this chapter are basically repeated for the head area. Create a stencil using a light table, cut it out, put the inside part or inner stencil into place, cut up the outer stencil, and place the pieces around the inner. Here that process is seen on the head.

HANDY HINT

For big projects that are flat surfaces, it's easy to keep dust off the part when it's not being worked on. I taped two pieces of masking paper together to keep a clean cover on the hood. Then, I laid my tracing paper drawing over that and the original decal for the bird. This arrangement kept those pieces from becoming damaged when I wasn't working on the hood..

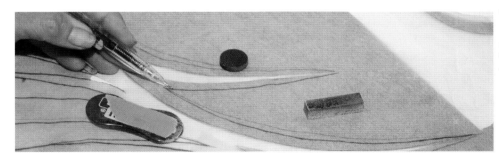

With the stencil for the head in place, I placed the bird tracing paper over the area and transferred the gold parts of the inner feathers by tracing, like I did for each outer feather group.

Here you can see the gold area taped off. It runs along the edges of the inner feathers and connects with the head. Now, to mask off the areas that will remain brown.

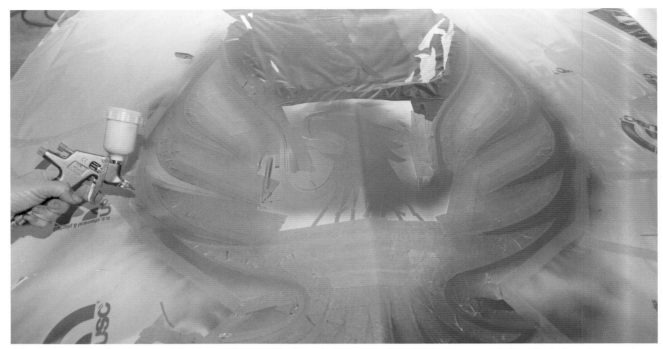

Using the SATA 20b artbrush, I sprayed #3 gold onto the areas. The first color I'm spraying is the third color sprayed for the outer feathers, the second darkest gold. Don't go too heavy—get even coverage with the gold—but don't flood it over the area, as it will build up a thick paint edge.

Left: No two graphics job will be the same. There is no set process to it. You break it down into parts as you go along. The main area of the bird's head is the next gold, #4. Using the light table and the inside piece of the head stencil, I traced the line of that part of the head onto the stencil piece and cut it out. On the left side of the photo, you can see where I've already starting putting the stencil pieces into place around the inner stencil. I placed the stencil around the head, then removed the head piece, masked off the area, and sprayed the #4 gold. The stencil pieces and masking are removed after being sprayed. **Above:** The next section to be sprayed is the yellow highlight color that runs alongside the gold wing and tail feathers. This yellow also runs along the bottom of the bird's neck, that zigzag area. Here I have already taped and started masking the yellow that runs along the edges of the wings.

Left: And finally the yellow highlights around the neck zigzag were taped and masked. Using SATAgraph airbrush, I sprayed them yellow. The yellow color was easy to mix. I started with white PPG DMD1684 and added an orange tint yellow toner DMD 641, a green tint yellow toner DMD1602, and a touch of black DBC9700. **Right:** The eye, nostril, and the stripe-patterned flame by the beak were applied using the same trace, tape, mask, and spray technique. The hood is now ready to be clearcoated then wet sanded with 800 grit. Any uneven lines will be reworked and the hood will be ready for final clearcoat.

Continued from page 219

TRANSFERRING GRAPHICS

Here's a quick and easy low-tech way to transfer graphics. This example uses a motorcycle saddlebag, but the technique can be used for any size of graphic. Just tape together the tracing paper and have plenty of magnets to hold the paper in place. Be sure to take reference measurements around the graphic to reference points on the part or vehicle.

continued on page 238

On the left is the factory painted saddlebag with the graphic. On the right is the new aftermarket saddlebag painted to match and then sanded with 800. Note how the new saddlebag is different. It's an extended bag, which means the lower part of the bag is longer than the stock saddlebag.

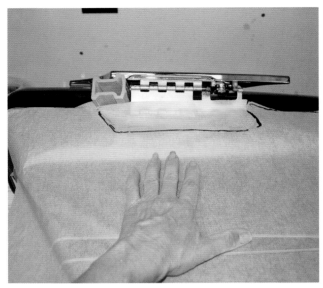 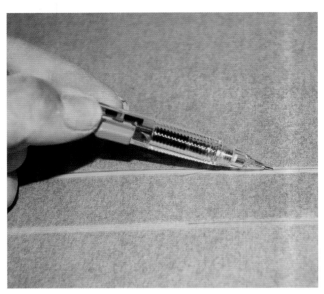

Left: I wrapped a piece of tracing paper around the stock bag. I lined up the top edge of the paper with the top edge of the saddlebag. There's an inset area for the saddlebag latch. This area serves as a reference point, so I drew around it. This will make it very easy to perfectly line up the drawing on the new saddlebag. **Right:** I carefully traced around the graphic. Look closely at where I am tracing the line. I'm tracing midway through the pinstripe around the graphic. This is really important. The reason why? The graphic will be striped. I want the pinstripe to cover the edge of the painted graphic. So the graphic will be $1/16$″ wider than what is seen on the stock saddlebag. This way, when I paint the pinstripe, the paint edge of the graphic will be under the pinstripe, covering that extra $1/16$″, leaving a sharp, clean edge against the graphic.

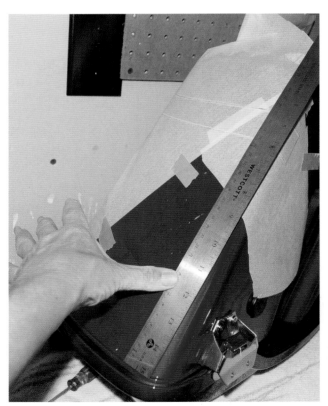 

Left: I added piece of tracing paper to the paper already on the bag, where the graphic goes around the back edge of the bag, then completed the tracing. I took a reference measurement from the bottom of the top edge lip of the bag to the top edge of the traced graphic. **Right:** I flipped the paper over and traced along the back side of the lines.

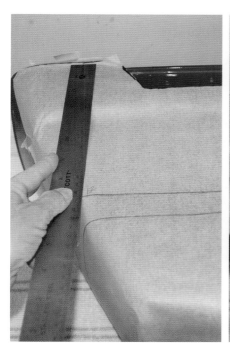

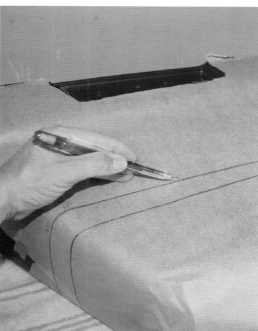

I turned the paper over and put it in place on the saddlebag. After double checking the reference measurements, I taped the paper in place. Then I traced along the line with a pencil. The pencil on the back side of the drawing leaves an image of the design on the surface.

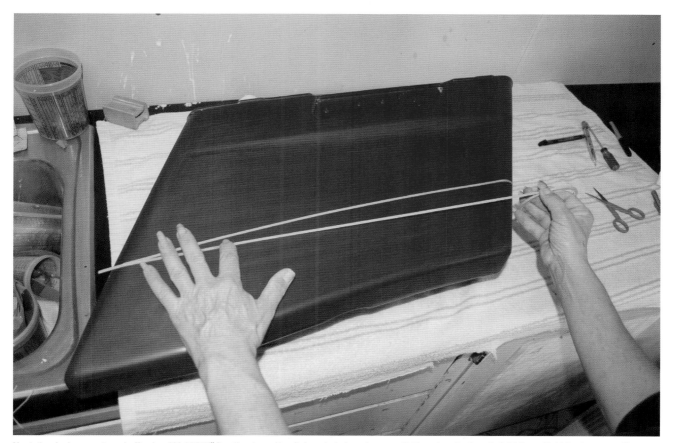

Next, the design was taped off using 3M 218 ⅛″ fine line tape. Here's how to help get a smooth line when taping straight lines. Hold the tape over the reference line and let your other hand gently run over the tape, pressing it into place. This takes some practice. You might not get it perfectly straight the first or second time. It usually takes me a few attempts to get the tape line very straight with no little ups and downs.

GETTING THE KINKS OUT OF THOSE LINES

The left side shows a kink or unevenness in the tape here around the corner. A quick and easy way to fix that is to run another piece of fine line tape next to the uneven area, but run this piece evenly. You'll want to run this tape all the way to one end of the first line. Now, starting at the end you ran the new tape to, rerun the first line of tape using the new tape as a reference, running the old tape right up against the new tape. The right side shows how the old tape now goes evenly around the corner. This method can be used to straighten out any length of taped line.

For taped lines on a car or truck, simply sight down the line from an angle. Then, using a pencil, mark the uneven areas on the tape line. Next run a new tape line up against it, paying attention to run it straight in those areas. Finally, rerun the old tape line against the new one. You don't have to be a taping expert to run straight tape lines.

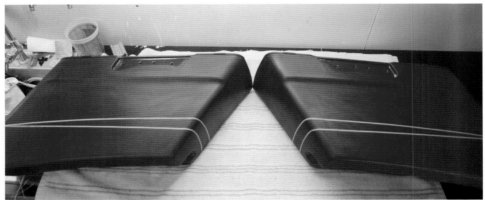

Here are the new saddlebags all taped off and ready for masking and painting. It was easy to transfer the graphic to the other saddlebag. I simply flipped the trace drawing over, used the reference marks and measurements to line up the drawing, then traced along the lines. After I was done painting, I checked carefully and removed any pencil marks that were left on the surface. To see the end result photo of this paint job, refer to chapter 8 (page 78).

REVERSING AND TRANSFERRING A GRAPHIC

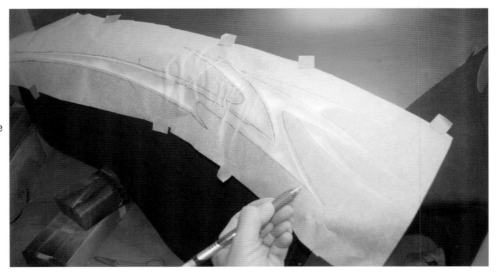

Ever wonder how painters get those amazing mirror reversed graphic effects to look so perfect? Using the previous technique makes it pretty simple. For this motorcycle fairing, I needed the graphic on the right side of the fairing to match the left side. The end result design will be split down the middle of the fairing. A piece of tracing paper is taped over the taped off design. I traced along the tape edge.

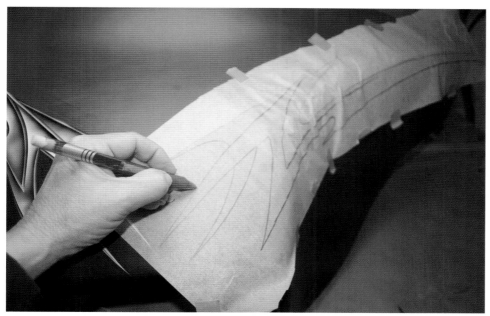

Then, I flipped the paper over and put it in place on the other side of the fairing and traced along the pencil lines. Using the reference lines on the surface, now I can just tape, mask, and spray the design.

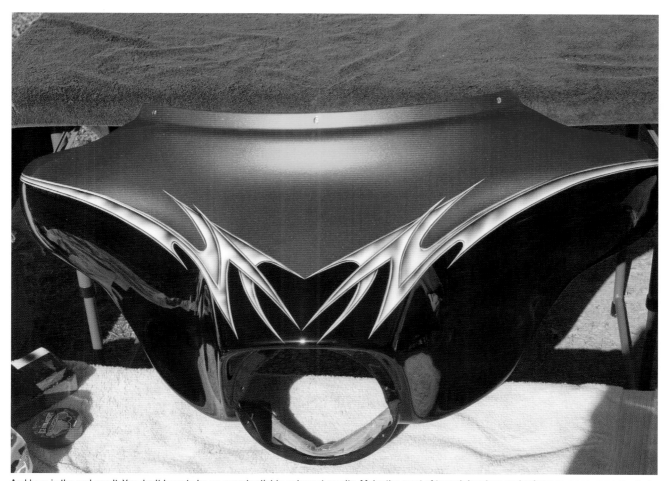

And here is the end result. You don't have to be an expert artist to get great results. Make the most of traced drawings and reference measurements. Just be sure to go back and remove any pencil marks that are left before you clearcoat.

This transfer method is a great way to transfer designs from one side of a vehicle to the other side. Simply flip over the drawing on the other side of the vehicle or part.

Continued from page 233

MULTIPLE LAYER GRAPHICS WITH WATERBORNE PAINT

When dried properly, waterborne paint dries quicker than solvent-borne paint and works great for doing graphics. Once waterborne is dry to the touch, it's dry all the way down and tape will not leave marks on it, which can sometimes be a problem on solvent-borne paint. But unlike solvent paint, all the water must be

dried completely from each application of waterborne paint before the next layer is applied.

One factor that makes waterborne ideal for doing graphics is its concentrated pigments; they give better coverage with less paint applied. That means thinner coats, thinner paint edges, and less clearcoat to level out those paint edges. A painter can get through a graphic paint job in less time using fewer materials. PPG's Paul Stoll and Frank Ruiz show how they take a car from primer to ready for the track using PPG's Envirobase High Performance waterborne.

Ever wonder how they do those wild, multilayer racecar graphics? It's simpler than it looks.

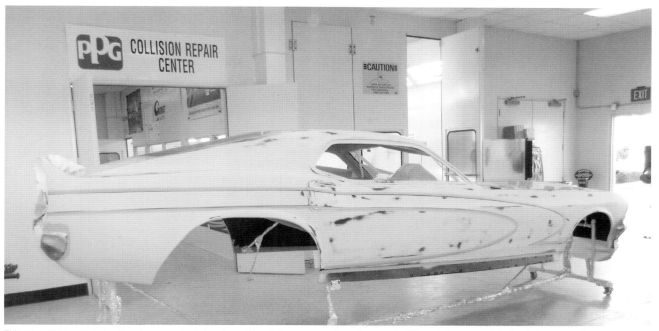

This is what they started with, a funny car body in primer. The dark areas are where they sanded through the primer into the dark epoxy primer underneath. Because waterborne doesn't penetrate as aggressively as solvent, and because in racing, the clock is always ticking, they skipped applying a sealer. The highly concentrated waterborne paint will cover any tonal inconsistencies in the surface and flow right over any sanded-through edges without irritating them.

The guys transferred the design to the surface and taped and masked off the first layer, which will be white. Note how wide the layer is compared to the white in the previous photo. The silver layer will be part of the application of white.

NO CHEATING!

One of the most critical pieces of advice this author can impart about doing any kind of painting with waterborne is that *you cannot cheat when spraying it!* Cheating refers to any one of these shortcuts:

- Piling on heavy coats
- Not waiting long enough in between coats, allowing the paint to flash
- Trying to flow out a surface flaw by applying thick or too many coats of paint

The reason that avoiding cheating is so important is that when doing graphics, the wet waterborne can rewet the waterborne layer on which you are applying graphics, allowing paint to actually flow under the edge of the tape and go into the paint that is taped and masked off. The paint is then trapped until you remove the tape. At that point, the tape will pull up the paint. The end result is not good.

Every painter tries to cheat. And as we always find out, it's not worth it. So don't cheat, not with solvent, and especially not with waterborne. It's not needed.

Frank sprayed the first coat of white on the car. Look closely at the white. Notice how it doesn't look overly wet. Yet, it's not dry. He applied a medium to light coat. As soon as he finished spraying, he turned on the air blower towers in the booth to dry the paint. He could have also used a hand-held air dryer to dry out the water. He would have started at one end, worked his way around, drying out the water as he went. It doesn't take that long. The average flash time for solvent basecoat is 10 minutes, and that is about how long it would have taken to use a hand-held dryer to dry the first coat of white, and it's completely dry, not just flash dry.

Frank has applied three coats of white EHP T400 (Envirobase High Performance) reduced 30% with T494 Waterborne thinner, to the body. It covered any color differences in the undercoat better than three coats of solvent basecoat. This was followed by a few coats of a waterborne white pearl. This formula consisted of 150 parts VWM 5556 Vibrance waterborne midcoat clear mixed with 50 parts T 4000 Crystal Silver and 2 parts VM 4141 White Flamboyance. This was also reduced 30% with T494. Now, the surface thickness of these coats is less than solvent base would be. That means less of a paint edge. All the masking has been left in place and the silver part of the graphic has been laid out and masked. The silver will use the white, which was just sprayed, as an undercoat. Always try and plan your graphics.

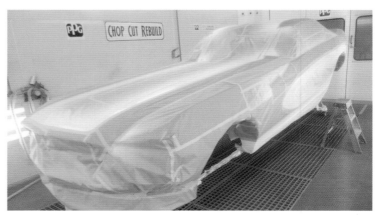

HANDY HINT

It always helps to draw renderings prior to doing the artwork. You can create a blank by whiting out the car on an enlarged copy of a photo of the vehicle. Then, simply make copies of the blank and draw up as many versions as needed until you find the rendering that works for you. On top, you see the drawing Paul did for this race car. On the bottom are two versions of the artwork I did on my truck.

HANDY HINT

When using waterborne or solvent paint, always reduce your paint depending on the temperatures and conditions in the shop. Refer to chapters 10 and 11 for more details.

Frank next sprayed the silver, using PPG's EHP T 475 mixed 1:1 with T 476 Coarse Lenticular Metallic. Note the gun's distance to the car. Gun distance is critical when it comes to waterborne. It dries fast, and if the gun is too far away, some of the paint droplets might dry before they reach the surface. Next, the masking over the white was removed and VWM 5556 Vibrance waterborne midcoat clear mixed with T510 Engine bay converter was layered over the two colors.

Here's what they have so far. It can seem confusing, but once you break down the elements of a design, it becomes easier to understand. The pearl white and silver were sanded with 800 grit. Now, it's time for the black tones.

Left: All the silver and white have been masked off, leaving the areas for the black tones. Paul mixes up 100 parts EHP T409 Black with 1.5 parts T 476, reduced 30% with T494. **Right:** Two coats of the dark metallic black mixture have been sprayed onto the car. Now they do several simple stripes in the black. Different widths of fine line tape are run side by side across the black areas. The wider middle sections are removed.

Paul mixes up a lighter black metallic using 100 parts EHP T409 Black with 15 parts T476 Coarse Lenticular Metallic, reduced 30% with T494. A light coat is sprayed over the taped off area. This picture shows what it looks like after the tape was removed.

All the masking has been removed. A gold pearl will be used as base for the red candy. Having a warm color under the red candy will give it a bright, hot glow. They mix 30 parts EHP T477 Extra Coarse Metallic with 30 parts EHP T479 Coarse Silver Dollar Metallic and 40 parts EHP T426 Warm Yellow, reduced 30% with T494.

242

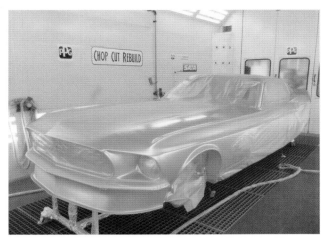 

Left: Frank sprays three coats of this mixture on the car. **Right:** Picking a point halfway down the side of the car, Frank tapes off the bottom portion of the yellow and does several fade stripes. These are pretty easy. Simply line up a few rows of fine line tape. Using an airbrush, spray along the top edge of the top piece of tape. Then, remove that piece of tape and repeat the process, spraying then removing the tape. Frank used 43 parts of EHP T479, 23 parts EHP T435 salmon red, and 6 parts EHP T409 black mixed together and reduced 30% with T494.

Left: Frank repeated this process all around the car, creating what will be a slick ghost effect, once the red candy has been layered over the yellow. In fact, many very cool graphic paint jobs are done using only this kind of effect, painting the graphics directly on the basecoat under the candy. This can also be done with flames or murals. **Right:** Frank's not done yet. He masks off another series of stripes and paints them with the white pearl waterborne mixture.

The finishing touch is five coats of candy red sprayed over the gold areas. Vibrance solvent-based paint is used. For the first three coats, 600 parts of VWM5555 is mixed with 19 parts of DMX 212 red candy. For the last two coats the amount of DMX 212 is doubled. Both of these mixtures are catalyzed with 3610 hardener according to the P sheet. Then all masking was removed and Frank sprayed four coats of EC 700 clear, which he let dry and then dry sanded smooth with 500/600 grit paper. The car shell was then recleared.

Above: Here's a look at one of the ghost effects. The silver stripes on top actually appear darker than the candy. **Right:** One cool detail is to make the graphics go into the around the door jams on both the doors and quarter panels.

The techniques in this chapter can be used to create just about any kind of graphics you want, like these very sleek graphics on this classic Chevy.

Or you can use them to create a graphic that separates a two-tone paint job. This graphic uses a simple beveled edge.

Chapter 22
Faux Finishes: Stone Effect, Wood Grain, and More

Faux effects are some of the most fun techniques to paint. The reason why is that there are very few rules. Many times, wicked cool effects and techniques are discovered by accident. It's a great way to get creative and come up with something different and eye catching. And you don't need to be a great or even a good artist to paint these effects. Faux effects are all about relaxing and creating. It's very much like arts and crafts.

The examples here are just to get you started. As you explore these techniques, you'll find that faux effects can be used in paint design in a number of ways: maybe a small detail along a trim line, a layer in a graphic, or a stone effect panel in a two-tone paint job. Then there's always doing wood-grain framework to make a vehicle look like an old Woody. Make sure to always learn, practice, and test your techniques on a practice panel before you try it on a car, truck, or bike.

STONE EFFECT

Many painters are familiar with the old way of creating a stone effect. You start off with a gray surface, then load various tones of white, gray, and black into an airbrush, then aim the airbrush at the pointed end of a paint stick in front of the gray surface. The paint hits the stick and tiny drips of paint spatter onto the gray surface, creating a speckled granite effect. But a new invention from Mike Lavallee has made it possible to create a different type of stone effect that has great deal of depth. Artool Killer GrungeFX is basically a freehand airbrush template in a can. It's fairly easy to use and you can build up as many layers as you want. Also try using it with pearl colors to create a surreal multitoned effect that has tons of depth.

WOOD GRAIN EFFECTS

Waterborne paint is the perfect paint for creating wood grain effects. Using waterborne has completely changed the way I paint wood grain. Try these EHP colors: dark red brown and T442 Woody Brown are mixed 8:1 with T430 Green. For the darker brown, add a small amount of T407 to the mix. These mixtures are reduced 15%.

Continued on page 249

This is not wood, it's metal trim painted to look like burlwood. This effect was done with a dipping method. The part was painted with a brown base then dipped into black and dark brown paint, which was floated on the surface of some water. It's a tricky technique and takes a good deal of practice to perfect. But there are a number of easier ways to create the illusion of a wood, stone, or metal surface.

The traditional granite effect is a black, white, and gray speckled surface. A variation of this effect can also be created by using sponges dipped in paint, and dabbing the sponges on the surface. This creates more a marbled effect.

Left: Here's what I started with, a panel painted with gray solvent basecoat. And I mixed up four different tones of gray basecoat, varying in degrees of darkness. From light gray to a dark, almost black gray. The Killer GrungeFX comes with two tips, the Fat Splat and Fine Splat. I'm going to start out with the Fine Splat. The can is shaken up good; in fact, the can needs to be shaken before each application of Killer Grunge. Have some clean dry paper towels handy. **Right:** Spray the panel, trying to distribute the Killer Grunge somewhat evenly over the surface. This was my first time using it. I shook the can as I sprayed the product on the surface. Immediately after spraying the Killer Grunge, using a SATA jet 20B artbrush, I sprayed the lightest of the gray basecoats in a light coat. I used a low air pressure, about 20 psi. High pressure will blow the product around on the surface, and you want it to stay in place.

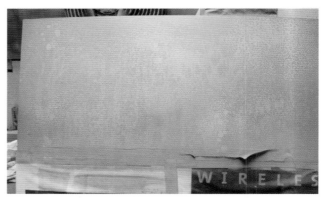

Left: After the basecoat had flashed, I wiped the surface with a clean paper towel removing all the Killer Grunge. Different kinds of paints, acrylic basecoats, and urethanes have different flash times, so be sure not to wipe too soon or the paint may smear. It's just the first coat, and it's already looking good. **Right:** I repeated the first two steps, spraying the Killer Grunge, painting color on it, and wiping it, only using a darker gray. This is the second round.

Left: The process was repeated three more times, until I used the darkest gray. The effect is pretty wild. It looks like a stone surface but a completely different effect than the traditional granite effect. Next I masked off half the panel to try something different. I went in the opposite direction and wanted to try spraying a very light gray, which was reduced down so that it would be transparent. I changed the nozzles and used the Fat Splat. I shook the can as I sprayed and got a pretty even layout of material. **Right:** Light gray was sprayed on the surface and the Killer Grunge was wiped off. This is the end result. Pretty easy stuff, as this was my first attempt using it.

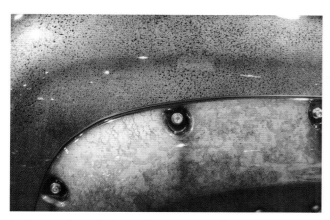

And here's a stone effect using Killer Grunge from the innovator himself, Mike Lavallee. This is a close-up shot from the Duck Truck he painted in 2012. He used the Fine Splat tip on the body of the truck and the Fat Splat tip below it on the fender flare.

The truck is pretty incredible with so much detail. Notice how the lettering on the front of the hood looks as if it's stamped into the surface. Check out the rivets that are airbrushed around the edges.

TOOLS FOR WOOD GRAIN

Painters and artists have a number of tools they like to use for wood graining. And that is one of the fun things about creating faux effects—there are no real rules. Play around and see what you can come up with.

For example, the following technique was pioneered by Charley Hutton. He was doing some wood graining, wiped his hand across the panel by accident and created one of the best wood graining techniques. You can also use sponges to dab the paint on the panel. Or use a brush to dry brush the paint. Or airbrush the rings or grain in the wood. Most of the time, I use a combination of all these tools. The bottom line is to use what works for you.

I started out with a panel, which I sprayed with a pale yellow. The panel will have a three-plank panel effect painted on it. I planned on doing each plank with a different wood grain effect. I used FBS ⅛″ tape #48710 to space out the planks. FBS ProMasker is used to mask off the individual planks as each one is separately painted.

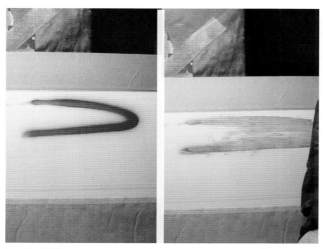

I used a SATAgraph 4 airbrush and sprayed a sharp curve on the board. Then wearing a disposable glove, I wiped the side of my hand across the still wet paint, dragging it back across the surface. And that is the basic technique: spray some paint and drag it across the surface. This creates the rings in the wood grain.

HANDY HINT

When using waterborne, for most transparent tones you'll need to reduce the colors by mixing in some clear basecoat. Try Evirobase T490 or Vibrance VWM5556 waterborne midcoat.

Left: Here, I repeated the technique using the lighter, more transparent brown, sprayed the curve, then dragged it, wiping it across the surface. **Right:** The beauty of waterborne is once the water dries out of it, you can add as many layers as you like over it and manipulate each layer as you like, while minimally or not disturbing the layer under it. Just make sure to dry out each layer as it's sprayed. Here, you can see where I started spraying the curves on the top of the previous layers, and then wiping them, forming more rings. I also used a paint brush on the sticky surface, dry brushing it across. Then, I dipped the brush in some of the red brown tone and dragged across a piece of paper, leaving most of the paint on the paper. Finally, I brushed across the painted surface, adding more lines of wood grain.

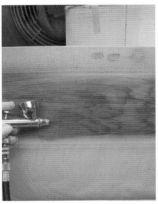

Left: On the left, the surface is starting to get a little sticky. This allowed me to get a more defined ring when the freshly sprayed paint was wiped. On the right, once the rings were all done, I airbrushed some very transparent red brown on it to richen up the tones. **Right:** I created three different kinds of wood grain on the panel. For the top plank, most of the grain was created using the hand dragging method and some dry brushing. The middle plank was created by using an equal combination of hand drag and dry brush technique. For the bottom plank, the technique combination was using the spray and hand drag to create the rings, using an airbrush to accent the rings, then dry brushing to accent the grain of the wood.

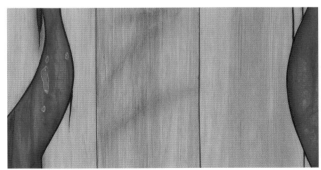
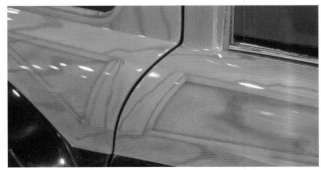

Left: Charley Hutton painted the wood grain on this surfboard for SEMA Show 2008. The effect is a combination of most of the techniques explained in this chapter. **Right:** Here's an example of wood grain created by airbrushing the lines of grain. Notice the inset beveled panel effect. This was done by taping off the bevels, airbrushing the grain, and then shadowing.

Continued from page 245

BRUSHED ALUMINUM EFFECT

Knowing how to create a bare aluminum brushed-metal effect can come in handy. This effect is very easy to create. There are two ways to create this effect. The first way will be shown in the step-by-step photos and involves using a very fine silver pearl and working on a urethane clearcoated surface. The other technique is spraying a very fine silver and then using a red scuff pad to scuff lines across the painted surface. The trick is to get the lines as straight as possible.

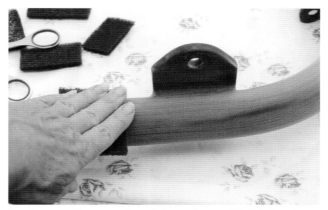

Here, I was working on a motorcycle frame. It was painted black and then cleared coated with PPG DBU2021, which was mixed 2:1:1 with DCX61 hardener and DT885 reducer. Once the clear had dried, I used 3M Scotch-Brite 7747 to scratch straight lines all across the surface. After the scratching was done, I thoroughly cleaned the surface with a precleaner like PPG DX320 to remove any sanding residue.

Next, I sprayed a very fine silver pearl or metallic over the scratches. PPG Vibrance Liquid Metal VM4201 is perfect for this. I sprayed two very fine coats. Do not spray medium or heavy coats. You don't want to fill the scratches with paint. Here is the effect on the frame compared to an actual piece of brushed aluminum.

Here's the finished brushed aluminum effect on a motorcycle tank after it's clearcoated. Like I said earlier in the chapter, this effect can done in reverse when it needs to be done over basecoat. Simply spray silver basecoat and scratch the lines in it with a scuff pad. The result is a little different, but it still has that brushed metal look.

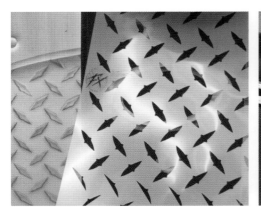

On the left, this brushed metal effect can also be used to create a wicked cool diamond plate effect using Artools' KFX 4SP Diamond Plate Template. On the right, here's another example of using faux effects on a paint job; a stone effect trim line on a Nova.

Chapter 23
Checkered Flag Ghost Graphics: Techniques and Tricks for Ghost and Any Kind of Graphics

Painting a ghost graphic is not quite as simple as it may sound. Ghost graphics can range from fully ghost—where very little paint is applied and the graphic can only be seen from some angles—to more of an easily visible ghost—where more layers of paint are applied and the graphic is somewhat transparent but readily visible.

Chapter 19 showed the process of doing a full ghost flame. In this chapter, we'll be doing a checkered flag graphic that is visible but still somewhat transparent. Please remember that the techniques and tricks in this chapter can be used with any graphic design, especially large-sized graphics and flag graphics. Look it over and apply them to any kind of design you want to do.

Here's the car we'll be working on. The customer wants a checkered flag running down the sides of the doors, coming from the cove or scoop on the side. I'll use this photo to create a blank drawing of the car (because the car is silver, this is easy to do). To make a blank drawing of your own vehicle, scan or download a photo of it into your computer. Use a graphics program like Microsoft Paint or Photoshop to render it black and white and then lighten the photo. Not skilled with a computer? Simply take the photo to a copy store, hit the button for a black and white copy, then lighten it up, and make copies. Most copy machines have a setting for lightening or darkening a picture. You can even use Whiteout Correction fluid to paint out the sheetmetal, then make a copy.

After trying six variations of a checkered flag design, this was the drawing the customer picked. It has a balanced, natural flow to it. The trick with crafting flag- or fabric-styled graphics is to keep it simple but effective. There are two folds in the flag—just enough to give it that illusion of dimension. Having too many folds looks overdone. Note how the checks are not all square; take a checkered flag and stretch it as though it were being ripped by the wind. For more ideas on how a checkered flag looks, go online and use a search engine. There are hundreds of images of checkered flags to look at and use for reference and ideas. Never neatly line up the squares. Now use the blank drawings to play around with the design and see what suits you and your vehicle.

Next, there are two ways to proceed. I can simply draw the same graphic onto the car and then tape that off. Or, to save time and make sure my graphic is the same as the drawing, I can enlarge the graphic to mimic the actual size it will be on the car. In this photo, I have marked off a few measurements needed to do this. I find the measurements of these areas on the car, then crop the drawing so it is only as long as the blue arrow. Using the measurement of the blue arrow, I enlarge the drawing to the actual size it will be on the car. Then I can take the image file to a copy store and print a large-format copy.

CORVETTE DESIGN TIP

Many times, designs on Corvettes look great if they make good use of the coves or scoops on the sides of the car. This is especially true of simple designs and graphics. If you're only doing a small amount of artwork on a Corvette, try running it out of the cove.

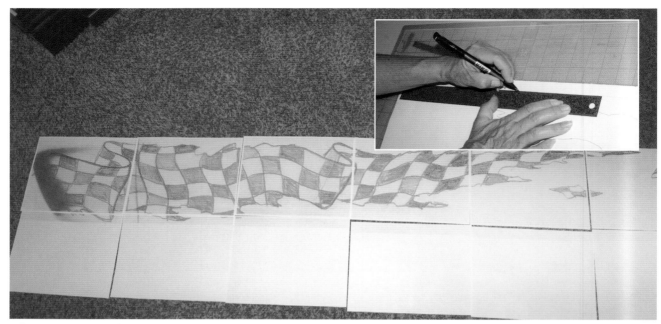

Left: I can also use the Microsoft Paint program on my computer, make sure it is printing at 100% of the size, print a series of 11″ x 8½″ pieces of the drawing, then tape the pieces together using regular household tape, just like taping puzzle pieces together. The next step is to cut a piece of either stencil or Frisket paper that is the same size as the drawing, tape it to the drawing, and put it on a light table or window to trace the entire design onto the stencil paper. But if you are familiar with vector drawings and have a plotter that cuts stencils, another option is to create a plotter-ready vector drawing and simply cut your stencil using the plotter. If you don't have a plotter, you can take the vector file to a sign shop and they can cut one for you. To create the stencil for the other side of the car, simply flip over the enlarged drawing and repeat whatever method you used. Here, you see the pieces of an enlarged drawing waiting to be taped together. Always use a low tack stencil film like GerberMask. I prefer it because it does not leave adhesive residue behind when used over acrylic enamel basecoat. Inset: In this photo, I created a vector drawing and cut out a stencil on the plotter. Make sure to trim the edges of the stencil so that they are neat, even, and square to the design. Having extra stencil material beyond the design makes it more difficult to work around, so trim away any unnecessary material. Carefully measure around the graphic and cut off the extra material.

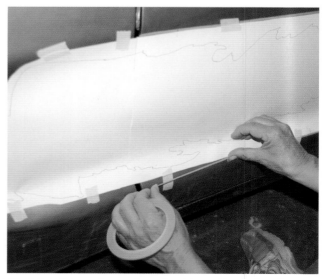

Left: Tape the stencil to the side of the car. Trace around the cuts of the design with a pen so they can be seen from afar, giving an idea of where the graphic will look best. **Right:** Once the stencil is positioned properly, use ⅛″ or any narrow masking tape and tape around the stencil. This will make it easier to place the stencil after the backing paper is removed. Make sure the stencil is pressed flat against the surface. If you are working on a metal surface, you can use magnets to help hold the stencil in place while you line it up. The stencil needs to be cut along the seam of the fender and door. These pieces will go on separately as the stencil needs to wrap around the edges of both panels.

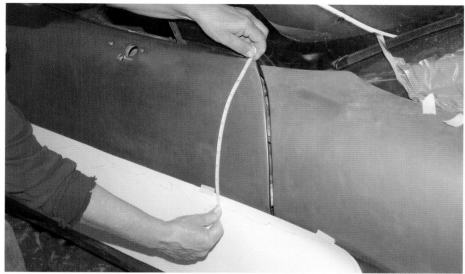

To ease placing the stencil on the other side of the car, simply take a few measurements of the placement of the stencil. For this, I used the measurements from the top of the stencil to the top of the door and to the front and rear of the door. Here, I measured on the passenger side and lined up the stencil. Make sure your stencils are both trimmed the same way or they won't line up.

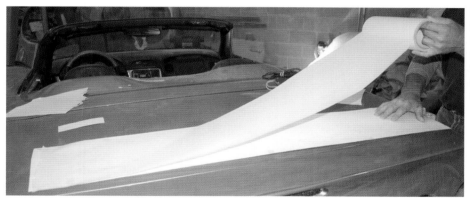

Here's an easy way to handle and apply large stencils. This works for any kind of large stencil. Apply transfer tape to the top of the stencil. Run a squeegee across the surface to remove any air bubbles, then trim off any excess transfer tape that extends beyond the stencil.

Next, preclean the surface of the car with a cleaner like PPG's One Choice SX1005. Spray it on a clean wipe cloth like PPG's Prep-All towels and wipe across the car. With another clean wipe cloth, wipe and remove the cleaner from the surface, making sure to remove all the cleaner. Next, run a tack rag along the surface. Applying the stencil to the surface of the car can be a little difficult, but here's a trick to make it easier (this will work with any long or large stencil). Flip the stencil over and peel away the backing halfway. Don't remove it all. Then, cut it halfway and put the cut material back in place. Now you have a cut in the backing halfway across the stencil. Tape the stencil back in place on the surface and use the tape outline to line it up. Place a piece of masking tape halfway on the stencil, leaving one edge loose to act as a hinge.

Now for the tricky part—this will require a helper. Lift up the loose end of the stencil, peel away the backing, and remove it. Make sure you save the backing and any other backing pieces you remove. Have your helper hold up the end of the stencil, keeping it from touching the surface of the car. Using a squeegee, and starting at the hinge point where that midway line of masking tape is, carefully start pressing the stencil onto the surface. Always start at the middle and work to the top and bottom.

HANDY HINT

Don't try to make your X-Acto blades last. They get dull fast, so don't hesitate to change them often. They are very inexpensive, so stock up and make sure you have a nice sharp blade ready to go.

STENCIL TIP

To help in lining up the stencil, draw lines running from the outline tape to the stencil. This trick makes it easier to line up the stencil.

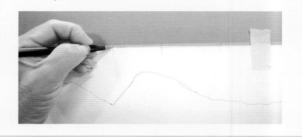

Have your helper hold the back of the stencil up and in place while you work the squeegee. Start working down the stencil using the squeegee in the center of the stencil, working your way to the sides, pressing out the air bubbles as you go.

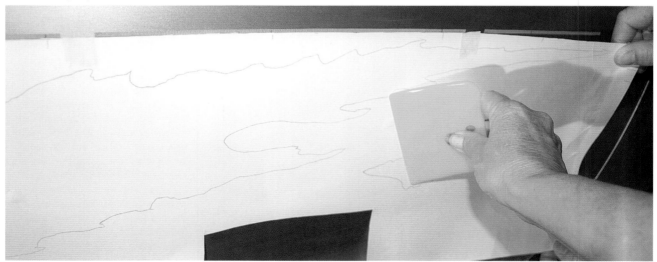

Once half of the stencil is stuck to the car, remove the masking tape hinge and any other tape holding the other end in place. Lift up the stencil and remove the backing.

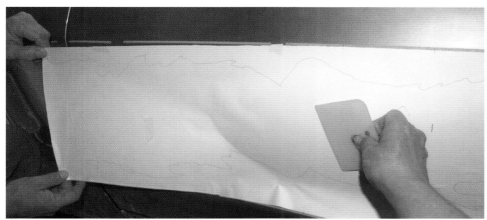

Using the squeegee and starting at the hinge point in the middle of the stencil, carefully press the stencil down. Make sure your helper is holding up the end of the stencil and not letting it touch the surface of the car.

Left: Use the same hinge technique to apply the smaller stencil behind the cove. Now repeat the technique on the other side of the car. **Right:** With the stencil in place, mask off the car with masking paper and plastic. Using the drawing as a guide, remove the black checks in the flag using a pair of tweezers. Remember those backing pieces you saved? Now is when you will need them. Carefully place the removed check pieces on the shiny side of the backing paper in a pattern somewhat similar to how they are arranged in the flag. You'll need them later.

Sometimes the stencil doesn't get fully cut. Keep an X-Acto knife handy and use it to hold down any difficult edges while you are peeling the checks; then, carefully cut any places that are not cut. Take care to only cut through the stencil material and not into the surface of the car.

Left: The stencil may not go around the edges of the panels, but for a cleaner and more finished look, simply extend the stencil with fine line and masking tape. Here, I use a pair of scissors to push the masking tape down past the edge of the panel. **Right:** At the front of the stencil where it abuts the cove of the vehicle, part of the stencil needs to be trimmed, as it does not extend far enough. It's easy to take an X-Acto Knife and cut and extend the checks.

Here, you can see how it looks after I extended the black checks. Now I have to extend the masking on the other checks using masking tape.

Left: Once all the masking is done, spray the black checks with black pearl paint using an airbrush. Before spraying the real thing, though, spray a test panel that is the same color as the car. Lay a piece of tape on it and test your colors to fine tune the mixture. Next, gently wipe the surface with a PPG SX1070 tack rag to remove any dust or debris. Spray a very light coat of black pearl on the car. Then, using the tweezers, lift up a corner of one of the masked-off checks and judge if you have sprayed enough black. Always remember that it's much easier to apply more paint than to remove it if you've sprayed one coat too many. **Right:** Once the black checks are sprayed, it's time to mask them off. Grab the check pieces you saved. Using the tweezers, place each check piece where it belongs. It can get confusing, so take your time and think of it as a jigsaw puzzle, putting pieces into place. The stencil material does stretch so you may have to trim any checks that have stretched out of shape.

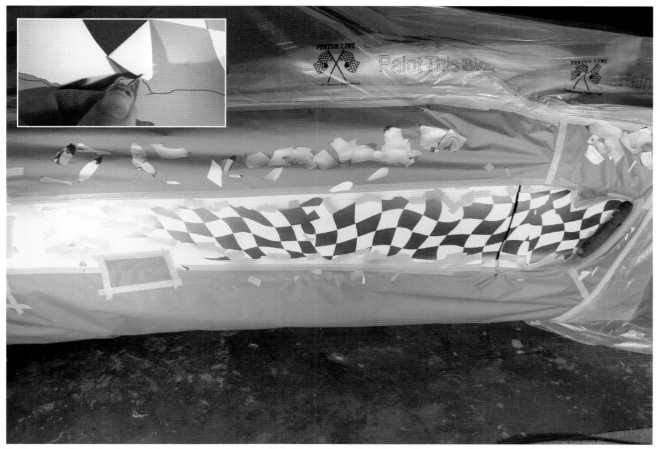

Inset: Remove the white checks of the stencil using tweezers. **Main image:** Remember to tape off any exposed seams of the black checks, especially in the front of the cove where the stencil does not extend far enough. Lightly spray the lighter pearl color, using the same technique as used with the black.

Here, I've created a template for the shadow in the front side of the fold and sprayed a little black. Remember this is a ghost image, so don't spray too darkly. I then sprayed the rest of the folds in the flag using the same technique.

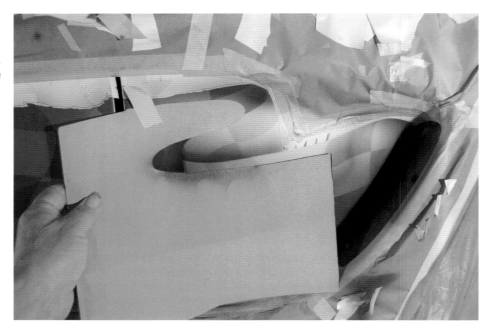

Once the folds are shadowed, it's time to spray the highlights and shadows on the flag. This is where any image research you did will come in handy. If you printed any of those images, look them over; see how the shadows and highlights fall across the surface of the flag fabric. Start airbrushing those shadows and highlights very lightly. For the highlight colors, *slightly* lighten up the color you used for the white checks. Here, I picture where my shadows are and airbrush them in, creating an area of the flag that seems to puff or billow outward. Note how the shadows tend to have a highlight that runs next to them. Here is another area where a test panel comes in handy. If you don't have much experience with airbrushing, play around on your test panels, trying to duplicate the effects you see in your reference pictures. Always remember that softer, lighter shadows and highlights are far more effective than darker or brighter ones.

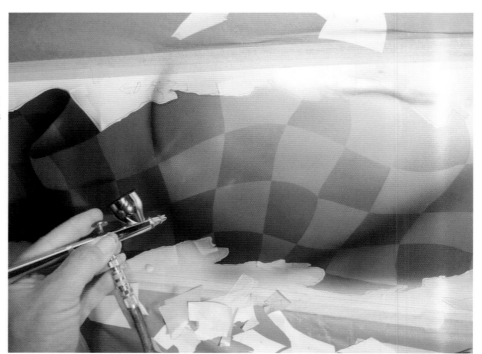

PICKING THE MOST EFFECTIVE COLORS FOR GHOSTING

To find the right color for your ghost color, start with the color you are painting over. You'll want to take that color and vary it just slightly. This Corvette is a silver pewter color. So for the darker checks, I'll use a black pearl, but I'll thin it down so it is very light. The black pearl was created by mixing PPG's PLRX2 Crystal Silver Pearl and DMD1683 Black. For the lighter checks, I'll use a silver pearl that is just slightly lighter than the car's color. In most cases, it's helpful to make a test panel to test your color mixes before spraying them. So make sure you have a test panel ready to go! For more info on ghosting colors see chapter 18.

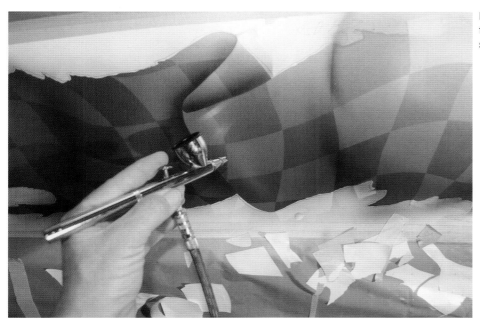

Here, I'm airbrushing a highlight along the top surface of a fold. Note how light and soft the highlight is.

Look over your work, making any adjustments or touchups. Once both sides are done, it's time to remove the stencils. See if any of the paint got past your masking—if so, lightly sand the surface to remove it. Also wipe around the area with precleaner to remove any leftover adhesive from the stencil. Now you're ready for clearcoating. Make sure your first coat of clear is not heavy. Do a light to medium coat of clear, allow it to flash, and then apply several more medium coats. Here is the finished result. Remember that you can go as ghost or as solid as you want, depending on how the paint is applied. Play around and have fun with this effect.

Chapter 24
Going Retro with Graphics

These retro graphics may look complex but they are actually easier than you may think. A number of different graphic techniques are combined on the surface of this power chair cover.

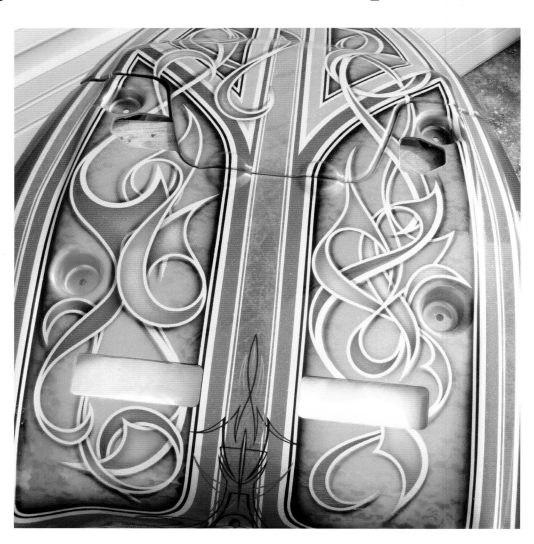

Andy Anderson is one of the pioneers of custom painting. In the '70s, I would drool over his paintwork in the magazines. Andy is a great guy and good friend. He has graciously agreed to share some of his knowledge and pass on a few of his techniques here in this chapter. Andy goes over lace painting, drop shadows, paneling, fades, and more. This is the cover for a power chair, and Andy already had it based in silver flake, cleared, and sanded—ready for artwork. Much of the artwork and candy colors you see on flake paint are done over the clearcoat. So here's Andy!

This was a fun project for me. During the 1970s about 75% of all paint jobs I did were metal flaked with candy color graphics. It seems there's a little resurgence in the flake jobs from those days. Maybe they really never went away, but given the opportunity to do a paint job for a friend, I chose an old flake paint job. I hope you enjoy this process as much as I enjoyed doing this job. The material list is comprised mainly of House of Kolor products.

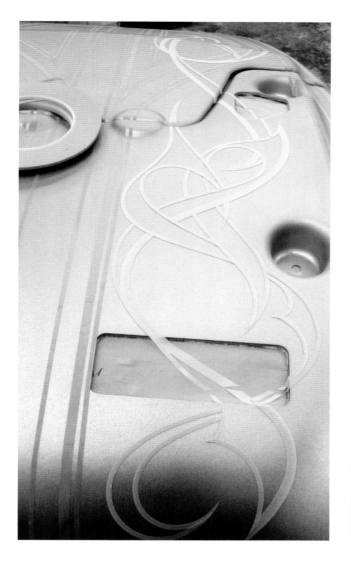

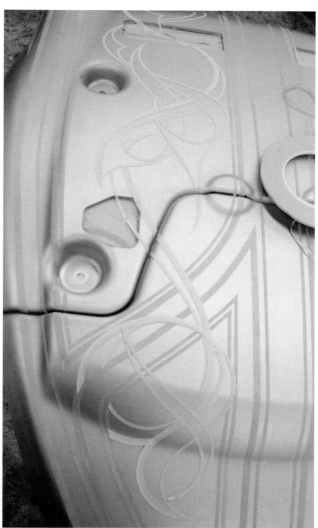

MATERIALS & EQUIPMENT

Paints are not listed as many different colors may be used depending on your project. The paints I used here are noted in the text.

Materials
Plastic mixing cups
Gerson Blend Prep tack cloths
PPG Prep Plus wipes
PPG DX320 precleaner
¼″, ⅛″, 1/16″ fine line tape
¾″ masking tape
Automask masking material
Evercoat paint mixing cups
Lace (found at any fabric store)

Tools
SATA Minijet 3000B spray gun
SATAgraph 4 airbrush
SATAjet 20 B artbrush
X-Acto #11 stencil knife
Solvent proof plastic bottles
Artool Essential 7 templates

Above left: I start this sequence with the silver flake and clear already applied on the wheelchair cover. This is for a long time customer of mine that is slowly becoming disabled. He always had the nicest vans and motorcycles so he asked if I'd paint his wheelchair cover. No problem! I began with ⅛″ and ¼″ tape masking tape to layout the curvy part of my design. This is all freeform—no pre sketch or layout. I just started taping and whatever works for me was what I went with. You can use a pattern made from a drawing or just freehand like I did. For the straight lines, 1/16″, ⅛″, and ¼″ 3M 218 fine line was used. Note how the freehand design crosses over the paneled areas.

Above: This photo gives a better idea of how the curvy design weaves over and under the paneled areas. It's pretty easy to do. Where the freehand design goes over the straight tape of the panels, the straight tape is cut and trimmed away from the inside of the freehand design. Where the freehand design goes under the straight line of the panels, the tape of the freehand design is trimmed away. One thing to keep in mind concerning the freehand/curvy design: the areas the masking tape lines cover will not have any candy paint on them. They will end up being the silver stripe that borders the curvy design. Compare this picture to the first picture in the chapter and it should help you understand. Take your time examining these photos to understand how it works. For your first retro design, draw two very simple designs and weave them over and under as seen above.

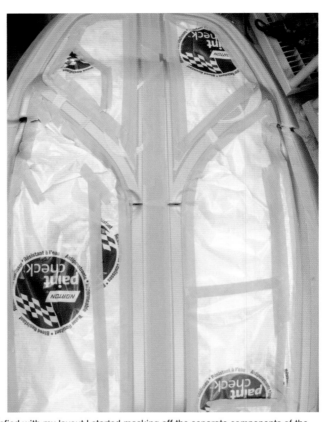

Left: I used a combination of panels and interweaving ribbons. Once I was satisfied with my layout I started masking off the separate components of the design, using masking tape and transfer tape. Here, I have masked off the curly design with transfer tape. Next, I'll mask the panels separately. When doing this on a vehicle, make sure to wrap the tape and masking around any edges like between fenders and doors. **Right:** The panels are masked, leaving the outside borders ready to spray.

Starting with Magenta Kandy Koncentrate mixed with SG-100 basecoat clear, I carefully faded the magenta, front to rear, using my SATA mini jet gun.

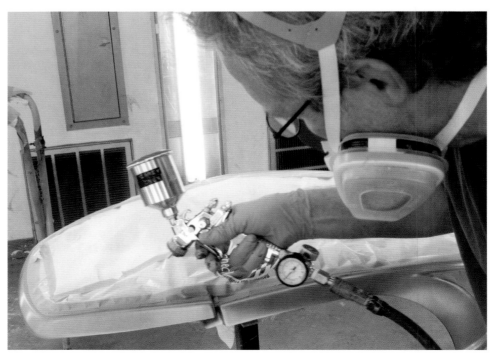

THE FADE FACTOR

Good, even fades with great transitions from one color to the other are not easy. They take practice. Know that the paint will always travel farther than you think and go past the point where the gun is stopped. Practice your fade technique until you know you have a good feel for it. Spray one light/medium coat of one color a little more than halfway across the fade area; then, at the opposite end, do the same with the other color. Then make another pass with the first color but don't go as far as the first pass. Keep repeating with each color until you get the desired result.

Take care where the two fades meet. The spray will be light there, and the surface may tend to get bumpy or gritty looking. This is where practicing comes in. The fade mixture must be reduced enough to blend well but don't overdo it. As each paint is different, there is no universal answer on how much to reduce the paint. Test your fade technique until you get a smooth, even fade.

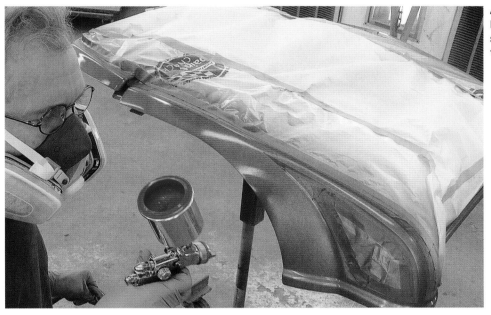

At the rear, I mixed Purple Kandy Koncentrate and started building color strength to fade toward the front into the magenta.

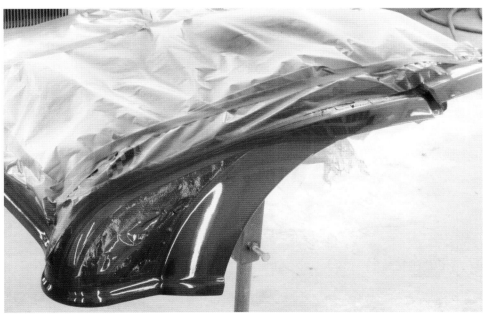

After the fades have dried (I also put two coats of basecoat clear over the fade or any area I spray in steps). After it's dry, I will mask off this area.

After the sides were masked off, I sprayed the magenta to purple fades on the top surface of the cover, using the same blending technique. I reversed my fade on the top border area, going with purple at the front and magenta at the rear. I'm using the FBS orange tape here, which I discovered in the middle of this project. Great product! I wish I had found out about it before I had the whole piece laid out.

Above: I unmasked the magenta and purple fades on the sides. Here, you can see the end result of the magenta and purple fades. **Below:** Next, I unmasked the inner border that will have a candy yellow to orange fade.

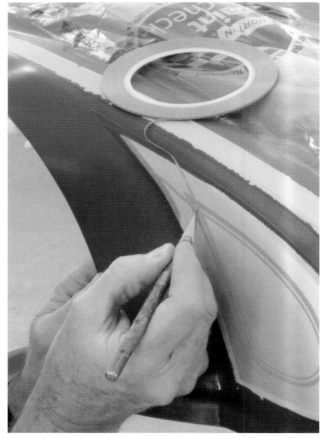

The side panel has the additional taping finished and the teardrop panel on each side is getting an inner ⅛″ tapeline. Using a #11 X-Acto knife, I carefully cut the tape after it was in place. Be careful to only cut through the tape and not into the paint.

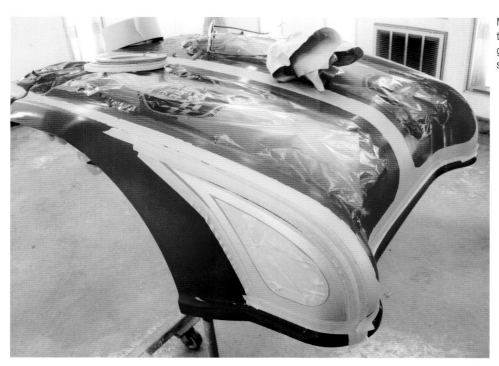

Next, I masked the inside of the teardrop panel. This photo gives a good idea of what the paint looks like so far.

I ran ¼″ masking tape around the edges of all the magenta/purple panels and masked them off.

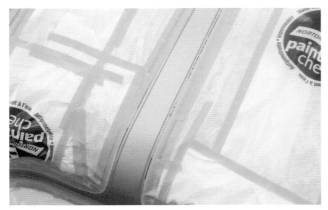

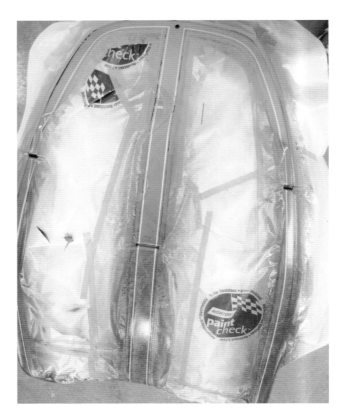

Above: The top is getting an inner ¹⁄₁₆″ tape line. To help space the line from the panel, I ran ¹⁄₈″ tape along the panel; then, the 1/16″ tape was run alongside that. The ¹⁄₈″ spacing tape was then removed. **Right:** For this border, I used HOK Kandy Koncentrate Spanish Gold faded to tangerine and magenta. I added a little texture first before the tangerine was sprayed, then started with my Gold Kandy and faded that back to Tangerine Kandy. Next, I lightly sprayed Magenta Kandy cut with SG-100 basecoat clear over the rear of the area to strengthen the tangerine. Note: I use the HOK SG-100 Intercoat Clear for mixing my Kandy Koncentrates. I mix the clear and Kandy per HOK recommendations. See their tech manual for details. On some applications I may overreduce the Kandy with clear to weaken the color. This helps to build the color a little slower when spraying. It may take a few more coats but it allows for greater control.

TEXTURED EFFECTS

Spraying a textured effect is simple and fun. Just find a web-like fabric (like lace) or an item (like peacock feathers, drywall tape, or a webbed bag that onions come in). Lay it over the area, and spray your paint. Look for more about lace painting later in this chapter.

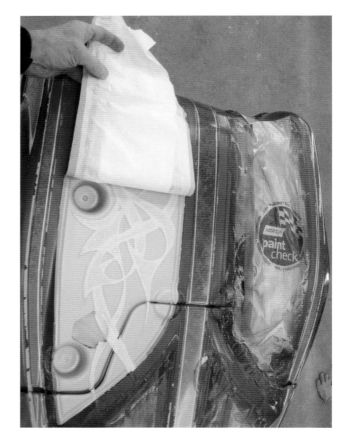

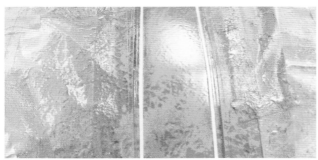

Above: Here's a close-up shot of the textured effect. I used lace for this, but I only put the lace over the tangerine part of the fade. Note the ¹⁄₁₆″ silver stripe in the orange. It was created by putting down the tape line before spraying the orange. **Right:** I pulled the mask off the next set of panels to be sprayed to prepare them for the next stage. Before I sprayed these panels, I have to tape off the areas that have already been painted. Make sure before you tape over any painted area, that it is thoroughly dry. Otherwise the tape will leave marks in the soft paint!

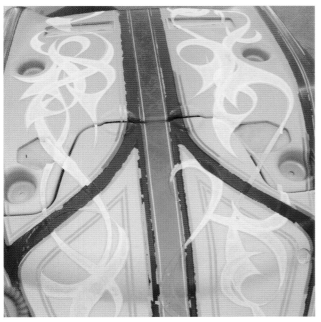

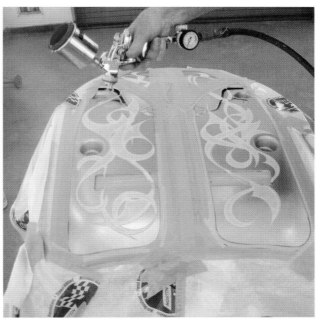

Left: Now I'm ready to mask off the magenta and purple panels. **Right:** The outer panels are now masked and the inner panels are ready for color. I put a coat of basecoat clear over the ribbons to help seal the tape edge. Because I used the old crepe/masking tape on these, I know there will be some paint that will creep under the edge. Don't ask why I used that product! The FBS tape would have yielded a clean tape line. The other choices of tape have limitations on a project like this. I had to leave this project, sometimes for many weeks, and come back. So any tape that would crawl or shrink was out of the question. In the end the crepe worked fine.

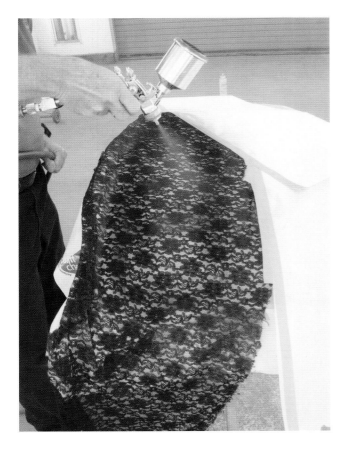

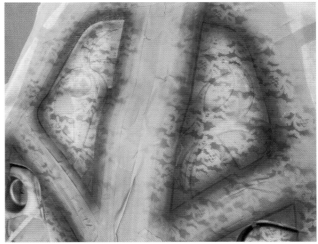

Left: The inner top panel is getting a lace texture. I taped a piece of lace down and began with my Kandy Organic Green, spraying around the edges using a SATAjet 3000 B mini gun. SATAjet 20 B artbrush would also work. Here's a little trick: if you have access to a mist textile adhesive, spray it on the side of the lace that will be against the paint. It holds perfectly, and any residue can be wiped up with a light wax and grease remover like PPG's DX320. Sometimes you can find it at fabric stores or hobby/art supply stores. You don't want a strong adhesive. No industrial strength. If you find some, make sure it will work by experimenting before you try it on your job. All manufactures' adhesives are not the same. Test, test, test! **Above:** I airbrushed the Organic Green Kandy solid around the edge after I pulled up the lace.

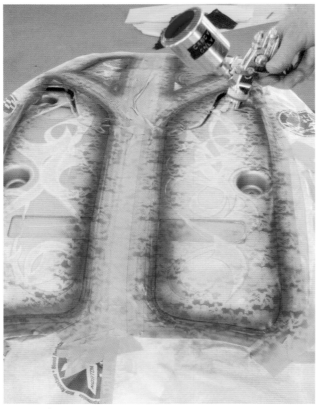

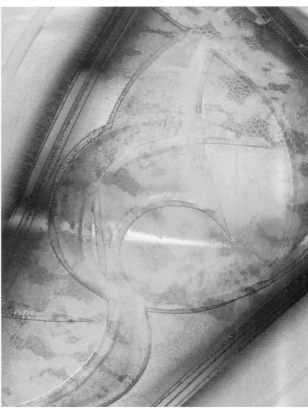

Left: Here you can see the Organic Green border. The next step is spraying the inner area of the panel with Candy Lime Gold. I sprayed on enough coats to get the tone of yellow I wanted. **Right:** A closer photo of the inner panel shows the completed fades in the lace. Next, I airbrushed black around the edge. The black will help define the panel by adding more contrast.

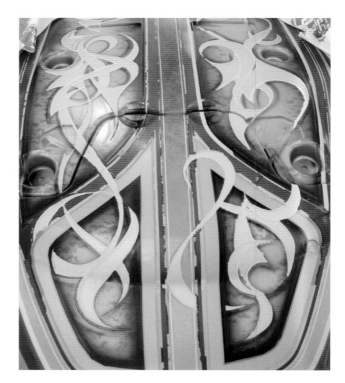

Above: This photo shows the shadows being airbrushed off of the ribbons. For the shadow color, I mixed Organic Green Kandy with some black and a touch of Kandy Purple. This will help to gray the color. The shadow color was cut with basecoat clear. Cutting the color strength with clear helps to gradually build the strength of the color when airbrushing. **Right:** I unmasked any tape that covered the ribbon areas. But only that tape. Look closely; see how the tape for the main panels remains in place. Now I'm ready for taping of the ribbons for individual color spraying.

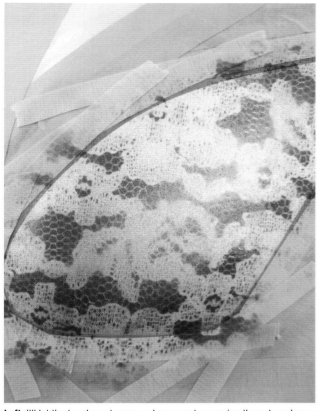

Left: I'll let the top dry out more and move onto spraying those tear drop panels that I taped off earlier on the sides. I airbrushed candy green over a lace pattern. Spray a little coat, lift one edge, and peek under to see if you have the desired amount of color. If not, you can always add more. **Right:** I repeated the candy lime gold and black airbrushed edging on the teardrop panels.

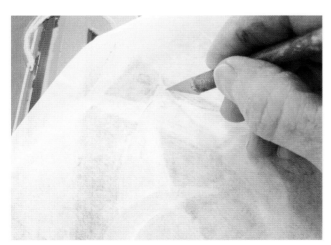

Above: The masking material has been removed from the ribbons; now they will be sprayed. I masked the ribbons with Automask masking material. Automask is easy to cut and doesn't leave any residue. I cut out the ribbons using an X-Acto #11 blade, using care to only cut through the mask and not into the tape below. **Right:** The first set of ribbons to be airbrushed were the yellow to tangerine. Spanish Gold Kandy was faded to tangerine at the ends. I added a touch of magenta at the tips to build color strength. Once the yellow/gold/orange ribbons are all done, the masking over them was removed.

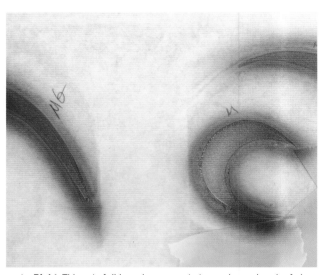

A PAINTING RULE

You can always add more paint. Just spray another coat. It's much more difficult, if not at times impossible, to take paint away.

Left: Here's what it looks like so far. Now to mask off the ribbons that will be magenta. **Right:** This set of ribbons is a magenta to purple candy color fade. I airbrushed magenta candy over the ribbon, and the ends are airbrushed with purple candy. Once these ribbons are completed, I unmasked them and repeated the masking and airbrushing for the blue candy ribbons.

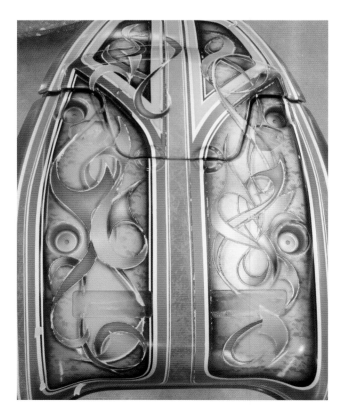

Above: I added a little more detail in some of the ribbons. This photo shows me airbrushing the tips of the yellow/orange ribbons with Magenta Kandy. **Right:** I finished all the main color work, and it's time for the detailed drop shadows over and under ribbons.

GOING RETRO WITH GRAPHICS

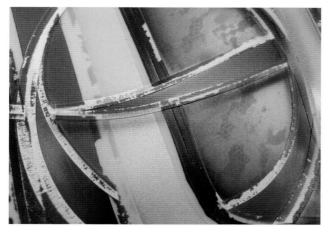

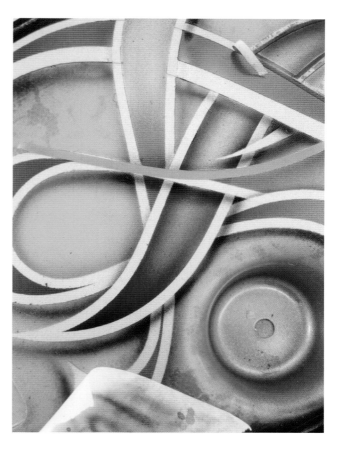

Above: The shadow over the lime gold border is made with Kandy Purple and black and a little organic green. Test your shadow mixtures before you airbrush on the cover. Make sure they are not too dark. Remember, you can always add more shadow. If you need to, hold a shield, such as an Artool template, next to the tape that you're spraying against. You can also make some shields yourself by cutting some simple curves in posterboard. This will help to keep the paint on the side of tape where it's being sprayed and not landing on the other side of the ribbon. **Right:** This is a good shot showing the tape that is pulled up (upper right corner) for airbrush shadowing. Here the shadow runs across a blue ribbon. I'm also airbrushing a shadow over the silver too. When I shadowed the ribbons, I pulled tape from an area that is usually the bottom ribbon. I pulled up tape all the way to the outline tape on the top ribbon so that it could be airbrushed. This part is a little tedious, so take your time.

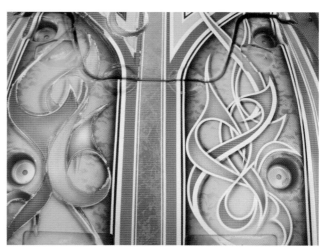

Left: Note the light purple candy used for shadowing over the silver. The soft, not overly dark, shadowing helps build depth in the design. **Above:** This photo shows the right side of the panel with all of the shadowing done and the tape pulled. The left side still needs airbrush shadow work.

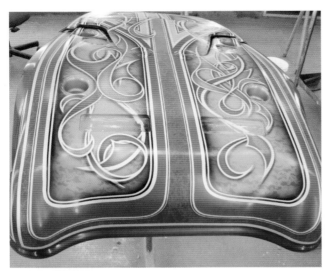

Above: All shadowing has been finished and all the tape has been removed. This is what the project looked like before I sprayed three coats of urethane clear. Now is the time to make corrections or repairs if needed. **Right:** The clear really brings out the color. I will wet sand the panel using wet or dry #500 paper and do this clearing and sanding process one or two more times until I achieve a flat surface over all the taped lines. I added a little personal touch for my friend: his initials in variegated gold leaf and a little pinstriping design. Once you are satisfied with the last coat of clear, you are now ready for the final sanding and buffing process.

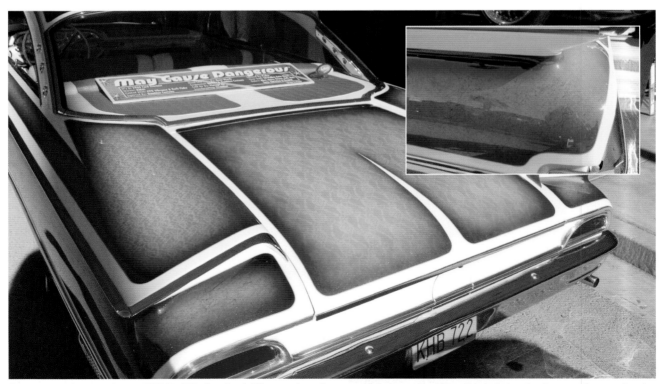

Here are some lace panels on a 1960 Ford Starliner. Inset: Other panels on the same car feature cobwebbing. This technique involves spraying unreduced paint at very low pressure.

This is one wild wagon. The retro artwork here is known as spaghetti striping or endless line. The technique uses 1/8″ or 1/16″ fine line tape to form geometric designs. Painting these require no special skills—just paint the desired background color, run a continuous line of tape, and airbrush the cover color. Some custom painters add a fogged accent to the endless line by spraying a third color, carefully following the tapeline, before the tape is removed.

Above: The custom paint is continued into the door and trunk jams, making for a show-winning paint job. **Right:** Here's another example of spaghetti striping and shadowed panels. The design carries under the windshield and onto the dashboard. Even the roof of this car has artwork.

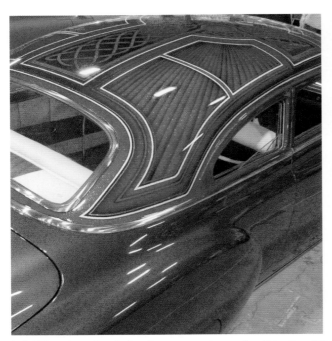

Left: This roof was done by layering green candy over silver flake, then doing black graphics. It was a great idea to two-tone it with a solid gray base paint.
Right: Here is a simple retro design that features simple shaded panels with lace texture.

This is a classic lowrider-style paint job. Note the use of the flake paint in the graphics. Complex designs are simply a matter of breaking down the elements of the design, creating the order in which the elements will be painted, and then, one by one, painting those elements.

Chapter 25
Lettering

Lettering can be easier to do than you might think. You don't need to be an expert at hand lettering with a brush or even an artist. This chapter shows how to use a stencil and an airbrush to create very cool lettering. There are two ways to create a stencil for lettering: using a computer and by hand.

USING A COMPUTER TO CREATE A STENCIL

It helps to know a little about using computer programs like CorelDraw or Adobe Illustrator. If you are familiar with these programs or have a friend who can help, then all you need to do is draw or plot out the lettering or logo you want by creating a plotter-ready vector drawing. For lettering, simply choose a font and type out what you want in either Corel or Illustrator. It's just that simple.

Then take or email the drawing to a sign shop. They will use a plotter to cut the stencil in stencil mask

Simple but effective lettering gives this '37 Ford a great nostalgic look.

material. I recommend using GerberMask Ultra II. But some sign shops prefer using Avery Paint Mask, which is also a good product. Plotter-ready vector drawings for popular images are sometimes found online. Shop around and you may find what you are looking for.

CREATING A STENCIL BY HAND

Chapter 21 shows how to create a stencil by tracing a drawing or lettering onto stencil material by using a window or light box. The example in that chapter is a logo. But you can also trace lettering onto stencil material, cut it out, and use it. Either a hand-cut stencil or computer stencil can be used for the following technique.

I am recreating the lettering on a black panel to demonstrate the process I used on this truck. I fed an Adobe Illustrator vector drawing into a Roland Plotter,

HANDY HINT

If you have a sign shop cut your stencil, be sure to tell them not to weed the stencil! Weeding the stencil is a technical term for removing the cut-out pieces from the stencil. Make sure they leave everything in place. Depending on what airbrush technique you use, these pieces might be needed during the artwork process. So don't lose them or throw them away.

which cut two stencils with the lettering. Once you have the stencil made, the first step is to use a ruler to draw lines around the lettering. This makes it easier to level the stencil and line it up. The lettering will have a border around the letters. This border will be the bevel for the metal effect.

Here's the lettering design and the truck being lettered: a 2013 Ford Raptor. The lettering will be on the back doors as other artwork has been planned for the front doors.

LETTERING

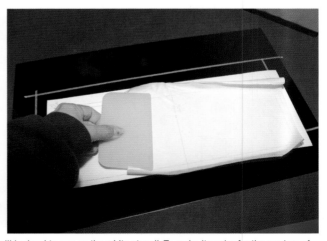

Left: I placed the stencil on the panel/door and taped it in place. The lettering will be hard to see on the white stencil. To make it easier for the readers of this book, I have ghosted the image of the cut letters over the stencil. In reality they would not be seen this easily. I ran fine line tape around the stencil and drew a few lines from the stencil to the surrounding tape. This makes it easier to line up everything later on. **Right:** The stencil was removed from the surface. Next, I placed transfer tape or film on top of the stencil. This helps keeps everything in place after the adhesive backing is peeled off the stencil. I ran a plastic spreader across the surface, forcing out any air bubbles trapped under the surface. Don't worry if it's not too neat; it's just temporary anyway.

Left: Next, I very carefully peeled away the adhesive backing. Sometimes it's easier to peel away half of it, cut that part off, then peel away the remainder. Refer to Chapter 23 for more information on handling stencils and an easy technique for applying them. I next lined up and put in place the stencil with the transfer paper. I started at the top, holding the stencil up and away from the surface. I lined up the top edge so that the lines I drew matched up. Then I pressed down the top of the stencil. Working from the middle top, I carefully pressed the stencil down to the surface. **Right:** Next, I masked off the rest of the surface around the stencil. The middle of the letters were then removed using tweezers; each letter was carefully pulled up. Keep a small ruler or other flat edged tool handy to hold down areas of the stencil that might want to pull up with the lettering. If you have a cut border around your letters like this one, make sure to leave it in place. I placed the removed pieces/letters on the pieces of backing that were removed from the back of the stencil, saving them.

Metal effect lettering has reflections, but the reflections are most effective when they are soft and even. Notice the diagonal lines I drew on the stencil. The lines make it easy for all the reflection lines to have the same angle across the lettering. I then reduced white basecoat to about 1:1 with reducer and loaded a SATAgraph4 airbrush. I airbrushed light strokes across the letters and concentrated on the left side and lower edges of the letters.

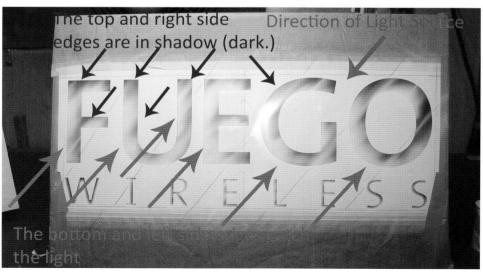

This photo shows as well as explains how the white/reflection areas are airbrushed. The technique is pretty simple: white on two edges and dark shadows on the other two edges. I airbrushed the top and bottom letters the same way.

This photo shows me airbrushing the lettering on the actual Fuego Raptor. Note how I first airbrushed the reflection lines in white. Then I sprayed white on the edges. One trick is to have a reference photo to work from. Keep it nearby your work area to look at while you're airbrushing.

With the white/reflections done, I airbrushed the darks/shadows. I mixed black basecoat 1:1 with reducer. If the black sprays grainy or rough, mix a little more reducer into it. I airbrushed the right and top edges with black. And some black was airbrushed along with the white diagonal streaks. The bottom letters are very thin, so I held the airbrush close to the surface and sprayed a fine line of shadow on the bottom and right edges.

REMEMBER THE LIGHT SOURCE

Whenever airbrushing a 3D effect like metal letters, remember where the light should be coming from. In this Fuego lettering, the light is coming from the upper right. Think about how the light hits the objects. It tends to put some edges in shadow, usually the top edges, and reflect light on the other edges, usually the lower edges.

Airbrushing the bevel is the same principal as airbrushing the middle of the letters. Think dark shadows and light reflections. The same process as before will be repeated for the bevel, only in reverse.

Left: I airbrushed the white edges very lightly with white once more. Don't overdo this step. **Right:** Next, I peeled off the outer border of the stencil lettering.

Left: Here is why you had the sign shop cut two stencils. Place the inside pieces of the letters over what has been airbrushed so far. If you are using a hand-cut stencil, use the pieces you saved from the earlier step. Place the pieces over the letters covering what was airbrushed. **Right:** This photo shows the result of the step I'm about to do next. The uncovered area around the letters will become the beveled edge. The letters on the right have had the bevels airbrushed. The next photos show how to airbrush that edge.

Using a business card or card with a straight edge, hold the card across a corner of one of the letters and airbrush white on the topside of the corner. Repeat this with each top corner of the letters. Then airbrush white on along the inner edges of the border where the light would hit it. You want to have the inner edge of the bevel or border contract against either the black or white of the masked off letter. Here, I'm spraying along the inner edge of the border on the top part of the U. Give the border of each letter a light dusting of white.

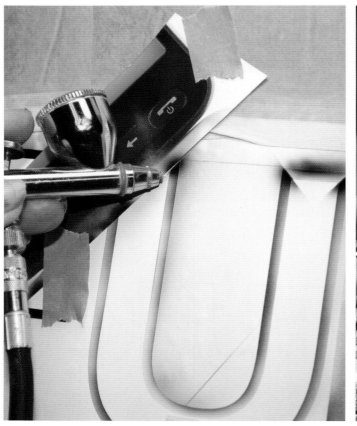

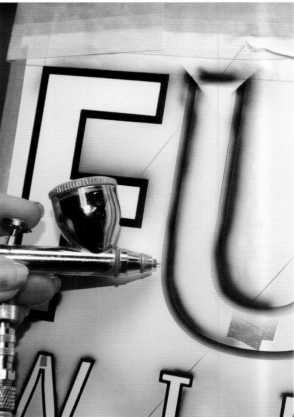

Next, I repeated the process with black, only I sprayed the areas that were not sprayed with white, like the downside of the corners.

Left: After I did the top and bottom letters with the black shadow, I softly went over the white reflections again—very lightly. There will be a little overspray from the black on these areas. This last step covers that black. **Above:** Here's the finished result before the stencil is removed. Do any rework or touch ups before you remove the stencil.

SIMPLE LETTERING WITH A BORDER

The previous technique can be used to create nearly any style of lettering, not just metal effect. Here's a quick and easy way to use those techniques to create simple one- or two-color lettering. The variations with airbrushed stenciled lettering are endless.

And here is the result once the stencil has been removed. Now it's ready for clearcoat.

The Raptor is finished. Now you can see why I did the lettering on the rear doors.

Left: The stencil has been laid out and set up on the doors of a '40s Ford truck and masked off. The inner pieces of the letters are removed as well as the cut borders. The inner pieces of the lettering are saved and put aside. The border pieces are thrown away. The lettering is sprayed with black basecoat.
Right: Next the inner pieces that were removed from the stencil are put back into place inside the letters. Each piece is centered so that the space around the letter is the same all the way. These pieces will cover the center of each letter. White or a contrasting color is airbrushed around the lettering.

Here is the finished lettering, which is part of the logo for Nu Relics Power Windows.

This is some wicked cool lettering on this '50s Chevy ¾-ton truck. Is it really old or was it painted to look old? It's hard to tell. To give your lettering an old worn-out look, simply brush it with a Scotch-Brite pad. You can decide exactly how much to scuff away.

Chapter 26
Understanding, Applying, and Buffing Clearcoats

Show quality clearcoat needs to be perfectly flat, without any orange peel or imperfections. The entire surface should as if it were dipped in liquid glass. It's easier than you think, but it requires a great deal of time and patience.

In Chapter 10, we went over the various kinds of clearcoats and their uses. Now we are going to spray urethane clearcoat on our project Firebird. The first applications will be to protect and level out the artwork, and then it will be applied as the final finish on the car and buffed to a show quality finish.

Spraying clearcoat is not that difficult. But like any other paint product, it's always easier to learn on practice panels. This rule applies especially to painting clearcoat on vertical surfaces. It's easy enough to paint clear on a flat surface. Spray it heavy, and it will flow out easy enough. But if you have the slightest angle, then runs and sags may result.

Spraying urethane clear is an art form in itself. You need the right combination of products and techniques to achieve that glassy finish. And what is the perfect combination? There is no one answer for that. Like any paint, temperature plays a very significant role in what is used and how it's applied. That is where experience comes into play. Yet even experienced painters get runs and sags and pinholes in their paint. Why? Most of the time when experienced painters run into problems with their finish clear, it's because they did not follow the rules. They let the faith in their past experiences fool them into thinking they could take a shortcut or not pay enough attention to the task at hand. For investigating problems relating to clearcoating, please refer to Chapter 15.

CLEARCOATING OVER ARTWORK

The first coat over artwork is always a light coat, yet more than a dusting. You want to cover the artwork but not flood the paint over it. If too much clearcoat is applied in the first or second coat, it can disturb the artwork by grabbing at the paint and dragging it around as it flows. This problem is especially evident on vertical surfaces. The artwork can literally run with the paint as it flows downward, creating a smudge.

The real fire flame artwork has been completed on the Firebird. Now it must be clearcoated to protect and level out the layers of the artwork.

One task that should not be overlooked is to check for overspray, paint drips, or anything on the surface around the artwork. For example, the fire is limited to the center of the hood. It would look funny to have orange dots from the artwork on the side areas. Some paint from the artwork may have strayed outside of the artwork area and appears flawed. So I carefully look to locate exactly the outside edges of the artwork. Then just a few inches beyond those edges, I wet sand the area with 800 grit. This way, anything that has landed on these surfaces will be removed. This is one of the reasons I like to use urethane clear over my color and under the artwork. It provides a barrier, a little insurance in case something goes wrong. Spilled paint or whatever can be sanded off and the color underneath will not be disturbed. So carefully go over the vehicle or parts, and check to make sure the paint surface is free from any defects.

HOW PAINT WORKS

This is a very simple truth about painting clearcoat over artwork: the more layers of artwork you have, the more layers of clearcoat it will take to level them out. There is no hard and firm answer of how many layers will be required. Each situation will be different. In general, the thicker the paint edges are, the more clearcoat will be required to level it out. For example, take three different kinds of flames:

- Ghost flames. One thin layer of artwork paint. Slight paint edge. Not much clear required to level.
- Real fire flames. Multiple, thin layers of artwork paint. Soft edges. Three to four coats of clear to level.
- Traditional flames. Thick solid layers. Hard edges from being taped. One to three separate rounds of three to four coats of clear, depending on if the flames are one solid color, candy or pearl, or metal flake with candy fade.

The important fact to remember is don't overdo the leveling clear. Don't flood on six coats of clear in one round. Spray three to four medium coats; allow them to dry. Sand or scuff, and then repeat the processes until the paint edges are flat.

The second coat is a light to medium coat. The last two coats are medium. On the last coat, an experienced painter may try and flood the edges with a little extra clear. But be warned: this action can lead to more problems. So if you are tempted to do that, think twice. Clear applied too heavily can result in solvent popping and other issues depending on the brand or kind of clear being used. This is why it's good to know your products and have experience with them before you try to push the limits.

One big fact to remember when sanding clearcoat over artwork is that each situation will be different. It's not a one size or technique fits all. This is where common sense is one of your best tools. For thick paint edges like those on traditional flames or complex graphics, don't try to sand the artwork edge until it is flat. Many times, if you try to sand a thick paint edge completely flat, you'll not only sand through the clear, but you might also sand into the upper and lower layers of the artwork.

Sand the surface but don't sand through the clear. Once the surface is taken down as much as it can be without going through, stop. How can you tell? When you sand clearcoat, the residue from the clear is white. Once you start to sand through, you will start to see some color in that residue. That means don't sand

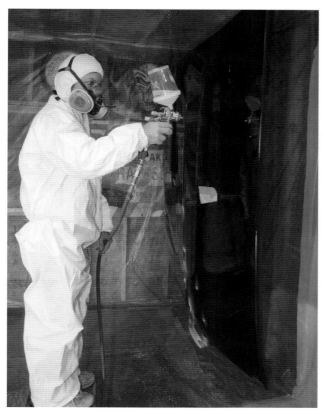

Like most show cars, the Firebird is clearcoated in pieces. The hood, fenders, trunk lid, and small parts are painted off the body of the car. Here I am applying four coats of clear on the hood using PPG's DCU2021 with a SATA 4000 RP with a 1.3 nozzle. The 2021 is mixed 4:1:1 with DCX61 hardener and DT870 reducer in a SATA RPS cup. I'm using the 2021 because I have a great deal of experience with it; I know how it reacts under many different situations. It's a great all-purpose clear—very painter friendly, nice and thick—yet it flows like glass when used as a finish clear and buffs like a dream. Most painters have their favorite clear; this is mine. Always wear a respirator when spraying any kind of paint. I'm using a Gerson One-Step respirator #8211P.

A PAINT TRUTH

Building up very thick layers of clearcoat can lead to serious problems that add many hours to what would have been a quick step in the paint process. This problem is not limited to painting hot rods. On motorcycle parts, the clearcoat may build up along the edges of the fenders and run, creating drips on the bottom of the tank. And because the paint is so thick, the top surface skins over before the bottom layers gas out. These trapped solvents create pinholes, known as solvent popping. These tiny trapped bubbles are very visible and do not go away on their own. They must be carefully sanded away to be removed, adding hours of labor and stress to the job. It's better to do several separate rounds of medium layers of clear rather than pile on many thick layers in one round.

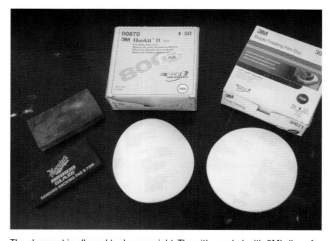

The clearcoat is allowed to dry overnight. Then it's sanded with 3M's line of purple finishing film discs. First the surface is dry sanded with 600 grit to take down any areas of orange peel. I'm not trying to take it all the way flat, just halfway. For flat areas, I wrap the sandpaper around a hard block like the Norton Holey Block #03729. For slightly curved surfaces, I use my favorite all-purpose block: a Meguiar's Sanding Backing Pad #E-7200. For rounded and curved surfaces, I simply fold the paper in half and sand by hand. Next, I further sand using 800 grit. Then for any areas that show the ultra-low point in the orange peel that the sandpaper did not get, I'll use a 3M Gray Scotch-Brite ultra-fine pad #64660. I also use the #64660 on shiny edges of artwork and any edges of the parts or recessed areas that are difficult to sand with the paper. These steps can also be done by wet sanding.

anymore in that area. Sanding clearcoat can seem kind of boring, but once you sand through, its anything but boring and you will give anything to be able to go back and pay close attention to your sanding. So, look carefully as you sand, and hopefully, if you do sand through, it's not too deeply and not in a critical area. See chapter 15 for more information.

For thick edges, once you've sanded as much as you can, you'll see a shiny area along the edges of the artwork. Those shiny areas need to be scuffed. Using a scuff pad like 3M's Gray Scotch-Brite ultra-fine pad #64660, sand along the shiny areas until they are dull.

If the surface is completely flat and the paint edges cannot be felt, move to the next step. If there's still an edge, repeat the clearing and sanding process until the edges are flat. Most of the time, I do two separate rounds of clearcoating and sanding to get the edges flat. This time, as the layers of the fire flames were not very thick, I was able to get it done with one round (four coats in that round) of clear.

APPLYING THE FINISH CLEARCOAT

If you're ready for finish clearcoat, then all the old masking materials must be removed from the vehicle. That means everything. Some painters will simply tape over the old materials with fresh ones, but no one is perfect. Chances are there might have been a mistake made when taping the car the first time. This is the time to find that mistake and fix it. So, unless the world will end if you do not get the clearcoat done by a certain time, take the time to check every edge to make sure it's clean and crisp and that no misplaced pieces of tape left ragged edges. Fix any flaws you find.

Then clean the paint area. If you're working in your garage or using a professional booth, this is the time to clean your area. Once everything is clean, then place the vehicle or parts in the paint area and blow out every crack and crevice. Have the fans running in the paint booth. Give the area time to clear. Then wipe the vehicle or parts down with a post painting precleaner, like PPG's DX320. Look for sanding residue in any

Some areas will need special attention, like these ventilation slots on the dashboard. To sand these, I wrapped 800 grit around a paint stick and individually sanded each slot. Then with a scuff pad, I went over the whole area. But be prepared to sand through the clear in those areas. Use common sense; if you're concerned about sanding through, then don't sand. Just get rid of the gloss with a scuff pad.

recessed areas, and wipe it away. Also make sure to wipe away any precleaner. This is a hard and fast rule if you are using a waterborne precleaner. Next, it's time to remask the vehicle.

The car is blown off again while the fans are running. Next, the car is carefully tack wiped with a Gerson Blend Prep tack cloth to remove any dust or debris that remains on the surface. The car is now ready for finish clearcoat.

BUFFING THE CLEARCOAT

An often asked question is how long to wait before the paint can be buffed out. It's also a question that has a number of variables to consider before it can be answered. Here are a few of the factors that determine how long you should wait to buff clearcoat:

- The temperature of the shop. The warmer it is, the quicker that clear will dry. Shops that have bake booths can speed up dry and cure times.

continued on page 290

HANDY HINT

Between rounds of leveling clear is the perfect time to rework any artwork. Look over the artwork. Are any places in need of a little help? Like maybe the airbrush spattered, a line needs to be a little straighter, or a fade is not even enough? Work on the little things when you have some downtime between tasks.

MIXING FINISH CLEAR

Mixing finish clear is not a step to be rushed through, as multiple variables need to be considered. Because each brand and kind of clearcoat is different, consult the P sheet for your clear and mix the product according to your shop conditions. For example, my shop was on the cold side with temperatures around 65–70°F. So, I had to use a fast reducer with my clear. I mixed four parts DCU 2021 urethane clear to one part DCX61 hardener and added one part DT870 reducer.

Here is a Ford Raptor sanded and ready for finish clearcoat. The masking has all been removed. Dust and sanding residue like to gather in areas like the recesses around these hood vents. I'll use cotton swabs to clean out narrow areas like this and use the air gun to blow them out. Sure it's a pain to remask them, but it's well worth it in the long run. Now the truck is ready to be remasked and finish clearcoated.

Here's how I masked the Firebird for finish clear. Please note that the next four photos were taken after the clear was done due to the fact that if I had not gotten the finish clearcoat done by a certain time, the world would have ended. There is no glass in the car, and the trunk lid, hood, fenders, fender extensions, and lower front valance were painted off the car. The rear window and trunk openings are masked off. To mask off the trunk, I ran American Tape's 2″ aqua mask around bottom edge of the drip channel. Then, I cut out a piece of USC #38018 masking paper in the shape of the opening and laid it on top of the tape that stuck out past the drip channel. For the rear window opening, I simply taped along the edge. The urethane for the window will cover the edge.

Unfortunately, due to the SEMA Show deadline, there was no time to clearcoat the doors off the car, so I had to get creative with my masking. Masking is all about common sense. You have to know what will show, and what will be covered by chrome and trim. Hopefully, you took reference pictures of the vehicle before it was taken apart. If not, then go online and find pictures of your vehicle and see exactly what shows. You want the clearcoat to flow under the edges of any trim pieces. After the show, the doors were removed from the car and the doors and door jams on the body were recleared.

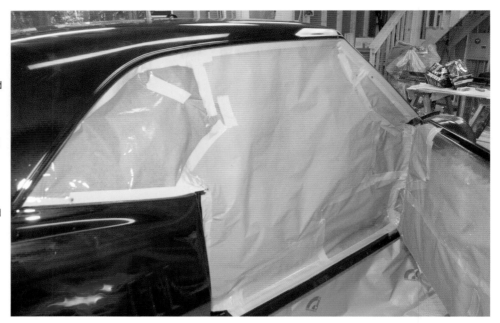

There was a special coating under the car and in the wheel wells, and I did not want clearcoat or overspray to get on these areas. So they were masked off. The masking paper was allowed to hang down and it was taped to the floor. This completely masked off the underside of the car. I also would make sure to mask off the undersides of the hood and trunk if the paint on those areas had been completed.

HOW PAINT WORKS

While temperature is important when painting, it is absolutely critical when it comes to spraying clearcoat. A poor decision here can add untold hours to the job after the clear is sprayed. The colder the shop is, the more the paint will flow. In fact, it can flow right off a panel or part, creating runs and sags. Be sure to use the proper temperature of reducer in your clear. The colder the temps are, the faster the reducer needs to be. The hotter the temps are, the slower the reducer needs to be.

Clearcoat will take longer to flow and dry when it's cold. That means it's more prone to run and sag. If you have a booth with heat, then you can fine-tune the temperature while painting. If not, then you need to pay attention to make sure you are mixing and applying the clearcoat to best suit the temperature in the paint area or booth. Never flow out heavy coats of clear in colder temps. Spray the first coat medium and see how much it flows during the recoat window. Then adjust your spraying technique accordingly.

Note how the dash area was masked off. I picked a line several inches under where the dash pad ends. This way the clear would flow under the pad once the pad was installed.

This picture was staged as I did not want to get overspray on the camera. Because it was cold, I had to pay very close attention to the material as it was landing on the surface. It needed to have a consistent flow out, not bumpy, but not perfectly flat. I knew the cold would make it flow for minutes after I was done spraying. I'm applying three coats of clear. The first two are sprayed medium wet. I watch carefully to see how much the clearcoat flows out in the minutes after each coat is sprayed. This lets me know how thickly I can apply the final third coat. Not wanting to risk getting any runs, I sprayed the last coat a medium to heavy thickness. Any slight or even heavy orange peel can be sanded and buffed to perfection. But sanding and buffing runs and sags are risky. It's easy to sand through the layers of finish clearcoat as you attempt to remove heavy runs.

Left: This photo shows the gun distance I used when spraying the clear. Don't be afraid to get up close. When using this SATA 4000 RP, I spray it about 7˝ from the surface. Getting used to how a gun sprays is another good reason to practice on test panels. Take the time to know how the product sprays with the equipment you're going to use. **Right:** Hanging parts have their pros and cons. The advantage is, dust or debris is less likely to land on the surface if it's vertical and the parts take up less space. The disadvantage? It's not as easy to flow out the clear as if the surface were flat. If the paint is applied on the heavy side and the paint area is cold, then slow hardening clear will be more likely to run or sag. I chose to hang the parts because I did not have much room, and I knew I would be buffing them anyway, so some light orange peel was no big deal. I did not have to try and get the clear flowed completely flat.

Here are the hood, front fenders, and running boards for a '39 Ford arranged for clearcoating in a downdraft spray booth. Sure it can be tricky assembling a vehicle after clearcoat, but the end result is amazing. The clear will flow seamlessly past joints and appear very professional. Note how the underside of the hood is taped off.

Continued from page 286

- The kind of clearcoat being used. Some urethane clears are "speed" clears. They dry fast and can be buffed in hours. But should they be?
- The speed of the hardener of catalyst used with the clear. Some clears have fast hardeners and slower ones. It all depends on which one was used.
- How much clearcoat was applied. Two coats of clear will dry faster than four coats of clear.
- How thickly the clear was applied. Thick clear will take longer to cure than thin clear.

This is where the P sheet comes in handy. Information such as how thick each coat should be, how much time the clearcoat needs to sit before it can be buffed, the temperature required to harden in that allotted time, the selection and requirements of which hardeners or catalysts needed for the painter's situation, and more can be found in the P sheet. The urethane clearcoat on the Firebird needed at least two days to cure before it was buffed.

Here again, experience with a product comes into play. Because I have been using the same product for years, I know how quickly as well as how long I can allow the clearcoat to sit. Some clearcoats have to be buffed within a certain timeframe or they become very hard and then difficult to buff. If you are unfamiliar with a product, then it's essential to follow the P sheet.

Twelve hours after the clearcoat was sprayed, all the masking was removed from the car. When masking is removed after the paint is completely cured and hard, the paint on the masking splinters and cracks. Bits of it pop off and go everywhere. Then you have to carefully tack and blow off this debris. If the paint is still somewhat soft, it remains on the masking and pulls cleanly away, leaving a neat edge. The paint on the

HANDY HINT

If you don't have experience with a buffer, here again, it's a good idea to practice so you can get used to how buffers work. Find the settings on the buffer or polisher that work best for you. Don't be stubborn enough to learn on your actual project. Spend an hour or so playing around with an old car part, fender, or bike tank. No matter what kind of buffer you are using, get to know the machine or products on your new paint. Don't spend countless hours and material on your paint only to buff through the clearcoat.

A PAINT TRUTH

The closer clearcoat is to being properly cured, the easier it is to buff. Of course, there's no clear cut surefire way to tell if your paint is hard enough to buff. But chances are if you're wondering if it's hard enough, there's a good chance it's not!

Most of the time with show cars, we have a few days to allow paint to dry. In a production body shop, that's not the case. But then again a body shop is not looking for a mirror, glassy, show car finish. So here's a quick, unofficial way to help gauge if your clear is hard enough to buff fairly easily. Take a piece of 1500 grit sandpaper and wet sand a small area of the surface. Then look at the paper. Is paint material loading up on the paper, clogging it up? If so, then the surface is going to be a pain to buff as it's on the soft, not-cured-enough side. If the paper doesn't load up and sands easily, then it should buff fairly easily as well.

While the paint was curing, Gary from Quackt Glass installed the windshield and rear window as well as the window trim. As I did not want to chance scratching the new Dynacorn window trim or get debris from the buffer in any painted areas like the trunk or wheel wells, those areas were taped and masked off again. Sure I could have left on the old masking, but it did not take that long and the result was well worth it.

The first thing was to place a Meguiars 1500 disc on the Summit Racing DA using a hook pad. A hook pad is a pad on the DA that has a Velcro-like surface. Hook-style sandpaper attaches to these pads. Next, I sprayed the surface being buffed and the sanding disc with water. Just a light spray will work. This step can also be done by hand using a sanding pad with 1500 paper.

Slowly work the pad over the surface, sanding down any flaws or orange peel. Be careful, it's easy to sand through. Work on one area at a time. For example, I divided the door into four areas: the upper left and right and the lower left and right. Go easy and take your time. Every few minutes, stop and wipe down the surface to check your progress. Stay away from any sharp corners or edges. Look at the previous picture to see where I sanded and did not sand on the side of the Firebird. The 1500 will remove any heavier peel and dust nibs. Next, I remove the 1500 disc and place a Meguiars 3000 foam pad on the DA, repeating the process, removing any scratches from the 1500. The foam pad reaches down into the lower parts of the orange peel that the 1500 did not get. Keep the DA steady; sometimes it wants to jump around. Look carefully for any little round swirls.

DA SWIRLS

Anyone who has used a DA for sanding knows what a DA swirl is. It's a round, corkscrew-like scratch across the surface after using a DA. What happens is a piece of grit or debris gets caught between the sanding disc and the surface and digs into the surface, leaving a long swirly scratch. DA swirls can be hard to see, and most of the time, a painter won't see them until the buffing phase. The only way to fix them is to sand them out, either by hand or with the DA. To avoid this problem, I rinse the DA pad every time I start sanding. I spray a good deal of water at the sanding disc to rinse away any grit. I also spray and wipe the surface often to remove anything that might have landed on it.

Firebird needed 24–48 hours to cure. So, the 12-hour mark was the perfect time to unmask.

Once you're done buffing, lightly spray the area with water or #34 and wipe off any leftover compound with a microfiber towel.

Keep in mind that you will have to go back and rebuff areas. You may even find scratches you miss the first time around and have to sand those again. Take your time, don't try to race through these steps.

Now that the surface is smooth, it's time to buff. The 3000 is a very fine grit and leaves a surface that buffs fairly easy. The wool pad is placed on the Flex Polisher and it's lightly sprayed with a little Meguiars #34 Final Inspection Spray. A small amount of Meguiars #100 is poured onto the surface. I use a mid-range speed on the polisher, about a 4. The wool pad is placed flat against the surface and I go easy on the trigger, keeping the speed slow to work the 100 into the pad. Once the material is on the pad, I slowly begin to work it across the surface. I work one area at a time, just like I did when I was sanding. If I run into a deep scratch, then I stop and sand the scratch with 1500 and/or 3000 and buff again. It's very important to keep the pad moving across the surface. Don't let it sit in one place as it may "burn" into the paint. It's also better to keep the surface somewhat damp. Keep the water spray bottle handy and spritz the surface from time to time. Here, I'm doing one final buffing pass on the trunk lid. The picture is posed so compound doesn't get on the camera.

Now for the fun part: using the Meguires 205 on the Meguiar's DA Polisher. The DA is very easy to use. Spread some 205 on the surface, give the foam pad a spritz of water or #34, and polish away. Start slow to pick up the material on the pad, and work the pad across the surface. After a few minutes, stop and wipe the surface with the microfiber towel. The surface should be like a mirror by now.

Here's the Firebird all assembled and on display in the Dynacorn booth at the 2013 SEMA Show. It's easy to see how it was well worth all the hard work and long hours that went into the metal work and the paint! Notice how the car looks almost black. In fact, some people thought the car was black.

But in the sun, the purple pearl in the paint becomes very visible. Keep in mind that while I made the paint samples on a sunny day, I did not get to see the car in the sun until the car was completed and on its way to SEMA Show.

Chapter 27
Troubleshooting Airbrush and Artwork Problems

Problems are going to happen when you airbrush. You can't escape them. Weird, irrational problems will crop up, and most of the time, there's no obvious reason for the problem. This can stress out the calmest person. The main thing to do when problems pop up is to remain calm, research the problem, use common sense, and fix it. The following problems are common occurrences when doing custom artwork.

DRIPPED OR SPILLED PAINT ON A FRESHLY AIRBRUSHED SURFACE

Let it dry. Or if it's a heavy drip, use a soft, lint-free wipe to gently blot the very top of the bubble of paint. Don't push down on it and smear it onto the surface. Just blot away most of it. Then maybe gently sand away the rest of the drip after it dries. Then, retouch the surface with your airbrush. Don't worry if an outline of the drip can still be seen. After you clearcoat, just retouch that area again with the airbrush and it should disappear. But what if the drip or spatter lands where there's no artwork being done? Hopefully there's lots of clearcoat layers protecting the basecoat color. Damp sand off any paint on the unairbrushed surface. If the drip or spill is on the clear, just let it dry and wet sand it off. Sometimes it can be quickly wiped off.

PULLING UP TAPE AND PAINT COMES WITH IT

Say a prayer that this problem happens only in this one spot. Then, look at the edges of the spot. Poke the broken edge with a stencil knife to see if the whole layer is lifting. Hopefully you did everything correctly, like thoroughly

Don't let airbrush problems get you down. Thinking through the problem and factoring out causes can fix any kind of problem. Worst case scenario, you may have to start over completely, but that is very rare.

sanded all the coats that needed to be sanded and used the proper grit paper. If so, then this may just be an isolated incident. If so, featheredge sand the area. Make sure to remove all lifted or loose paint. If the spot is really deep, fill the pit with polyester filler, tape it off, spot prime, spot paint, rework the artwork. If shortcuts were taken or you're not 100% sure of the adhesion of the paint layers, or if someone else did the basecoats, you may have a serious problem. Stick 2″ tape on the part, let it sit a while, then rip off the tape. In short, test the area to see if it keeps happening. If it does, remove all the paint.

WHAT NEVER TO DO

Never, never, never bake paint in the sun. I tried it once. Extremely bad idea. That was 8 years ago. Ever since I dry my paint in my shop, but only after the paint is dry enough to leave the booth. As a rule, I tend not to bake paint that has artwork on it. Some painters do; some don't. If you are a newcomer to custom painting, it might be a good idea to let custom-painted parts or vehicles air dry.

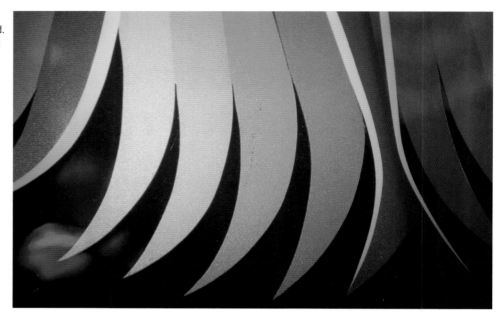

This is a flaw in the artwork on a TA hood. I have no idea how it happened. But something disturbed the paint on this section before it was completely dry. I had to mask off this small section and respray the color. This is why it's always a good idea to mix plenty of paint for artwork. Chances are it will be needed for touchups like this.

UNEVEN FADES

Another common problem for newcomers is getting a consistent and even fade when doing candy fades on flames and graphics. The airbrush or mini spray gun must be moved at an even speed, and the movement itself must smoothly follow the line of graphic. If the airbrush has a jerky or irregular movement, the fade will be uneven. There are two ways to fix an uneven candy fade.

1. You can try to softly retouch the center of the fade. For example, to fix yellow hot rod flames with an orange fade along the edge, take an airbrush and softly spray some yellow along the center of the flame. Then redo the orange fade.

2. For candy fades where the center cannot be touched up, such as with a metallic or pearl base, one option is to use the candy to extend the fade close to the center of the flame or graphic. Hopefully, this will even up the fade.

HOW TO REPAIR A PROBLEM

So what do you do when a part of the artwork gets messed up? The first thing is don't freak out. Allow the paint to dry, and think the problem through. In some cases, you can spray some base color over the affected area, which will cover up the flaw, and repaint the artwork in that area. But above all—think! Sit back, relax, and think the problem though.

THE REALITY OF REWORK

Like it or not, most automotive or motorcycle artwork will need some rework. Paint sneaks past tape lines, metallics look uneven, the airbrushes spit out blobs of paint. The best thing to do is to recognize that reworking is part of painting and plan on spending a day or more doing rework after the first round of filler clearcoat has been completed. This happens on most paint jobs and to most custom painters. And the more artwork that is done, the more rework will be needed.

Don't get frustrated when you see small flaws appear. Print out photos of the artwork after it's done. Then go around the vehicle with the photos and mark on the photos the areas that need reworked. This way you won't miss any spots. It's an awful feeling to be completely finished with a paint job, after the final clear has been done, and see a small flaw that would have taken five minutes to fix had you seen it before the finish clear had been done.

AIRBRUSH PROBLEMS

How to specifically remedy an airbrush problem depends on the airbrush being used. But keeping the airbrush very clean is the best way to keep it working fine. At the start of each airbrush session, I remove the needle and give it a quick wipe with thinner. And I always protect the business end of the airbrush by keeping protective caps in place when brushes are not being used. Here are just a few problems and their causes and remedies.

Airbrush spray is grainy.

Problem: Instead of a smooth, soft distribution of color, the paint hits the surface and appears grainy or spotty. In some cases the paint actually spits in bits out of the airbrush.

Remedy: The paint is either too thick or the pressure is too low. Look at your paint. Is it already very thin? Then turn up the air pressure a few pounds. Also check if the spots, or "spit," are coming from the tip of the airbrush. Sometimes paint can build up on the crown cap or spray regulator, which will cause spitting. Unscrew the crown cap/regulator and clean it with a cotton swab dipped in thinner. And while you have the crown cap off, carefully clean the area around the tip.

Paint comes out of airbrush even when the trigger is not pulled back.

Cause 1: Something—maybe dried paint, a hair, or a fiber—is caught in the tip causing the needle not to close into the tip properly.

Cause 2: Wear and tear on the needle and/or on the tip is causing paint to escape through those gaps. (It also be caused by paint leaking into the air passages past the head seal.

Remedy 1: Remove the needle and tip, and clean both thoroughly. Very carefully, use an old airbrush needle or airbrush reamer to poke into tip to see if anything is caught in the passage.

Remedy 2: Replace worn parts. Replace needle first. If problem is still present, replace the tip.

Tips are held in place by threads, and a little wrench that comes with the airbrush must be used to unscrew the tip. Other tips are simply pushed in place and held there by friction. Take care with those, as they can fall out very easily when you are working on the airbrush. Work over a towel. That way the tip won't roll away and be lost forever.

No paint comes out of airbrush, or the trigger must be pulled back farther than normal to get paint flow.

Cause: Something is caught in the paint passages.

Remedy: Remove the needle and tip and clean them and the paint passages in the airbrush body thoroughly.

Air flow is not consistent.

Cause: The spray regulator or airbrush head is not sealing properly, causing outside air to affect air flow. The head could be loose or, with some airbrushes, the head washer could be worn.

Remedy: Remove the spray regulator or head. Look to see if the sealing surfaces are clean and free of debris. Properly tighten regulator. Replace the head washer if applicable.

No paint comes out when using siphon-feed airbrush.

Cause: Either the tube or the siphon cap is clogged, or the air hole in the top of the cap is clogged.

Remedy: Check and clean the paint's passageway up from bottle and clear out the air hole.

The needle does not move smoothly when pulled back.

Cause: Paint may have leaked back past the needle seal and is sticking in the machinery that pulls the needle back.

Remedy 1: Remove the needle, and clean it. Replace the needle in the airbrush, and test it. If this remedy does not fix the problem, try Remedy 2.

Remedy 2: Remove the needle and needle chuck and spring assembly. Remove the trigger. Take apart the assembly, and thoroughly clean it. Clean out the airbrush body interior with cotton swabs. Use a small, round brush to clean out the needle chucking guide. Reassemble the airbrush.

If paint has been leaking into these areas, the seal or packing that seals the head from the body is worn. In some airbrushes, the seal is not too hard to replace; in others, it is a total pain. And in some airbrushes, like Badger and SATAgraph airbrushes, a set screw can be adjusted to tighten up the packing seal.

Very reduced paint will leak out faster than thick paint. Paint leaking into the airbrush body can also leak into the air passages. Clean out the body, and if possible, take apart and clean the air inlet. Remove the head assembly, reinstall the trigger, and blow air through the brush until it comes out clean. Basically, clean out every bit of paint from the airbrush.

Paint piles up on the tip of the airbrush.

Cause: This problem happens for several reasons. Lower air pressures are needed for fine work, but the lower the pressure is, the slower the paint flows through the airbrush. Slower paint flow means that the paint doesn't have enough velocity to keep bits of it from sticking to the end of the needle. This tends to be a pesky problem when working with water-based airbrush colors because they dry so quickly.

Solution: There is no easy answer here, but there is a simple solution, although it may not be the one you want to hear: always pay attention to the airbrush. When using auto paints, I have gotten into the habit

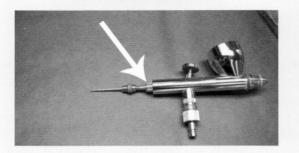

HANDY HINT

Many times, the airbrush just plain seems to be working incorrectly. Maybe paint comes out when it should not. Or the trigger feels funny. If you find yourself dealing with a problem that is hard to pin down and if you are using a dual action airbrush, try this. Remove the airbrush handle. Grab onto the needle chucking assembly. Is it loose? If so, simply tighten it up. For some unknown reason, this assembly has a habit of coming loose occasionally.

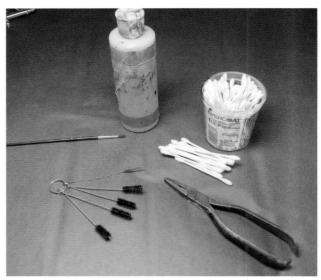

Here are the tools I use to keep my airbrushes happy and healthy: cotton swabs, narrow paintbrushes, small diameter soft round brushes, and a set of pliers with flat, yet toothed jaws.

of clearing out the airbrush before getting started on a new area of the painting. In fact, I'm not even aware of doing it anymore; that step has become an automatic move when I airbrush. For example, say I'm spraying yellow for a woman's hair. Next, I'll need to add white highlights. After I'm done with my yellow, I pick up the airbrush with the white. I point the airbrush toward my ventilation inlet and away from my painting surface. I pull back all the way on the trigger and give a good blast of paint out of the airbrush. This blast does two things: it takes away most of the paint that has built up on the tip, and it also clears away any wet paint that may have settled on the inside surface of the spray regulator or crown cap. This tip only works with solvent-based paints, as the solvent in the paint is so strong, it can soften the paint on the tip so that it blows away.

This tip will not work with water-based paint because it is already dry and does not react like a solvent-based paint. Once waterborne paint is dry, it must be picked off the tip. If you are using water-based paint, get in the habit of picking the paint off the tip each time you pick up the airbrush and every few minutes while you are airbrushing. It seems frustrating at first, but after a while, it will become something you automatically do.

CARE OF YOUR AIRBRUSH

Many airbrush problems will be due to poor airbrush maintenance. Airbrush days are long, and the last thing

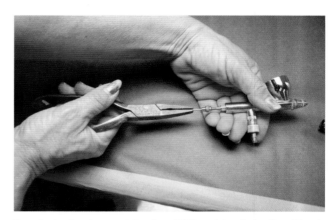

Here, I'm tearing down and cleaning a SATAgraph4, a dual-action airbrush. Twist off the handle. A knurled nut holds the needle in place. Loosen that and slide out the needle. If the needle does easily pull out, firmly grasp it with the pliers and pull it straight back. Make sure to pull it straight back, because if you pull it at any kind of angle, it will bend the needle. Take care; otherwise, you will be replacing the needle.

any artist wants to do at the end of a brutal, frustrating day of attempting perfection is thoroughly clean the airbrushes. It's easier to fool yourself into thinking, "I'll just take a little break and come back later to clean the brushes." And then you wake up the next morning and sit down to airbrushes still full of paint. It happens to everyone once in a while. So take the extra five to ten minutes and clean those airbrushes.

Each brand of airbrush is different and will be slightly different in the way the inner workings are

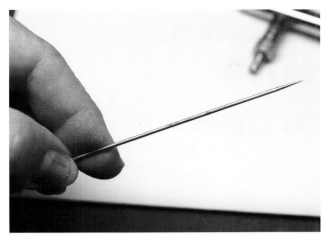

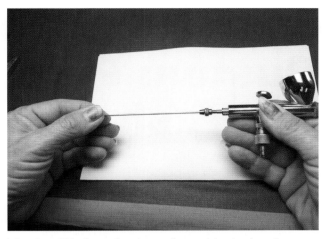

Left: Wow, look at all the paint residue on the needle! I'll wipe it with thinner and clean it until it's all smooth, using a cotton swab to wipe down the needle. **Right:** Now, simply insert the needle back into the airbrush. This is the tricky part. It takes a little experience to know when the needle is seated properly in the tip. Push the needle in too far and it will damage the tip. And if the needle is not inserted far enough, there will be space between the needle and the tip and paint will go through that opening, even if the trigger is not pulled back. So gently slide the needle and feel it settling up into the tip. It will stop when it is properly in place, so don't force it. Next, tighten the nut. Pull back on the trigger and make sure it has nice smooth travel. If not, then repeat the needle cleaning procedure.

designed. So don't lose or discard the little pamphlet that came with your airbrush. It will have a diagram that shows how the pieces inside your airbrush fit together. Even though the airbrush appears to be clean, you'll be amazed at the amount of stuff that gets left behind.

HOW TO CLEAN YOUR AIRBRUSH

Many times, even with proper cleaning, you'll go into the shop to airbrush, pick up the airbrush, and the trigger won't move or won't move smoothly. No problem, it happens all the time. Just pull out the needle and clean it. Much of the time, stuff forms on the inner diameters that surround the needle, and after a night of sitting, that material gets on the needle, causing it to stick. This happens very frequently if you are using automotive paints. In fact, I clean my airbrushes each morning before I start working and then clean them at the end of the day.

Auto Body, Fabrication, Custom Paint, and Airbrush Resources

For more information on the products used in this book, please check out these websites.

SATA Spray Equipment – www.satausa.com
Spray Guns, Airbrushes (www.sataairbrush.com), Air Systems, Breathing Protection, Air Filtration and more. They also have a Youtube channel with excellent how to videos, and a Facebook page: www.facebook.com/satausa.

PPG Refinish – www.us.ppgrefinish.com
High Quality Paint and Painting Products. Their website features the latest news and products concerning automotive paint and refinish.

www.Hypertherm.com
The finest plasma cutting systems in the world and they are very affordable.

www.Dynacorn.com
Replacement sheetmetal for classic muscle cars.

www.SummitRacing.com
Tools, Sanders, Sandpaper, Shop Equipment, Parts. The Summit Racing body and paint catalog is one of the most complete resources for painting your projects.

www.Millerwelds.com
Welding Machines, helmets, gloves and more

www.CP.com
Chicago Pneumatic Air Tools. See CP for your air tool needs. They have a great selection.

www.Meguiars.com
Meguiars Car Care Products. When it comes to taking care of your car's finish and its parts, this is the place to go.

FBS Distributors –www.fbs-online.com
Tapes, Sprayers, Masking Systems. I use a lot of their products.

www.crazyhorsepainting.com – custom painting
This is my website. From this site you can check out my Facebook pages and post questions, check out the latest work, and see custom painting news. You'll also find a link to my Youtube channel, which has a good deal of how-to videos posted on everything from metal fabrication to custom painting to airbrushing.

www.Evercoat.com
Evercoat products, like body fillers, bonding adhesives, and seam sealers are all through this book. Chapter 1 has more information. See their website for a full list of products and tech sheets.

Soft Sanders – www.softsanders.com
Specialized sanding blocks and sandpapers which contour to almost any shape. Made especially for doing autobody work.

Hutchins Sanders - www.hutchinsmfg.com
See Hutchins website to see the various sanders they make which help in saving time and materials when doing autobody work.

www.iwata-media.com/artool/
Artool templates are the handiest tool for anyone doing custom paint and airbrush work.

Gerson – www.gersonco.com
Tack cloths, respirators, strainer systems and more.

Coastairbrush.com
Coast Airbrush is a great resource for most kinds of painting tools, equipment, paint, templates, artist forums, galleries, and news about events, classes and how-to videos.

Quackt Glass.com
Superior Replacement Glass for factory replacement and restoration vehicle projects.

Index

INDEX